STRATEGIC NETWORKS

Strategic Management Society Book Series

The Strategic Management Society Book Series is a cooperative effort between the Strategic Management Society and Blackwell Publishing. The purpose of the series is to present information on cutting-edge concepts and topics in strategic management theory and practice. The books emphasize building and maintaining bridges between strategic management theory and practice. The work published in these books generates and tests new theories of strategic management. Additionally, work published in this series demonstrates how to learn, understand, and apply these theories in practice. The content of the series represents the newest critical thinking in the field of strategic management. As a result, these books provide valuable knowledge for strategic management scholars, consultants, and executives.

Published

Strategic Entrepreneurship: Creating a New Mindset
Edited by Michael A. Hitt, R. Duane Ireland, S. Michael Camp, and Donald L. Sexton

Creating Value: Winners in the New Business Environment
Edited by Michael A. Hitt, Raphael Amit, Charles E. Lucier, and Robert D. Nixon

Strategy Process: Shaping the Contours of the Field
Edited by Bala Chakravarthy, Peter Lorange, Günter Müller-Stewens, and Christoph Lechner

The SMS Blackwell Handbook of Organizational Capabilities: Emergence, Development and Change
Edited by Constance E. Helfat

Mergers and Acquisitions: Creating Integrative Knowledge
Edited by Amy L. Pablo and Mansour Javidan

Strategy in Transition
Richard A. Bettis

Restructuring Strategy: New Networks and Industry Challenges
Edited by Karel O. Cool, James E. Henderson and René Abate

Innovating Strategy Process
Edited by Steven W. Floyd, Johan Roos, Claus D. Jacobs and Franz W. Kellermanns

Entrepreneurial Strategies: New Technologies and Emerging Markets
Edited by Arnold C. Cooper, Sharon A. Alvarez, Alejandro A. Carrera, Luiz F. Mesquita and Roberto S. Vassolo

Strategic Networks: Learning to Compete
Edited by Michael Gibbert and Thomas Durand

Strategic Networks

Learning to Compete

Edited by

Michael Gibbert
Thomas Durand

Blackwell Publishing

© 2007 by Blackwell Publishing Ltd
except for editorial material and organization © 2007 by Michael Gibbert and Thomas Durand

BLACKWELL PUBLISHING
350 Main Street, Malden, MA 02148-5020, USA
9600 Garsington Road, Oxford OX4 2DQ, UK
550 Swanston Street, Carlton, Victoria 3053, Australia

First published 2007 by Blackwell Publishing Ltd

1 2007

Library of Congress Cataloging-in-Publication Data

Strategic networks: learning to compete/edited by
Michael Gibbert and Thomas Durand.
    p. cm.—(Strategic Management Society book series)
Includes bibliographical references and index.
ISBN-13: 978-1-4051-3585-6 (hardcover : alk. paper)
ISBN-10: 1-4051-3585-9 (hardcover : alk. paper)
1. Strategic alliances (Business) 2. Business networks. 3. Knowledge management.
4. Organizational learning. I. Gibbert, Michael. II. Durand, Thomas. III. Series.

   HD69.S8S785 2007
   658.4'038—dc22

                                                                    2006012848

A catalogue record for this title is available from the British Library.

Set in 10/12pt Gilliard
by Newgen Imaging Systems (P) Ltd, Chennai, India
Printed and bound in Singapore
by Markono Print Media Pte Ltd

The publisher's policy is to use permanent paper from mills that operate a sustainable forestry policy, and which has been manufactured from pulp processed using acid-free and elementary chlorine-free practices. Furthermore, the publisher ensures that the text paper and cover board used have met acceptable environmental accreditation standards.

For further information on
Blackwell Publishing, visit our website:
www.blackwellpublishing.com

Dedication

Sadly, Gerardine DeSanctis passed away after an illness while working on her contribution for this book (chapter 7). It is to Gerry's memory that we dedicate the present volume.

Contents

Notes on Contributors   ix

List of Figures   xiii

List of Tables   xiv

Foreword   xv
Yves Doz

Acknowledgments   xvii

Introduction   1
Thomas Durand and Michael Gibbert

1   Knowledge Types and Knowledge Management Strategies   8
    Hari Bapuji and Mary Crossan

2   Learning to Compete or Struggling to Survive? Objectives and Outcomes
    of Scale and Link Alliances   26
    Pierre Dussauge, Xavier Castañer, and Bernard Garrette

3   Teaching in Supplier Networks   40
    Lars-Erik Gadde and Håkan Håkansson

4   On the Challenges of Buyer–Supplier Collaboration in Product
    Development Projects   58
    Stephan M. Wagner and Martin Hoegl

5   Observing the Learning Process in an Interfirm Team   72
    Thomas Durand

6   *Consocia et impera*: How French and Italian Fabric Producers Cooperate
    to Conquer the "Dominant Design" in the Fashion Industry   88
    Diego Rinallo, Francesca Golfetto, and Michael Gibbert

7   Online Social Networks and Knowledge Exchange   107
    Siyuan Huang and Gerardine DeSanctis

8   Bramble Bushes in a Thicket: Narrative and the Intangibles of Learning
    Networks   121
    Cynthia F. Kurtz and David J. Snowden

9   Competing and Collaborating in Networks: Is Organizing Just a Game?   151
    Max Boisot and Xiaohui Lu

10 Networks and Some Limits to Managing Them   171
    J. C. Spender

Index   191

Notes on Contributors

Hari Bapuji is an assistant professor in the Business Administration Department at University of Manitoba, Canada. His research examines the strategies that help organizations to use intangible resources and capabilities to achieve performance that benefits all the stakeholders over a longer time period. His research appeared in the *Best Paper Proceedings of Academy of Management* and *Management Learning*.

Max Boisot is adjunct professor at INSEAD, Fontainebleau, France, Associate Fellow at Templeton College, Oxford University, and a visiting scholar at the Wharton School's Sol Snider Entrepreneurial Center. His research interests are centered on the flow of knowledge and information within and across organized populations as well as on China and the Chinese economic reforms. He has published in *Administrative Science Quarterly, Organization Science,* and *Research Policy.*

Xavier Castañer (PhD, Minnesota) is an assistant professor at the Strategy and Business Policy Department of the HEC School of Management (Paris). His research interests are corporate strategy and value creation, M&A synergy sources and performance, governance choice and dynamics, and organizational integration and innovation. He has published in the *Administrative Science Quarterly* and the *Journal of Cultural Economics.*

Mary Crossan is a professor of Strategic Management at the Richard Ivey School of Business located at the University of Western Ontario in London, Canada. Her research interests are in organizational learning and knowledge management as they relate to strategic renewal. Her research has appeared in such journals as the *Academy of Management Review, Strategic Management Journal, Organization Science,* and *Journal of Management Studies.*

Gerardine "Gerry" DeSanctis, died August 16, 2005 after a long struggle against cancer. A member of Fuqua's management area since 1994 (and area coordinator 1996–99), DeSanctis became the Thomas F. Keller Professor of Business Administration in 2001 and served with distinction. She held major editorial board positions with an array of prestigious journals, including *Management Information Systems Quarterly, Information Systems Research, Management Science,* the *Journal of Organizational Behavior,* and *Organization Science.* Her areas of expertise and recent research interests were on electronic communication, distributed teams, virtual communities and organizational learning.

Yves Doz is the Timken Chaired Professor of Global Technology and Innovation at INSEAD. His research on the strategy of multinational companies and on strategic alliances led to numerous publications, including four books (among these: *From Global to Metanational: How Companies Win in the Knowledge Economy* co-authored with José Santos and Peter Williamson (2001); *The Multinational Mission: Balancing Local Demands and Global Vision*, with C. K. Prahalad (1987); and *Alliance Advantage* with G. Hamel (1998)). Professor Doz was most recently elected Fellow of the Academy of Management (2006) and received an appointment as "Inaugural Fellow of the Strategic Management Society" (2005).

Thomas Durand is professor of Business Strategy at Ecole Centrale Paris, France (www.ecp.fr). His research interests focus on technology strategy, the management of innovation, and organizational learning and knowledge. He is a founding member of the European Institute of Technology and Innovation Management (www.eitim.org). He also heads CM International, a management consultancy which he founded, with 40 staff in France and the UK, working for large corporations and public organizations (www.cm-intl.com).

Pierre Dussauge is a professor of Strategic Management at HEC School of Management. His current research focuses on the topic of global strategic alliances. He is the co-author of *Cooperative Strategy: Competing Successfully through Strategic Alliances* (J. Wiley & Sons, 1999).

Lars-Erik Gadde is professor of Industrial Marketing at Chalmers University of Technology in Gothenburg, Sweden. His research is focused on distribution network dynamics and buyer-supplier relationships, in which areas he has been involved in the publication of several books and journal articles.

Bernard Garrette is Associate Professor of Strategic Management at HEC, Paris. He has been an executive with Valeo (1987–88), a visiting professor at London Business School (1997–99) and a consultant (Senior Practice Expert in Corporate Finance and Strategy) with McKinsey & Company in 2000–2001. His research focuses on strategic alliances between competitors.

Michael Gibbert is an assistant professor at the Institute for Business Management at Bocconi University in Milan. Prior to joining the faculty at Bocconi, he held appointments at Stellenbosch, INSEAD, Yale, and St Gallen, where he also studied for his PhD.

Francesca Golfetto is professor of Marketing at Bocconi University in Milan, Italy. Her research interests focus on value creation and marketing communications in industrial markets. She has worked as a consultant for the trade show industry in many European countries. She has published in *Harvard Business Review*, *Journal of Business Research* and *Industrial Marketing Management*.

Håkan Håkansson is the NEMI Professor of International Management, Norwegian School of Management in Oslo, Norway. He is one of the founding members of the IMP Group and has published a number of books and articles within industrial marketing, purchasing, innovations and technological development.

Siyuan Huang is a PhD student in the Management Area of the Fuqua School of Business, Duke University in North Carolina, USA. Her research interests are online communities, social network analysis, social capital, learning, knowledge management, and innovation diffusion. She has an MBA degree and MS degree in Information Systems from the University of Arizona. She has worked in China as a business consultant for several years.

Martin Hoegl is a professor at WHU – Otto Beisheim School of Management, Vallendar, Germany, where he holds the Chair of Leadership and Human Resource Management. His main research interests include leadership and collaboration in organizations, management of R&D personnel, knowledge creation in innovation processes, the management of geographically dispersed and interorganizational collaboration, as well as the influence of cross-cultural differences on individual and team behaviors in organizations. He has published in leading international journals including the *Academy of Management Journal, Decision Sciences, Human Resource Management, Organization Science, Journal of Management, Journal of Management Studies, Journal of Product Innovation Management, Research Policy*, and others.

Cynthia F. Kurtz is Principal Researcher of Cognitive Edge. She began her career as an evolutionary biologist and ethologist, then spent several years designing educational software for informal science education, then spent another phase researching organizational narrative, only to cycle back and combine all three elements in her current work on decision support in complex environments.

Xiaohui Lu is a PhD candidate at the Management Department of the Wharton School. Her research interests are network formation and dynamics, firm strategy and capability development under economic transition and overseas M&A of Chinese firms.

Diego Rinallo is a research fellow at Bocconi University, Milan, Italy. He received his PhD from Bocconi University. His current research interests include the role of representations in the social construction of markets.

David J. Snowden is founder and Chief Scientific Officer of Cognitive Edge. He was a former director of IBM's Institute for Knowledge Management and founder of the Cynefin Centre with IBM before he left to create Cognitive Edge as an independent research group focused on naturalistic sense making, the development of emergent research methods and the creation of an open source movement for consultancy methods. He is associated with several universities around the world as fellow or adjunct professor and a principal editor of E:CO.

J. C. Spender is a visiting professor at Leeds University Business School. Prior to his retirement in 2003 he was Dean of the School of Business and Technology at FIT/SUNY in Manhattan. His research interests revolve around knowledge-based approaches to management and the theory of the firm. His prize-winning PhD thesis was published as *Industry Recipes* (Blackwell, 1989).

Stephan M. Wagner is professor of Business Administration and the Kuehne Foundation Endowed Chair of Logistics Management at WHU – Otto Beisheim School of Management, Vallendar, Germany. Recent research projects have been devoted to supply chain risks, the management of interfirm relationships in marketing channels (e.g., supplier switching, supplier development, knowledge-sharing), and the integration of suppliers in the innovation process.

Figures

1.1 Knowledge types   13
1.2 Knowledge management strategies   14
3.1 Suppliers involved in the development of the electrical system   53
5.1 Community and complementary modes of cooperation   75
5.2 A four-stage model of group learning   85
6.1 The textile-apparel supply chain   92
6.2 The concertation process   95
6.3 The trend area at *Moda In*, February 2004   98
6.4 *Première Vision*: pattern of network expansion 1973–2002   102
7.1 A coffee house in Cleveland, Ohio   108
7.2 Star network structure   113
7.3 Social network visualization of "Intellectual Knowledge Management
     Discussion"   114
7.4 Core-periphery structure   115
7.5 Social network visualization of "Knowledge Management Initiatives"   116
9.1 Four different network structures   161
10.1 A typology of organizational forms   175
10.2 Coleman's notion of social evolution   178
10.3 A typology of socioeconomic networks   178
10.4 Distribution of types of network   180

Tables

1.1	Definitions of knowledge management	11
1.2	Distinctions among the four KM strategies	19
2.1	Scale versus link alliances	33
6.1	*Première Vision* and *Moda In*: key facts	94
6.2	*Première Vision* and *Moda In*: exhibitors by country of origin (February 2004)	102

Foreword

Strategic networks are an increasingly important phenomenon, yet a relatively poorly understood one. Part of the challenge has been for two hitherto separate literatures and research traditions to converge: that of network structure analysis, emerging from sociology, and that of strategic alliance analysis, emerging from economics and strategic management as perhaps the most critical variable in network value creation. The various essays in this book integrate these two perspectives around a key issue – knowledge sharing – and constitute a valuable and commendable effort. The importance of knowledge transfer, or even sharing, and of its efficiency and equity, in strategic networks has been increasingly well recognized.

Network structural analysis has the advantage of having grown as a well-defined set of methods, finding and exploring an increasing range of issues around the configuration of relationships, mostly at the individual level. In that perspective, the value of an individual's position in a network, her or his social capital, combines structural, cognitive, and relational aspects. Yet, the evolution of relationships, and therefore of network structures, the transposition of these individual level conceptual developments and analytical methods to the inter-institutional levels, and the dynamics of learning in networks have faced difficulties, despite some of the best research academics devoting themselves to the area.

Strategic alliance analysis has been hampered by a twin problem: its origin in transaction cost economics, and its attendant focus on bilateral exchanges. Knowledge sharing across contexts, although a relatively new area of attention, has also shown itself to be a complex research area, in particular because knowledge complexity and the dependency of knowledge interpretation and use on context have been difficult to research. Their very nature makes them important but elusive phenomena.

This book, and the remarkable group of contributors coming from different perspectives it brings together, is therefore a valiant effort. Building an integrative framework between these perspectives is quite important, across a wide empirical territory of customer–supplier alliances, networks of complementers and alliance webs.

Perhaps the most important contribution here is to demonstrate how taking that integrative perspective challenges our conventional wisdom assumptions about strategy (market competition vs. network influence-centrality competition), about organizational boundaries (what are the units and the locus of learning in a network), about competitiveness (what about the collaborative capacity of firms and nations), about learning between partners (an objective, a reality, a windfall). This is an important contribution.

Yves Doz
May 2006

Acknowledgments

This book has benefited from many interactions facilitated by the Strategic Management Society's Interest Group Knowledge and Innovation. We are indebted to Dan Schendel and Mike Hitt for entrusting this volume of the Blackwell Series to our care. And we would like to thank Albert Angehrn from INSEAD for many discussions about the technological side of strategic networks. Rosemary Nixon and Karen Wilson at Blackwell have been most helpful (and patient). Funding from SDA Bocconi, the Bocconi School of Management, is gratefully acknowledged. Last but not least, a special thanks to our contributors for the time and effort they put into their chapters.

Introduction

Thomas Durand and Michael Gibbert

This book is about learning in and from networks. This is about maneuvering strategically in networks with the purpose of extracting, co-constructing and appropriating knowledge to improve competitive posture.

The idea for this book came from practice. One often has some prefabricated ideas about networks in mind such as the split between vertical and horizontal partnerships, or the differentiation between the emphasis on either enhancing existing knowledge/capabilities of each partner (e.g. Kogut, 1988; Cohen and Levinthal, 1990; Hamel, 1991; Inkpen and Beamish, 1997), or allowing access to complementary capabilities of others while focusing on exploitation of existing capabilities within each firm (e.g. Quinn, 1980; Powell et al., 1996; Dyer and Singh, 1998). However, some of the neat borderlines we draw in academia stop looking so crisp as one enters practice. Consider the following quote:

> Our people claim that they want to co-innovate with external partners. Well, if we keep behaving as we currently do, talking to our partners the way we do business with our tier one suppliers, in a master-executants relationship, we got it all wrong. Innovation requires creativity, flexibility, joint work, acceptance for trial and error. This is not compatible with our usual demands for strictly pre-defined deliverables, imposed standards, fixed conditions according to our own rules. If we want to learn from a network of partners, we can no longer behave as the dominant player, literally placing orders on the other guys. Something in our culture has got to change around here.

The Vice President for Engineering of this European car manufacturer clearly makes the point. It is neither easy nor natural for such a large dominant firm to learn from the company's network of vertical "partnerships," a positive word for client–supplier asymmetric relations. Yet, most would agree that a key intent of a strategy of networking is to try to learn from the ecosystem surrounding the firm. This is what we mean by the subtitle of this book, "Learning [how] to Compete." Consider another voice from practice:

> We, in the American chemical industry, are not used to cooperating across the sector through the professional associations as you do. This is an oligopoly but we essentially compete. You, Europeans, tend to have a more collaborative behavior in the sector, competing on the market but lobbying jointly the governments and the EU Commission or promoting the industry in the media through your professional associations. In order

to reach the same level of industry influence, we would need to build something which we do not have today.

This manager of a large US based multinational in the chemical sector clearly hints how cooperative behaviors in horizontal networks can support the strategy of some of the players in the industry. This, however, requires a history of social interactions among the competitors – a mindset and challenge well known to we academics at least since the publication of Hamel, Doz and Prahalad's article in the *Harvard Business Review* nearly two decades ago (Hamel et al., 1989). The issue here is not how practice lags behind theory, or, indeed, why practice apparently doesn't pick up what we academics like to think of as classical concepts. The issue is one of revisiting some of the neat borderlines we have drawn and continue to draw. One manager told us:

We do not fully understand why our company entered this incredible partnership agreement with Microsoft. We view them as a competitor. We are not used to cooperating with a competitor. Of course we may learn a lot from them. But how are we going to protect our own knowledge base? This is scary. How are we going to manage the dynamics of the relationship?

The manager of this large IT company expresses – some would say – a classical issue. A partnership means learning for all partners, leading to the usual concern, but who will be the fastest learner of the network? Consider Procter and Gamble. On their website, Procter and Gamble openly invite any contributor worldwide for proposals for new ideas (products, services, processes). The aim is clearly to reach out for ideas, learning not only from the "usual suspects," that is, the first layer of the ecosystem surrounding the firm, but also from the rest of the world, as technology permits. "Not all smart people work for us," as Paul Polman, Vice President for P&G Western Europe, put it. This goes beyond vertical and horizontal partnerships, to reach out in the web, the network of networks enabled by IT. Is this another way for firms to try to learn from extended networks whose boundaries are difficult to draw? Has the Open-Source approach finally left its cozy home of software development? We think yes. The phenomenon is not limited to Procter and Gamble. On easygroup's website, CEO "Stelios" asks anyone with a business idea that is in line with the yield management approach the company espouses to share this idea with him – and eventually become a partner in the business. Some would say this is internal corporate venturing turned inside out. Or rather, outside in.

Ever since the argument about knowledge and competence came out (Prahalad and Hamel, 1990; Wernerfelt, 1984), the issue of managing knowledge or at least managing learning has been on the agenda. Not surprisingly, this extended into the issue of leveraging networks strategically, since networks can be seen as one of the most powerful tools to share and distribute knowledge. The Strategic Management Society (SMS) created interest groups on specific topics. We built upon a session of the SMS Interest Group on Knowledge and Innovation to generate this book with the help of a panel of contributors in the field. Our objective with the book is to show that strategic networks as a tool for learning to compete go beyond the classic black-and-white distinctions we have grown so accustomed to. In particular, we attempt to show that:

- Learning from internal networks in multidivisional multinational corporations is as relevant as learning from external networks (Chapter 1).
- Not all alliances aim at learning. Some alliances are based on scale and mostly aim at survival (Chapter 2).
- In vertical buyer–supplier partnerships, each party may want to teach the other ones to ensure that their objectives will be better served (Chapter 3).
- In vertical buyer–supplier partnerships, new product development may benefit from the partners' involvement but some conditions are needed (Chapter 4).
- Horizontal networks among competitors require some minimum social base to be workable. This takes time (Chapter 5).
- Horizontal networks may be managed in a closed form to ensure commitment and convergence on shared objectives (Chapter 6).
- Technology now makes it possible to further reach out, beyond the usual networks of partners of the firm. High tech may partially substitute for high touch (Chapter 7).
- Yet, social interactions across networks affect three systemic attributes of organizations (managing identity, trust and conflicts), e.g. through narratives. High touch should thus not be abandoned (Chapter 8).

We believe that these contributions actually lead us to question whether the classical literature on strategy and organization is adequately addressing the issue of learning in networks. We thus end up with two theoretical chapters which seriously (as one would have come to expect from these authors) and quite profoundly upset some of our received wisdom:

- The firm's boundaries may be challenged as the internal/external dichotomy may be seen as a misleading construct to look at organizations and networks. The implication is that a new theory of organizing is needed, challenging mainstream definitions of strategy (Chapters 9 and 10).

The SKIN Framework and the Contributors in this Book

Allow us at this stage to introduce the authors and their individual contributions to the book. We do this by developing the SKIN framework (short for Strategy for Knowledge In Networks).

Thanks to Bapuji and Crossan (Chapter 1), we start with a mainstream model of strategizing in networks. Companies aim at learning from their networks. Yet, Bapuji and Crossan very relevantly suggest that learning covers not only the explicit but also the tacit knowledge. They also suggest to extend this type of logic to internal networks, especially within large corporations when inner boundaries are often more difficult to cross than external ones. The learning strategies vary accordingly: Capturing, appropriating, etc.

Ch. 1

Knowledge Management Strategies in Networks

	Internal	External
Explicit	Capture strategy	Appropriation strategy
Tacit	Learning strategy	Participation strategy

The mainstream argument: "strategizing to learn in networks"

This matrix helps to distinguish the type of priorities firms may have on their learning agenda.

Yet, Dussauge, Castañer, and Garrette (Chapter 2) rightly point out that not all alliances aim at learning. There are situations when players decide to enter a partnership essentially as a way to survive, building up scale together in search of efficiency. This thus appears as a useful caveat in our framework. Not all networks are a learning game.

Not all networks aim at learning

Ch. 2

Ch. 1

Knowledge Management Strategies in Networks

	Internal	External
Explicit	Capture strategy	Appropriation strategy
Tacit	Learning strategy	Participation strategy

The most natural way of leveraging the firm's networks is to go to the clients and suppliers and learn from them. Gadde and Håkansson (Chapter 3) suggest that teaching your vertical partners is in fact a good way to be in a position to learn more from them. Similarly, although from a slightly different standpoint, Wagner and Hoegl (Chapter 4) discuss how to call upon suppliers (and lead clients) into the development of new products (NPD). They argue that this is neither easy nor fulfilling but they suggest that there may be practical ways of doing it.

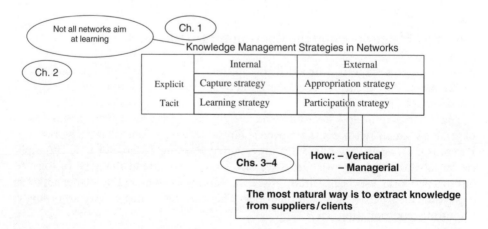

Not all networks aim at learning

Ch. 2

Ch. 1

Knowledge Management Strategies in Networks

	Internal	External
Explicit	Capture strategy	Appropriation strategy
Tacit	Learning strategy	Participation strategy

Chs. 3–4

**How: – Vertical
– Managerial**

The most natural way is to extract knowledge from suppliers / clients

Horizontal networks are even more difficult to handle. Durand (Chapter5) shows that horizontal cooperation among competing players need a social process to build recognition and legitimacy for the collaboration. Yet, once established, horizontal networks may be remarkably efficient to build power of influence on other players. Rinallo, Golfetto, and Gibbert (Chapter 6) show how a closed, well-coordinated network can play a decisive role in shaping the future of an industry.

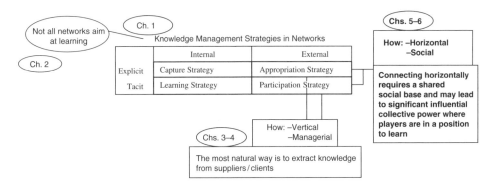

Technology opened up new venues for virtual interactions. Beyond the classical high touch way, some new forms of interactions in networks appeared. We call these the high tech connections.

These permit new forms of learning, reaching further out, beyond the "usual suspects." Huang and DeSanctis (Chapter 7) discuss the impact of electronic forums and the learning that takes place through this new form of virtual networking. In turn, this tends to blur the classical lines of divide between players, mixing the internal to the external, the close to the distant, the in-house to the unknown.

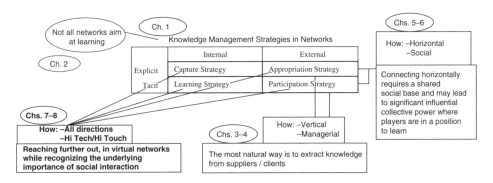

However, Kurtz and Snowden (Chapter 8) argue that learning in interorganizational networks affects three intangible and fundamentally social elements of organizations (managing identity and multiple identity, trust negotiation, productive conflicts). They further argue that the network operates as a mirror for the organization, thus contributing to changing these three elements of any participating organization. They suggest that narratives are a good way to support these forms of social learning in networks.

This thus takes us back to the high touch perspective, while contributing to question the essence of organizations, for example through the multiple identity argument.

All in all, the above framework as it unfolds through the chapters happens to be both detailed and weakened along the way. Indeed, as more in-depth insights are brought about by the contributors in their chapters, the very foundation of the framework vacillates. What exactly is an organization within a network (the individuals, the group of workers, the branch of a firm, the legal entity known as the firm, the association of various firms, a sub-network, the community of individuals connecting in a forum, etc.)?

And if the definition of the organization becomes uncertain, then what is strategy? This may call for a fundamental rethinking of what the concepts of organization and strategy mean. This is exactly what both Max Boisot and Xiaohui Lu (Chapter 9) and J. C. Spender (Chapter 10) are after.

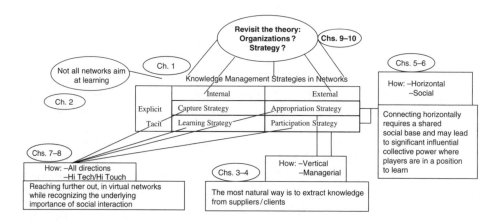

All in all, this discussion opens up quite a challenging research agenda for the future. Both in the mainstream part of the SKIN Framework, and in re-theorizing the concepts of organization and strategy.

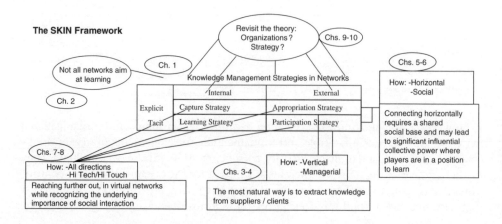

References

Cohen, W. M. & Levinthal, D. A. (1990) Absorptive capacity: A new perspective on learning and innovation. *Administrative Science Quarterly*, 35, 128–52.

Dyer, J. H. & Singh, H. (1998) The relational view: Cooperative strategy and sources of interorganizational competitive advantage. *Academy of Management Review*, 23(4), 660–79.

Hamel, G. (1991) Competition for competence and inter-partner learning within international strategic alliances. *Strategic Management Journal*, 12, 83–103.

Hamel, G., Doz, Y. & Prahalad, C. K. (1989) Collaborate with your competitors and win. *Harvard Business Review*, 67(1), 133–9.

Inkpen, A. C. & Beamish, P. W. (1997) Knowledge, bargaining power, and the instability of international joint ventures. *Academy of Management Review*, 22(1), 177–202.

Kogut, B. (1988) Joint ventures: Theoretical and empirical perspectives. *Strategic Management Journal*, 9(4), 319–32.

Powell, W. W., Koput, K. W. & Smith-Doerr, L. (1996) Interorganizational collaboration and the locus of innovation: Networks of learning in biotechnology. *Administrative Science Quarterly*, 41(1), 116–45.

Prahalad, C. & Hamel, G. (1990) The core competence of the corporation. *Harvard Business Review*, May–June, 79–91.

Quinn, J. P. (1980) *Intelligent Enterprise: A Knowledge- and Service-based Paradigm for Industry.* New York: The Free Press.

Wernerfelt, B. (1984) A resource based view of the firm. *Strategic Management Journal*, 5, 171–80.

CHAPTER ONE

Knowledge Types and Knowledge Management Strategies

Hari Bapuji and Mary Crossan

Knowledge Management Strategies in Networks

	Internal	External
Explicit	Capture strategy	Appropriation strategy
Tacit	Learning strategy	Participation strategy

The mainstream argument: "strategizing to learn in networks"

Abstract

In this chapter, we categorize knowledge into four types along two dimensions: tacit-explicit and internal-external and suggest that each type of knowledge can be managed using a different strategy. A capture strategy is suitable for managing internal-explicit knowledge whereas a learning strategy is useful for managing internal-tacit knowledge. For external-explicit knowledge, an appropriation strategy is suitable while a participation strategy is beneficial for managing external-tacit knowledge. By aligning knowledge categories with knowledge management strategies, this chapter seeks to expand the theory and practice of knowledge management to realize its potential benefits.

Knowledge has increasingly been viewed as a source of competitive advantage (Grant, 1996b; Spender, 1996; Grant, 1996a). Not surprisingly, organizations have turned their attention to managing it. Some researchers suggest that "as free natural resources and cheap labor are exhausted, the last untapped source of competitive advantage is the knowledge of people in organizations' (Davenport, 1997: 191). Some others argue that the need to manage knowledge increases proportionately with the service intensity of companies; and service intense companies represent a significant component of growth in the economy (Apostolov and Mentzas, 1999).

According to one estimate, global corporate spending on knowledge management services will increase from US$4.2 billion in 2003 to US$8.9 billion by 2006 (IDC Group, 2002). However, companies report very little satisfaction with knowledge management because it has not yielded the expected performance benefits (KPMG, 2000; Prewitt, 2005; Malhotra, 2005). Some scholars argue that shifting the current focus of knowledge management efforts from technology to people and processes will yield expected performance benefits (Davenport and Prusak, 1999; McDermott, 1999). Others assert that firms must develop a strategic approach to managing knowledge (Bierly and Chakrabarti, 1996; Zack, 1999). However, very little is known about the different strategies that firms can adopt to manage knowledge. In this chapter, we propose four different strategies to manage knowledge. We suggest that each of these four strategies is best suited to manage a particular type of knowledge.

Our central thesis is that knowledge can be categorized into four types based on whether the knowledge is tacit or explicit and whether the knowledge resides inside or outside the firm boundaries. We suggest that a capture-based strategy is best suited for knowledge that is explicit and resides in the firm boundaries. In contrast, a learning-based strategy is suitable for knowledge that is tacit and is inside the firm boundaries. For knowledge that is outside the firm boundaries and is explicit, an appropriation strategy is appropriate. On the other hand, a participation strategy is more suitable if such outside knowledge is tacit.

This chapter is organized as follows. First, we discuss knowledge management and associated issues to provide the necessary theoretical background. Second, we categorize knowledge using the dimensions of tacit-explicit and internal-external and discuss each of the four categories that arise out of the dimensions. Third, we propose four strategies to manage each of the four knowledge categories. Finally, we conclude with a discussion on the implications for research and the practice of knowledge management.

Knowledge Management

The expression "knowledge management" (KM), has been used in the literature for over a decade now. Its evolution has been traced by many scholars (Wiig, 1997; Ponzi, 2002). The KM literature has grown exponentially over the last decade (Ponzi, 2002; Crossan and Guatto, 1996). During the early stages of KM research (1991–5), the computer science discipline contributed significantly to KM concepts (Ponzi, 2002). The computer science literature viewed knowledge as an "object" that can be managed better with the help of IT. During the later stages (1996–9), the KM literature witnessed contributions from as many as 13 disciplines (Ponzi, 2002). During this period, there were significant contributions from organizational science scholars (i.e., Nonaka and Takeuchi, 1995; Argyris and Schon, 1978; Senge, 1990; Nonaka, 1994; Polanyi, 1966) who emphasized the social processes involved in knowledge management.

The contributions made by several disciplines have enriched the theory and practice of KM. They have, however, limited the possibility of a uniform approach. Not surprisingly, despite the voluminous literature on KM, there is no readily accepted definition of knowledge management (Earl, 2001). Some of the definitions found in the literature are presented in Table 1.1, along with a brief comment on the focus of each.

The definitions presented in Table 1.1 focus on managing the knowledge already existing within the organization. They place less emphasis on creating new knowledge within the organization and outside. Also, the existing definitions of KM focus more on making the knowledge available and pay little attention to developing the capabilities that are needed to utilize the available knowledge. Further, the extant definitions do not focus on the social processes within an organization that are necessary for learning and knowledge creation. In short, each of the existing definitions of knowledge management focuses on a limited aspect of organizational knowledge management.

The existing definitions of knowledge management are limited because they arise from different perspectives. During the formation period of knowledge management (1991–5), primarily two disciplines contributed to KM: computer science and business. During 1996–9 when KM witnessed an explosive growth several other disciplines including management science, information and library science, engineering, psychology, and operations research contributed to the growth of KM research. The engineering disciplines viewed KM from an artificial intelligence perspective whereas library sciences emphasized indexing and taxonomies. Armed with high power computing and communication tools, the information technology discipline viewed KM as a technical activity of providing IT, which stores the information. Some scholars in the organizational literature viewed knowledge as an asset and emphasized the need to leverage it. Other scholars in the organizational literature pointed to the importance of learning processes that create knowledge.

In both the theory and practice of knowledge management, very little effort has been made to integrate these different perspectives. Perhaps this is one of the reasons why much of the literature on KM has taken an IT approach viewing knowledge as an asset (Davenport et al., 1998), but the much needed focus on processes has been missing (Ruggles, 1998; McDermott, 1999). Accordingly, we combine the insights from various perspectives and define knowledge management as "a set of practices and processes to acquire both tacit and explicit knowledge from outside the organization, create knowledge inside the organization and apply knowledge to facilitate organizational operations."

In the definition of KM adopted in this study, the phrase "process of acquiring" is used to reflect the "process of acquiring knowledge and creating knowledge." Therefore, it includes the acquisition of existing knowledge from within and outside the firm boundaries. Further, it also includes the process of creating new knowledge. The phrase "applying" is used to reflect activities such as capturing, storing, accessing, and transferring knowledge that may be necessary before knowledge can be applied to fulfill organizational requirements.

In contrast to the existing definitions, the definition used here underscores that KM involves both processes and practices, rather than simply the practices and/or systems that capture knowledge. Further, our definition explicitly includes tacit knowledge and thus the learning processes associated with it, unlike the earlier definitions which emphasized explicit knowledge through their focus on identifying/creating, capturing, storing, and retrieving knowledge. In addition, unlike previous definitions

Table 1.1   Definitions of knowledge management

Author	Definition	Comment
Bassi, 1997	KM is "the process of creating, capturing, and using knowledge to enhance organizational performance" (p. 26)	A comprehensive definition; does not consider the types of knowledge and where it resides
Duhon, 1998	KM is "a combination of technology supporting a strategy for sharing and using both the brain power resident within an organization's employees and internal and external information found in 'information containers' (primarily documents). The goal of KM is to simultaneously manage data, information, and explicit knowledge while leveraging the information resident in peoples' heads (tacit knowledge) through a combination of technology and management practices" (p. 9)	Considers both tacit and explicit dimensions of knowledge, but does not consider knowledge that may be outside the organization
Gray, 2002	"KM practices are tools and approaches used to improve individuals' ability to access knowledge that is held by others in an organization" (p. 10)	Focus on the knowledge available within the organization
Knapp, 1998	KM is "a set of processes for transferring intellectual capital (IC) to value – processes such as innovation and knowledge creation, knowledge acquisition, organization, application, sharing, and replenishment" (p. 3)	Focus on organizational processes; Some of the processes such as knowledge creation and acquisition could include knowledge inside and outside the organization
Liebowitz and Wilcox, 1997	KM is the "ability of organizations to manage, store, value, and distribute knowledge" (Preface)	Focus on knowledge existing within the organization
O'Dell and Grayson, 1998	"The process of identifying, capturing, and leveraging knowledge to help the company compete" (p. 154)	Focus on exploiting the existing knowledge
O'Leary, 1998	KM is "the formal management of knowledge for facilitating creation, access and reuse of knowledge, typically using advanced technology" (p. 34)	Focus on creating and distributing knowledge within the organization
Spek and Spijkervet, 1997	KM is "the explicit control and management of knowledge within an organization aimed at achieving the company's objectives" (p. 43)	Focus on knowledge within the organization
Wiig, 1997	The objectives of KM are "(a) to make the enterprise act as intelligently as possible to secure its viability and overall success, and (b) to otherwise realize the best value of its knowledge assets" (p. 1)	Focus on firm's existing knowledge

of KM, our definition explicitly emphasizes the application of knowledge to facilitate organizational operations.

Our definition of knowledge management directs attention to the different types of knowledge and the varied practices and processes that may be needed to manage them. In order to derive benefits from KM, firms need to develop a KM strategy that "guides and defines the processes and infrastructure (organizational and technological) for managing knowledge" (Zack, 2002: 271). In developing a KM strategy, firms need to take into account the type of knowledge that is sought to be managed.

Knowledge Types

Knowledge has been defined by researchers in many different ways; from *what is known* to *what provides insight*. Among the most commonly found definitions are: (1) knowledge is justified true belief (Nonaka, 1994: 15); (2) knowledge is justified personal belief that increases an individual's capacity to take effective action (Alavi and Leidner, 1999: 109); (3) knowledge is a fluid mix of framed experiences, values, contextual information, and expert insight that provides a framework for evaluating and incorporating new experiences and information (Davenport and Prusak, 1999: 5); and (4) knowledge is information whose validity has been established through tests of proof (Liebeskind, 1996: 94).

The existing definitions of knowledge provide an insight into what knowledge is. In order to develop a KM strategy, however, we need to understand the dimensions of knowledge. Not surprisingly, the most common and popular conception of knowledge is that it consists of both tacit and explicit dimensions. The explicit dimension is knowledge that can be expressed in words, text, and diagrams. The tacit dimension consists of expertise, insights, intuition that cannot be explicated. The tacit dimension is often described as what people know but cannot tell (Nonaka, 1994; Polanyi, 1966).

The categorization of knowledge into explicit and tacit dimensions is important for developing a KM strategy because explicit knowledge can be acquired and distributed within an organization through organizational systems using technology. Tacit knowledge, however, cannot be acquired easily. Further, it poses several challenges in transferring (Szulanski, 1996, Simonin, 1999). An organization can manage its explicit knowledge through investments in technology but managing tacit knowledge requires investments in social processes such as communication and coordination (Anand et al., 1998).

In addition to the dimensions of knowledge, another important factor to consider is whether the knowledge is available within the firm boundaries or needs to be acquired from outside the firm boundaries. We refer to knowledge that resides within the firm boundaries as internal knowledge and knowledge that resides outside the firm boundaries as external knowledge. Internal knowledge is that knowledge to which a firm can stake a claim to own, or a right to use. In the event of a dispute, a firm has a basis to defend itself from any legal actions arising out of using internal knowledge. This definition, therefore, also incorporates knowledge such as traditional knowledge that is not owned by any particular entity but is available to all for usage. The knowledge that is external to a firm is held by outside agencies, such as suppliers, customers, competitors, industry associations, and research communities (Powell et al., 1996; Takeishi, 2001).

Managing external knowledge is important because firms create new knowledge in interaction with other firms (Powell et al., 1996; Tsoukas, 1996). Many researchers have acknowledged the limited utility of the knowledge residing within the firm boundaries and the need to acquire knowledge from outside the firm (Anand et al., 1998; Bierly and Chakrabarti, 1996). In fact, a firm's ability to interact with other firms and acquire knowledge is a distinctive competence that can yield competitive advantage (Leonardbarton, 1995; Lorenzoni and Lipparini, 1999; Takeishi, 2001).

In developing a KM strategy, the internal-external dimension is important because internal knowledge can be transferred within the firm whereas transferring knowledge, particularly tacit knowledge, from one firm to another is very difficult (Kogut and Zander, 1993). Given the importance of the dimensions tacit-explicit and internal-external, we put them together in a matrix and categorize the knowledge types.

As presented in Figure 1.1, knowledge can be categorized into four types. Internal-explicit knowledge consists of formal rules, procedures, policies, and all other information that can be codified and documented in reports, brochures, and directories. Internal-tacit knowledge comprises the belief structures in the company, the way things are done, and the knowledge about the relationships with suppliers, customers, and other business associates, for example. This knowledge cannot be documented but is available in the organization for employees to use as the need arises, that is, it will be revealed only in the organizational context and action (Cook and Brown, 1999; Orlikowski, 2002). External-tacit knowledge exists within other organizations as well and includes values, management practices, informal rules, projects under exploration, and experiences. Also, very useful knowledge about the relationships between players in the industry, informal rules, and unwritten codes of conduct remain in a tacit form. Finally, external-explicit knowledge includes the reports of other companies, industry reports, benchmarking studies, and public policy statements.

	Internal	External
Explicit	• Company procedures, routines, policy statements, directories, databases, and reports	• Patents, annual reports, and press statements of other companies • Customer/market/industry reports, news items, benchmarking studies, articles/research studies, public policy statements, and conference presentations
Tacit	• Belief structures, judgment, intuition, management practices, architectural knowledge (ability to integrate components), and informal routines and procedures • Knowledge about suppliers, distributors, customers, research institutions, consultants, competitors, other firms, etc.	• Preferences of other companies, exploratory projects, failed experiments, belief structures, values, culture, and new technologies under consideration/development. • Industry norms, culture, and relationships between players

Figure 1.1 Knowledge types

	Internal	External
Explicit	Capture strategy	Appropriation strategy
Tacit	Learning strategy	Participation strategy

Figure 1.2 Knowledge management strategies

In summary, the dimensions of tacit-explicit and internal-external enable a categorization of knowledge types that can be aligned with different knowledge strategies.

Knowledge Management Strategies

The strategies needed to manage tacit knowledge are different from the strategies needed to manage explicit knowledge. Similarly, the strategies that are useful in acquiring and using external knowledge are different from the strategies needed to acquire and use internal knowledge. In this section, we discuss four strategies that are appropriate for managing the four knowledge types. These four strategies are presented in Figure 1.2 and explained in the following paragraphs.

Capture strategy

The knowledge-based view (KBV) of the firm (Spender, 1996; Liebeskind, 1996; Conner and Prahalad, 1996; Grant, 1996a, 1996b) suggests that firms exist because they are superior to markets in managing knowledge. The KBV asserts that firms substitute superior knowledge of one individual for the inferior knowledge of another, through mechanisms such as instructions, directions, and routines (Conner and Prahalad, 1996). Consequently, firms try to "capture the knowledge of specialists in knowledge bases which other specialists or qualified people can use" (Earl, 2001: 218). Such efforts reflect a capture strategy that is *an orientation to codify organizational knowledge and store it in repositories.*

The capture strategy treats knowledge as an entity separate from the people who create and use it. The essence of a capture strategy is in capturing and storing relevant knowledge of employees. Many firms have approached the task of codifying and capturing knowledge with the help of information technology. In fact, information technology is considered to be one of the central drivers of knowledge management (Davenport and Prusak, 1999). Some scholars note that corporate efforts to manage knowledge is an important reason for the growth in adoption of technology tools such as intranets (Scott, 1998). Further, information systems planning methods have been deployed to implement knowledge management and to design its management processes (Kim et al., 2003; Gold et al., 2001).

The emphasis placed on IT in the KM literature and in practice has resulted in two types of KM activities: (1) those that are aimed at providing technology, and (2) those that are aimed at codifying employee knowledge. This distinction is well articulated by Bassi (1997: 26): "In general, two types of activities fall under the rubric of knowledge management. The most common are efforts to facilitate the sharing of knowledge. Typically, they are technology-based, and they rely on interactive software, such as groupware. The other type of activity involves efforts to codify knowledge by documenting and appropriating individual knowledge."

It is possible to manage a repository without IT tools. For example, a collection of research reports, presentations, and articles can be stored and retrieved in an old-fashioned library-like manner without the aid of IT tools. However, such visualization and management is impractical given the prevalence of IT systems in every aspect of organizational life. Therefore, IT tools have an important role to play in a capture-based strategy. The IT infrastructure, however, is perhaps a necessary but not a sufficient condition for capture; the efforts to capture, store, and retrieve are the sufficient conditions for a capture-based strategy.

Firms that employ a capture strategy view KM as a tool to exploit their existing knowledge. Such firms have the following objectives for managing knowledge: capturing lessons learned, avoiding repeating mistakes and capturing expertise before it is lost (Davenport et al., 1998). These objectives suggest that firms realize the importance of employees and the knowledge they carry. Not surprisingly, knowledge codification is pursued as one of the most important activities for managing organizational knowledge (Earl, 2005).

The capture strategy is well suited for capturing and distributing internal explicit knowledge because the organization can provide incentives to document the codifiable knowledge. The internal coordination mechanisms make it easy for the organization to identify which knowledge is valuable and encourage its documentation, distribution, and usage. Finally, the availability of IT infrastructure that spans the entire organization and connects its members makes it feasible to employ a capture strategy to manage explicit knowledge.

In short, the capture strategy emphasizes codifying organizational knowledge and storing it in repositories. The stored knowledge is made accessible to other organizational members. The capture strategy does not, however, manage tacit knowledge because tacit dimensions of knowledge are revealed only in social interactions. The aspect of social interactions and tacit knowledge transfer are reflected in the learning-based KM strategy.

Learning strategy

It is difficult to manage knowledge solely through databases and protection systems because knowledge is not only explicit, but also tacit (Polanyi, 1966). Further, knowledge is not only a resource, as viewed by the capture strategy, but a process of knowing (Nonaka, 1994; Spender, 1996; Zack, 1999). The literature on organizational learning has emphasized that learning is a process that creates knowledge (Vera and Crossan, 2003). The belief that learning is a means to create and manage knowledge is central to a learning strategy; that is, *an emphasis on organizational learning that occurs through a two-way interaction between individuals, groups, and the organization.*

The 4I framework of Crossan et al. (1999) suggests that learning occurs through four social and psychological processes: intuition, interpretation, integration, and institutionalization (the 4Is). The 4Is are connected through feed-forward and feed-back flows in the 4I framework. In order for the feed-forward flow to occur, learning at the individual level (intuition) must travel through the group and organizational level (interpretation and integration) to become institutionalized learning at the organizational level. It is such institutionalized learning (or knowledge) embedded in the systems, strategy and processes of an organization that helps firms to exploit organizational knowledge (Crossan et al., 1999). In other words, knowledge creation is very important for knowledge exploitation to occur.

For the feed-forward and feed-back flows to occur, certain facilitating conditions must be present. These conditions are represented in the Strategic Learning Assessment Map (SLAM), which is an operationalization of the 4I framework (Bontis et al., 2002). According to SLAM, high learning stocks at the individual, group, and organizational levels are necessary for organizational learning. Further, organizational support in the form of an open culture, tolerance for errors, sharing of ideas, critical examination of ideas presented by individuals, and transfer of learning from one group to another are some of the factors that influence feed-forward and feed-back flows (Bontis et al., 2002).

The process of organizational knowledge creation has also been explained by Nonaka (1994) in his framework of Socialization–Externalization–Combination–Internalization. According to Nonaka, individual tacit knowledge gets externalized in a social context and moves to the level of organizational knowledge through combination and internalization. In other words, meaningful conversations are central to creating and transferring knowledge (Crossan, 2003a, 2003b). Enabling such interactions is an integral part of a learning-based KM strategy. Therefore, the firms that follow a learning strategy define the objectives of KM in an overarching manner: leverage knowledge of the entire firm, share experiences, improve development process and embed knowledge in strategy (Davenport et al., 1998).

A learning strategy is appropriate for managing tacit knowledge within the organization because the tacit knowledge is revealed only in action. As organizations provide the context for knowledge creation and transfer, paying attention to learning processes can help a firm to manage tacit knowledge. The learning processes reflected in open culture, tolerance for errors, and importance of individual input into organizational decisions and actions generate the conditions for creating and transferring tacit knowledge.

In short, learning strategy facilitates organizational processes that help individuals to share knowledge in a group. Further, groups are encouraged to interact with each other to share their solutions. By defining the objectives of KM in an overarching manner, learning strategy enables people to look beyond what is known and create new solutions to organizational problems.

Appropriation strategy

External knowledge that a firm needs can be either explicit or tacit. External-explicit knowledge is not easy to capture, store, and distribute because identifying the knowledge that is valuable is a very difficult task. In the case of internal-explicit knowledge, the firm can identify valuable knowledge because it is within the firm boundaries and the firm thus has the information it needs to assess its usefulness. Often, the internal-explicit knowledge is known to the organizational members as valuable because they have witnessed its value. By contrast, the utility of external knowledge is not known to members and the members may often misjudge the utility and value of external-explicit knowledge. Therefore, firms need to scan their competitive environment closely, gather information, and acquire it from external sources. We define this appropriation strategy as "an emphasis on identifying and acquiring external knowledge from public domains through arm's-length scanning and monitoring."

Firms that adopt the appropriation strategy scan the environment for new knowledge and try to gather it. They monitor the patents that are granted to their competitors, the products introduced by their competitors, the new research published about their industry or products, the new policies introduced by the government, and any customer information that may be available. Unlike the internal-explicit knowledge, the external-explicit knowledge is vast and can be expensive to acquire, store and distribute within the organization. Therefore, the firm focuses only on the knowledge that is of immediate use.

External knowledge can be acquired through several means. A firm may locate itself in a location where it has access to a vast labor pool, research institutions, and government support (DeCarolis and Deeds, 1999). Firms that adopt the appropriation strategy access knowledge through interactions with those outside the firm (Almeida and Kogut, 1999; Saxenian, 1990). Further, firms can acquire knowledge of its competitors by hiring former employees of competitors (Almeida and Kogut, 1999). Similarly, they can acquire knowledge by attending conferences, by scanning the published research, and by reviewing the patents within an industry (Appleyard, 1996).

Appropriation strategy helps a firm to gain an understanding of the developments in its industry but does not help in internalizing those developments. Also, scanning from a distance does not provide a firm access to the tacit parts of that knowledge. For example, distant scanning can get a firm access to patent information but not to the failed experiments that shaped the final innovation. Similarly, a firm can learn that its competitor has implemented a new system to improve productivity but cannot learn about the troubles that it went through in implementing a new system. Knowledge of this nature is important and does not get published but gets disseminated through networks of informal social relationships that professionals form (Appleyard, 1996). Accordingly, to access external-tacit knowledge, firms need to employ a participation strategy.

Participation strategy

We define participation strategy as "an emphasis on developing external knowledge through active interaction with agencies such as suppliers, customers, competitors, and research institutions." Participation strategy emphasizes an active interaction between a firm and external forces such as suppliers, competitors, customers, and research institutions. It envisages active participation in the research programs of universities and other firms. Further, it entails participation in industry-benchmarking exercises. Such participation leads to creation of new knowledge in the industry.

As discussed previously, knowledge is both explicit and tacit. Knowledge that is tacit and not available within the organizational boundaries can only be acquired through communication, social interaction, and relationships (Lorenzoni and Lipparini, 1999; Takeishi, 2001; Yli-Renko et al., 2001). Therefore, firms access knowledge through their relationships with other companies (Lane and Lubatkin, 1998; Zollo et al., 2002), suppliers (Lorenzoni and Lipparini, 1999; Takeishi, 2001), universities and research institutions (Lee et al., 2001; Powell et al., 1996), industry associations/networks (Hanssen-Bauer and Snow, 1996; Lee et al., 2001), and customers (Yli-Renko et al., 2001). Moreover, firms form consortiums and networks to learn from each other and create new knowledge. For example, firms across various industries in Norway formed a network to learn from each other and develop a common knowledge base to deal with hyper-competition (Hanssen-Bauer and Snow, 1996).

Participation strategy entails active involvement of the firm in the knowledge creation activities occurring in the industry. As a result of the participation, a firm's relationships with others is strengthened. Such strong relationships help firms to acquire and internalize knowledge and adopt innovations (Abrahamson and Fombrum, 1994). Such external knowledge helps an organization to create new knowledge (Bierly and Chakrabarti, 1996; Danneels, 2002; Mowery et al., 1996). Additionally, it helps organizations to better utilize their internal knowledge because performance benefits from internal knowledge capabilities are higher in the presence of external linkages and the knowledge gained from them (Lee et al., 2001).

Firms that actively participate in the industry activities broaden their knowledge bases and can avoid learning traps, that is, paying too much attention to short-term and local conditions (Levinthal and March, 1993). Empirical evidence reveals that firms that learn from the experience of others avoid such learning traps (Baum and Ingram, 1998; Ingram and Baum, 1997) and also save on the costs of creating new knowledge (Schulz, 2001).

Participation strategy enhances the social relationships of a firm and increases its social capital, which helps to acquire tacit knowledge from outside the firm boundaries (Nahapiet and Ghoshal, 1998). Firms in the industry develop a shared language, industry norms, and industry standards through active participation of the various firms (Spencer, 2003). By being a party to the development, a firm can acquire that tacit knowledge very easily. Further, by being an active participant, a firm can develop a lot of goodwill and trust, which enables it to acquire tacit knowledge (Nahapiet and Ghoshal, 1998; Szulanski, 1996).

Distinguishing among the Four KM Strategies

The KM strategies discussed above can be distinguished from each other on a variety of factors such as the role of technology, beliefs about KM, type of knowledge managed, and the component of KM that each of the strategies emphasizes. These distinctions are presented in Table 1.2 and are explained in the following paragraphs.

Both the capture and learning strategies manage internal knowledge whereas appropriation and participation strategies manage external knowledge. Capture strategy focuses on the codifiable knowledge within the organization whereas learning strategy manages the tacit knowledge. Appropriation strategy focuses on the codified external knowledge, particularly the knowledge that is relevant and very useful to the

Table 1.2   Distinctions among the four KM strategies

Factor	Capture strategy	Learning strategy	Appropriation strategy	Participation strategy
Type of knowledge managed	Codifiable knowledge inside the organization	Tacit knowledge inside the organization	Appropriable codified knowledge	Tacit knowledge that is useful in the long run and across several settings
Type of technology	Advanced/specific; strong enabler	No specific technologies needed; moderate to weak enabler	Advanced/specific technologies to scan and store knowledge	Not important; but technologies could help participation
Focus of KM	Knowledge utilization through access	Knowledge creation and transfer through interactions	Knowledge appropriation	Creation of industry knowledge
Role of people	One-way input into technology	Dynamic with two-way interactions across people	To scan, evaluate, and store external knowledge	To be active in the industry and be industry leaders
Managerial challenge	Motivating employees to share knowledge	Fostering a learning culture	Identifying the relevant knowledge	Obtaining support for participation; protecting organizational knowledge
Definition of KM objectives	Capture employee knowledge before they leave; avoid repeating mistakes	Share experiences; embed learning into firm's strategic orientation	Acquire useful knowledge from outside; learn from others' mistakes	Share experiences; learn from each other in the industry
Level of awareness about KM	Knowledge sharing through contribution to repositories is important	Knowledge sharing is a social process	External knowledge is important to remain competitive	Creating external knowledge is key to survival in the long run
Direction of knowledge flow	One-way: from employees to organization	Two-way: from employees to organization and vice versa	One-way: from outside to inside the organization	Two-way: from outside to inside and vice versa

organization. Finally, participation strategy focuses on knowledge that can be created for the benefit of everyone in the industry. As a result of participation, a firm not only acquires industry knowledge but also can acquire the tacit knowledge of important players because of the social capital it has developed.

The capture strategy holds that employee knowledge is an invaluable resource, which the organization may lose when employees leave. Therefore, it focuses on codifying the knowledge of employees and capturing it in knowledge repositories and other organizational systems. With the learning strategy knowledgeable employees are the key to knowledge management. Knowledge is created and shared when employees are provided with a "space" to express their ideas. Therefore, the learning KM strategy emphasizes interactions between/among people and developing people to ultimately benefit the company. The appropriation strategy emphasizes the importance of external knowledge and the need to use it in organizational operations. The participation strategy takes a step further and emphasizes the need to actively participate in the industry and create industry knowledge.

Although technology may be common to all four strategies, the type of technology employed and its role varies with each strategy. In capture strategy, technology plays an important role, however the emphasis is more on codifying knowledge and exploiting it. For a capture strategy, IT tools offer a useful means for storing and retrieving codified knowledge. The technology employed differs and includes refined software and hardware to index, store, and retrieve knowledge. Likewise, the acquisition strategy needs refined and specific technologies. In a learning strategy, the emphasis is on interactions and processes. As a result, technology will not play an important role, but it will be used to the extent that it can facilitate interactions between people. Often, technology tools may decrease the rich face-to-face communication between organizational members and lead to a loss of knowledge. In contrast, the technology is likely to help in a participation strategy because the distances between organizations can be overcome with the help of IT tools.

In a capture strategy and appropriation strategy, the role of people is limited to identifying the relevant knowledge and storing it in repositories. As a result, the direction of flow in a capture strategy is from employees to organizational repositories whereas the direction in an appropriation strategy is from outside to organizational repositories. In learning and participation strategies, people are actively involved with others to create and share knowledge. Consequently, the flow of knowledge in a learning strategy is from employees to organization and vice versa because the organization actively supports the creation of knowledge. Similarly, the flow of knowledge in a participation strategy is from organization to the environment and vice versa.

The managerial challenge in a capture strategy is to motivate employees to document knowledge and store it in repositories whereas the challenge in an appropriation strategy is to identify the knowledge that is valuable to the firm. The challenge in a learning strategy is to foster a learning and knowledge sharing culture. Finally, the challenge in a participation strategy is to secure resources for participating in activities that do not have a visible and/or direct effect on the firm and may also have the potential to expose the organization to the dangers of knowledge leakages.

In summary, each of the four KM strategies is appropriate for managing a particular type of knowledge. Although these strategies are conceptually different from each other, they are not mutually exclusive. These strategies could complement each other in managing the different dimensions of knowledge in order to provide performance benefits from knowledge management.

Discussion

The strategies used by firms are often unstated (Mintzberg et al., 1998) and are best reflected in firm actions (Bierly and Chakrabarti, 1996). Accordingly, the knowledge management strategies of firms are revealed in the knowledge management activities of firms. The KM activities of firms suggest that they focus largely on internal explicit knowledge and to a very limited extent on external explicit knowledge. For example, a survey of 431 US and European organizations indicated that their KM activities included mapping sources of internal expertise and providing IT tools such as intranet, decision support tools, and groupware (Ruggles, 1998). Similarly, Davenport and his colleagues found that organizations managed three basic types of repositories: "(1) external knowledge, for example, competitive intelligence; (2) structured internal knowledge, such as research reports, product-oriented marketing materials, and techniques and methods; and (3) informal internal knowledge, like discussion databases full of know-how" (Davenport et al., 1998: 45).

The repositories and IT tools that firms develop and employ only capture the explicit component of employees' knowledge and experience. The tacit components of employee knowledge are revealed only through social interactions (Nonaka, 1994). Similarly, the repositories containing competitive intelligence only capture the explicit knowledge but do not capture the tacit knowledge that provides the meaning and context to that knowledge, both of which are important if the knowledge is to be useful for an organization. In short, the existing knowledge management efforts have so far focused largely on internal explicit knowledge and to some extent on external explicit knowledge. The focus on tacit knowledge has been limited. Perhaps, as a result, the firms have not been able to receive performance benefits from knowledge management. As prior research has indicated, knowledge management strategies such as learning and participation that focus on tacit knowledge enhance a firm's long-term performance (Bapuji and Crossan, 2005).

The four strategies presented in this paper appear to be complementary. However, a balance needs to be maintained in pursuing these strategies. The relative emphasis on each of the four types of knowledge and the sequence in which the strategies are implemented are very important factors that determine the success of knowledge management. The capture strategy has the potential to send negative signals to employees that the firm is interested only in capturing their knowledge, which could arouse mistrust and lead to insecurity in the minds of employees (Bapuji and Crossan, 2005). Consequently, the employees may not share knowledge, which is a voluntary exercise and cannot be forced on them (Davenport, 1997).

In developing our framework, we treated firm boundaries as identifiable and rigid. Further, we treated the firm as a single entity with one boundary. Although we do not view these boundaries as entirely rigid and identifiable, particularly in the case of large, multi-unit organizations which often have departmental and divisional boundaries, the strategies that we have suggested are useful for managing knowledge, however the boundaries are defined. Our framework, much like several studies in the past (Yli-Renko et al., 2001; Tsai, 2000, 2002; Burt, 1997; Burt et al., 2000; Koka and Prescott, 2002; Reagans and McEvily, 2003), suggests that social relationships and boundary spanning help to acquire knowledge that an entity does not have but needs for effective operations.

In this paper, we have provided a framework for strategic knowledge management by categorizing knowledge along two dimensions, that is, tacit-explicit and internal-external. We suggested that firms need to adopt a different type of strategy for each type of knowledge. Our conceptualization, therefore, provides a useful framework to approach knowledge management in a strategic manner.

References

Abrahamson, E. & Fombrum, C. J. (1994) Macro cultures: Determinants and consequences. *Academy of Management Review*, 19, 728–55.

Alavi, M. & Leidner, D. E. (1999) Knowledge management systems: Issues, challenges and beliefs. *Communications of the AIS*, 1, 107–36.

Almeida, P. & Kogut, B. (1999) Localization of knowledge and the mobility of engineers in regional networks. *Management Science*, 45, 905–17.

Anand, V., Manz, C. & Glick, W. (1998) An organizational memory approach to information management. *Academy of Management Review*, 23, 796–809.

Apostolov, D. & Mentzas, G. (1999) Managing corporate knowledge: A comparative analysis of experience in consulting firms. *Knowledge and Process Management*, 6, 129–38.

Appleyard, M. M. (1996) How does knowledge flow? Interfirm patterns in the semiconductor industry. *Strategic Management Journal*, 17, 137–54.

Argyris, C. & Schon, D. A. (1978) *Organizational Learning: A Theory of Action Perspective*. Reading, MA: Addison-Wesley.

Bapuji, H. & Crossan, M. (2005) Knowledge management strategies and firm performance. Strategic Management Society Conference, Orlando, October 23–26.

Bassi, L. (1997) Harnessing the power of intellectual capital. *Training and Development*, 12, 25–30.

Baum, J. A. C. & Ingram, P. (1998) Survival-enhancing learning in the Manhattan hotel industry, 1898–1980. *Management Science*, 44, 996–1016.

Bierly, P. & Chakrabarti, A. (1996) Generic knowledge strategies in the US pharmaceutical industry. *Strategic Management Journal*, 17, 123–35.

Bontis, N., Crossan, M. M. & Hulland, J. (2002) Managing an organizational learning system by aligning stocks and flows. *Journal of Management Studies*, 39, 437–69.

Burt, R. S. (1997) The contingent value of social capital. *Administrative Science Quarterly*, 42, 339–65.

Burt, R. S., Hogarth, R. M. & Michaud, C. (2000) The social capital of French and American managers. *Organization Science*, 11, 123.

Conner, K. R. & Prahalad, C. K. (1996) A resource-based theory of the firm: Knowledge versus opportunism. *Organization Science*, 7, 477–501.

Cook, S. D. N. & Brown, J. S. (1999) Bridging epistemologies: The generative dance between organizational knowledge and organizational knowing. *Organization Science*, 10, 381–400.

Crossan, M. (2003a) Altering theories of learning and action: An interview with Chris Argyris. *Academy of Management Executive*, 17, 40–46.

Crossan, M. (2003b) Introduction: Chris Argyris and Donald Schon's Organizational Learning: There is no silver bullet. *Academy of Management Executive*, 17, 38–9.

Crossan, M. & Guatto, T. (1996) Organizational learning research profile. *Journal of Organizational Change Management*, 9, 107–12.

Crossan, M. M., Lane, H. W. & White, R. E. (1999) An organizational learning framework: From intuition to institution. *Academy of Management Review*, 24, 522–37.

Danneels, E. (2002) The dynamics of product innovation and firm competences. *Strategic Management Journal*, 23, 1095–121.

Davenport, T. (1997) Ten principles of knowledge management and four case studies. *Knowledge and Process Management*, 4, 187–208.

Davenport, T. & Prusak, L. (1999) *Working Knowledge: How Organizations Manage what They Know.* Boston: HBS Press.

Davenport, T. H., Long, D. W. D. & Beers, M. C. (1998) Successful knowledge management projects. *Sloan Management Review*, 39, 43–57.

DeCarolis, D. M. & Deeds, D. L. (1999) The impact of stocks and flows of organizational knowledge on firm performance: An empirical investigation of the biotechnology industry. *Strategic Management Journal*, 20, 953–68.

Duhon, B. (1998) It's all in our heads. *Inform*, 12, 8–13.

Earl, L. (2005) *Knowledge Sharing Succeeds: How Selected Service Industries Rated the Importance of Using Knowledge Management Practices to their Success.* Ottawa: Statistics Canada.

Earl, M. (2001) Knowledge management strategies: Toward a taxonomy. *Journal of Management Information Systems*, 18, 215–33.

Gold, A. H., Malhotra, A. & Segars, A. H. (2001) Knowledge management: An organizational capabilities perspective. *Journal of Management Information Systems*, 18, 185–214.

Grant, R. M. (1996a) Prospering in dynamically-competitive environments: Organizational capability as knowledge integration. *Organization Science*, 7, 375–87.

Grant, R. M. (1996b) Toward a knowledge-based theory of the firm. *Strategic Management Journal*, 17, 109–22.

Gray, P. (2002) Knowledge sourcing effectiveness. PhD thesis – Business. Kingston: Queen's University.

Hanssen-Bauer, J. & Snow, C. C. (1996) Responding to hypercompetition: The structure and processes of a regional learning network organization. *Organization Science*, 7, 413–27.

IDC Group (2002) *U.S. and Worldwide Knowledge Management Services Market Forecast and Analysis, 2001–2006.* Framingham, MA: IDC Group.

Ingram, P. & Baum, J. A. C. (1997) Opportunity and constraint: Organizations' learning from the operating and competitive experience of industries. *Strategic Management Journal*, 18, 75–98.

Kim, Y.-G., Yu, S.-H. & Lee, J.-H. (2003) Knowledge strategy planning: Methodology and case. *Expert Systems with Applications*, 24, 295–307.

Knapp, E. M. (1998) Knowledge management. *Business and Economic Review*, 44, 3–6.

Kogut, B. & Zander, U. (1993) Knowledge of the firm and the evolutionary theory of the multinational corporation. *Journal of International Business Studies*, 24, 625–45.

Koka, B. R. & Prescott, J. E. (2002) Strategic alliances as social capital: A multidimensional view. *Strategic Management Journal*, 23, 795–816.

KPMG (2000) Knowledge management research report.

Lane, P. J. & Lubatkin, M. (1998) Relative absorptive capacity and interorganizational learning. *Strategic Management Journal*, 19, 461–77.

Lee, C., Lee, K. & Pennings, J. M. (2001) Internal capabilities, external networks, and performance: A study on technology-based ventures. *Strategic Management Journal*, 22, 615–40.

Leonardbarton, D. (1995) *Wellsprings of Knowledge: Building and Sustaining the Source of Innovation*. Boston, MA: Harvard Business School Press.

Levinthal, D. A. & March, J. G. (1993) The myopia of learning. *Strategic Management Journal*, 14, 95–112.

Liebeskind, J. P. (1996) Knowledge, strategy, and the theory of the firm. *Strategic Management Journal*, 17, 93–107.

Liebowitz, J. & Wilcox, L. (1997) *Knowledge Management and its Integrative Elements*. Boca Raton, FL: CRC Press.

Lorenzoni, G. & Lipparini, A. (1999) The leveraging of interfirm relationships as a distinctive organizational capability: A longitudinal study. *Strategic Management Journal*, 20, 317–38.

Malhotra, Y. (2005) Integrating knowledge management technologies in organizational business processes: Getting real time enterprises to deliver real business performance. *Journal of Knowledge Management* 9, 7–28.

McDermott, R. (1999) Why information technology inspired but cannot deliver knowledge management. *California Management Review*, 41, 103–17.

Mintzberg, H., Ahlstrand, B. & Lampel, J. (1998) *Strategy Safari: A Guided Tour through the Wilds of Strategic Management*. New York: The Free Press.

Mowery, D. C., Oxley, J. E. & Silverman, B. S. (1996) Strategic alliances and interfirm knowledge transfer. *Strategic Management Journal*, 17, 77–91.

Nahapiet, J. & Ghoshal, S. (1998) Social capital, intellectual capital, and the organizational advantage. *Academy of Management Review*, 23, 242–66.

Nonaka, I. (1994) A dynamic theory of organizational knowledge creation. *Organization Science*, 5, 14–37.

Nonaka, I. & Takeuchi, H. (1995) *The Knowledge-creating Company: How Japanese Companies Create the Dynamics of Innovation*. New York: Oxford University Press.

O'Dell, C. & Grayson, C. J. (1998) If only we knew what we know. *California Management Review*, 40, 154–75.

O'Leary, D. (1998) Using AI in knowledge management: Knowledge bases and ontologies. *IEEE Intelligent Systems*, 13, 34–9.

Orlikowski, W. J. (2002) Knowing in practice: Enacting a collective capability in distributed organizing. *Organization Science*, 13, 249–73.

Polanyi, M. (1966) *The Tacit Dimension*. New York: Doubleday.

Ponzi, L. J. (2002) The evolution and intellectual development of knowledge management. PhD – Library and Information Science, Long Island University.

Powell, W. W., Koput, K. W. & Smithdoerr, L. (1996) Interorganizational collaboration and the locus of innovation: Networks of learning in biotechnology. *Administrative Science Quarterly*, 41, 116–45.

Prewitt, E. (2005) CRM gains ground as a management tool. *CIO Magazine*, available at: http://www.cio.com/archive/090105/tl_management_report.html.

Reagans, R. & McEvily, B. (2003) Network structure and knowledge transfer: The effects of cohesion and range. *Administrative Science Quarterly*, 48, 240–67.

Ruggles, R. (1998) The state of the notion: Knowledge management in practice. *California Management Review*, 40, 80–9.

Saxenian, A. (1990) Regional networks and the resurgence of Silicon Valley. *California Management Review*, 33, 89–112.

Schulz, M. (2001) The uncertain relevance of newness: Organizational learning and knowledge flows. *Academy of Management Journal*, 44, 661–81.

Scott, J. E. (1998) Organizational knowledge and the intranet. *Decision Support Systems*, 23, 3–17.

Senge, P. (1990) *The fifth discipline: The art and practice of the learning organization*. New York: Doubleday.

Simonin, B. L. (1999) Ambiguity and the process of knowledge transfer in strategic alliances. *Strategic Management Journal*, 20, 595–623.

Spek, R. V. D. & Spijkervet, A. (1997) Knowledge management: Dealing intelligently with knowledge. In J. Liebowitz & L. Wilcox (Eds.) *Knowledge Management and its Integrative Elements*. Boca Raton, FL: CRC Press.

Spencer, J. W. (2003) Firms' knowledge-sharing strategies in the global innovation system: Empirical evidence from the flat panel display industry. *Strategic Management Journal*, 24, 217–33.

Spender, J. C. (1996) Making knowledge the basis of a dynamic theory of the firm. *Strategic Management Journal*, 17, 45–62.

Szulanski, G. (1996) Exploring internal stickiness: Impediments to the transfer of best practice within the firm. *Strategic Management Journal*, 17, 27–43.

Takeishi, A. (2001) Bridging inter- and intra-firm boundaries: Management of supplier involvement in automobile product development. *Strategic Management Journal*, 22, 403–33.

Tsai, W. P. (2000) Social capital, strategic relatedness and the formation of intraorganizational linkages. *Strategic Management Journal*, 21, 925–39.

Tsai, W. P. (2002) Social structure of "coopetition" within a multiunit organization: Coordination, competition, and intraorganizational knowledge sharing. *Organization Science*, 13, 179–90.

Tsoukas, H. (1996) The firm as a distributed knowledge system: A constructionist approach. *Strategic Management Journal*, 17, 11–25.

Vera, D. & Crossan, M. (2003) Organizational learning and knowledge management: Toward an integrative framework. In M. Easterby-Smith & M. Lyles (Eds.) *Handbook of Organizational Learning and Knowledge Management*. Oxford: Blackwell.

Wiig, K. M. (1997) Knowledge management: Where did it come from and where will it go? *Expert Systems with Applications*, 13, 1–14.

Yli-Renko, H., Autio, E. & Sapienza, H. J. (2001) Social capital, knowledge acquisition, and knowledge exploitation in young technology-based firms. *Strategic Management Journal*, 22, 587–613.

Zack, M. H. (1999) Developing a knowledge strategy. *California Management Review*, 41, 125–45.

Zack, M. H. (2002) Epilogue: Developing a knowledge strategy. In C. W. Choo & N. Bontis (Eds.) *The Strategic Management of Intellectual Capital and Organizational Knowledge: A Collection of Readings*. Oxford: Oxford University Press.

Zollo, M., Reuer, J. J. & Singh, H. (2002) Interorganizational routines and performance in strategic alliances. *Organization Science*, 13, 701–13.

CHAPTER TWO

Learning to Compete or Struggling to Survive? Objectives and Outcomes of Scale and Link Alliances

Pierre Dussauge, Xavier Castañer, and Bernard Garrette

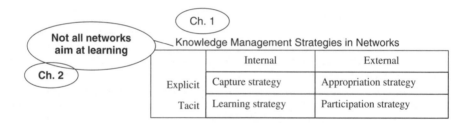

Abstract

Most of the literature on alliances and networks has emphasized learning and knowledge brokerage as a central issue in the formation, evolution, and outcomes of interorganizational arrangements. We propose in this chapter that this perspective on alliances and networks implicitly focuses on partner complementarity and thus on link alliances, while overlooking alliances aimed at achieving scale economies. We analyze the motivations, formation, dynamics and outcomes of such scale alliances and contrast them to those of link alliances. We argue that scale alliances are formed by weaker competitors, are aimed at survival, and exhibit poorer performance than single-firm projects.

Most of the literature on alliances and networks has emphasized learning and knowledge brokerage as a central issue in the formation, evolution, and outcomes of interorganizational arrangements. Because of this focus, the benefits and risks associated with alliance activity and firms' positions in network structures are viewed in terms of learning and loss of proprietary knowledge. We propose in this chapter that this perspective on alliances and networks overlooks a wide segment of cooperative strategies. Indeed, all alliances are not motivated by learning and thus all alliance outcomes cannot be assessed on the basis of resource and knowledge transfers between partner firms.

The literature on horizontal interfirm alliances has suggested that pursuing scale benefits and leveraging complementarities are two main motivations for firms to collaborate (Kogut, 1988). This has led to categorizing horizontal alliances as either scale alliances or link alliances (Hennart, 1988). Empirical studies have supported this distinction by showing that scale and link alliances are formed by firms with different attributes, and, more importantly, lead to contrasted outcomes. Partners in scale alliances are more similar in size and geographic origin than partners in link alliances; link alliances are less stable than scale alliances and lead to more asymmetric outcomes for the involved partners (Dussauge et al., 2000, 2004). While this categorization of alliances is widely accepted, research on alliance formation, management and outcomes has primarily focused, explicitly or implicitly on link alliances. As a consequence, conclusions derived from the analysis of link alliances are often assumed to be applicable to all forms of horizontal alliances. We propose that scale alliances are formed by firms exhibiting specific characteristics, raise particular management issues and lead to different outcomes.

The objective of this paper is to contrast the logic of scale alliances with that of link alliances, to explore why firms form scale alliances, how they manage them and what drives their performance. In doing so, we aim to lay the foundations of a theory of scale alliances.

Alliance Formation: A Focus on Complementarity

Early theoretical work on alliance formation suggested that two main motivations lead firms to enter into horizontal alliances: (1) increasing efficiency and/or market power, and (2) exploiting asset complementarity and/or acquiring new capabilities (Mariti and Smiley, 1983; Ghemawat et al., 1986; Porter and Fuller, 1986; Kogut, 1988; Hennart, 1988; Nohria and Garcia-Pont, 1991). These motivations are necessary drivers of alliance formation but could be achieved through other means (market transactions or industry consolidation through horizontal mergers). Transaction cost arguments have thus been introduced to justify when alliances become the preferred option (Hennart, 1988; Kogut, 1988). This has led to categorizing alliances as either scale alliances or link (i.e. complementary) alliances (Hennart, 1988; Dussauge et al., 2000, 2004). The scale/link typology categorizes alliances according to the partners' contributions to the joint activity. Scale alliances, in which partners contribute similar resources for the same stages in the value chain, aim at producing economies of scale for those activities that firms carry out in collaboration. Link alliances, in contrast with scale alliances, aim at combining different skills and resources from each partner. Link alliances include partnerships in which one partner provides market access to products or technologies that the other firm has developed. Scale alliances primarily produce efficiency gains by pooling similar assets from the partners, carrying out business activities in which both firms have experience. In contrast, link alliances organize the use of complementary resources in order to pursue expansion opportunities in new business areas (Dussauge et al., 2000, 2004).

Scale alliances can include joint R&D efforts, the joint production of components or sub-assemblies, or the manufacture of an entire product. The Sevelnord alliance that has associated Peugeot-Citroën and Fiat since 1988 to develop and manufacture a common minivan for the European market is an example of a scale alliance.

Link alliances include partnerships in which one partner provides market access to products that the other firm has developed. The 1989 CPW (Cereal Partners Worldwide) joint venture between General Mills and Nestlé that produces and markets cereal products originally designed by General Mills through Nestlé's distribution network in Europe and Asia, using the Nestlé brand, is an example of such link alliances.

Early empirical studies tried to discriminate between the two above-mentioned motivations. Results showing that larger firms had a greater propensity to form alliances provided support for a market power argument (Berg and Friedman, 1978) while the observation that firms forming alliances operated in slightly different industry segments supported the complementarity/capability acquisition rationale (Berg and Friedman, 1981).

More recent studies on alliance formation have focused on the main characteristics of those firms that have the highest propensity to form alliances. These characteristics include firm size, competitive position, product portfolio, and resource endowment (Shan, 1990; Mitchell and Singh, 1992; Eisenhardt and Schoonhoven, 1996; Ahuja, 2000).

Shan (1990) examined firm-level determinants that lead high tech start-up firms to team up with established companies to commercialize an innovation rather than to go to market alone. The results of this study show that smaller firms and industry followers are more likely to collaborate, while larger competitors and technology leaders tend to favor independent market entry. This suggests that the main driver of alliance formation is a lack of critical resources. All the firms examined in this study are high tech start-ups that provide their established partner with a valuable innovation, thus creating new business opportunities for this partner.

Mitchell and Singh (1992) focused on the other party in alliances, that is, industry incumbents that choose to collaborate with innovators to expand into a new technical domain. Their results demonstrate that stronger competitors are more prone than weaker players to form pre-entry alliances, suggesting that more attractive partners are presented with more alliance opportunities and can therefore more easily enter into promising partnership agreements. This appears to be contradictory with Shan's (1990) conclusions. However, Mitchell and Singh (1992) also showed that latecomers into the new domain are more likely to collaborate. This suggests that alliance formation is induced by both a need, as argued previously by Shan (1990), and opportunities stemming from a firm's attractiveness as a potential partner.

Eisenhardt and Shoonhoven (1996) have explicitly built on this view, claiming that alliance formation is driven by both strategic needs and social opportunities. In a study on entrepreneurial semiconductor firms, they have shown that firms tend to enter alliance agreements when they are in a vulnerable strategic position, either because they are competing in emergent or highly competitive industries or because they are attempting pioneering technical strategies, which the authors interpret as denoting a strategic need. Eisenhardt and Shoonhoven (1996) also found that the studied firms were more likely to collaborate when they were in "strong social positions," that is, led by large, experienced, and well-connected top management teams, which they interpret as creating greater opportunities for collaboration.

The above-mentioned studies examined alliances formed by small innovative firms with established industry incumbents. Such a context creates a high degree of complementarity between potential partners, suggesting in turn that this complementarity is the primary driver of alliance formation. The general conclusion of these studies is twofold: those small innovating start-ups most likely to collaborate are the weaker or more vulnerable firms; in contrast, those industry incumbents most likely to cooperate with such start-ups are the stronger competitors. Indeed, all start-ups are potentially attractive partners because of the innovation they can contribute to the alliance; those most likely to cooperate are the firms that are the least able to exploit their innovation on their own. Conversely, most established incumbents seek innovations with which to expand their business, those most likely to cooperate are those in a position to cherry-pick and exploit the most promising innovations thanks to their manufacturing and commercial capabilities.

Ahuja (2000) extended the same line of reasoning to alliance formation among leading incumbents in a mature industry. Consistent with the above argument, he found that industry incumbents with the highest propensity to collaborate are those that have greater technical or commercial capital. Based on the argument that alliance formation is driven by both inducements and opportunities, he also found that simultaneous ownership of strong technical and commercial capital reduced a firm's propensity to collaborate. In other words, firms most likely to collaborate are those that are strong in some resource categories and seek a complement in some other resource category. Again, Ahuja (2000) found that opportunities to collaborate are a function of the firms' attractiveness and that collaboration is induced by some resource need. Though complementarity between the partners is not predetermined by the context of this study, resource complementarity is nevertheless conceptually seen as the main driver of alliance formation. Indeed, when firms are strong in all resource categories, opportunities for complementary alliances vanish, resulting in a decreased propensity to form alliances. Ahuja's (2000) empirical results on alliance activity among leading chemical firms confirmed this view.

In sum, all these studies on alliance formation have in fact focused on complementary (link) alliances. One of the main findings of these studies on complementary alliances is that those industry incumbents most likely to collaborate are the leading competitors in the industry. However, as mentioned earlier, theories on motivations for alliance formation argue that access to complementary resources is only one of two possible alliance motivations (e.g. Hennart, 1988). Empirical work on alliance activity in various industries supports this view by showing that both scale and link alliances co-exist in most industry settings, are formed by firms pertaining to different strategic groups and lead to contrasted outcomes (Nohria and Garcia-Pont, 1991; Dussauge et al., 2000, 2004).

Alliance Performance and Outcomes: A Focus on Interpartner Learning

Several perspectives have examined alliance performance and outcomes (Uzzi, 1996; Gulati, 1998). A first stream of research has focused on the success of the alliance itself and has often used alliance stability and duration as an indicator of success. A second stream of research has examined the impact of alliance outcomes on the involved partner firms and has focused on interpartner learning. In this approach, a partner's success in an alliance is evaluated by how much it has learned from the other partner.

Most early studies on the outcomes of joint ventures tried to identify factors that influence their duration and stability. Several studies have investigated joint venture equity distribution between the parent companies (Janger, 1980; Killing, 1982, 1983; Beamish, 1984, 1985; Beamish and Banks, 1987; Geringer and Hebert, 1989; Blodgett, 1992), with somewhat contradictory results. Other authors (Harrigan, 1988; Kogut, 1988, 1989; Park and Russo, 1996; Park and Ungson, 1997) examined the influence on joint venture duration and survival of factors such as partner asymmetries, joint venturing experience, joint venture scope, industry structure, R&D intensity, interpartner rivalry, and governance structure. More recent studies have suggested that joint venture survival should not stand as an implicit criterion of success. Instead, the more important issue is how the alliance affects the parent firms.

In this second stream of research, the focus shifts from the fate of the alliance itself to the consequences of allying for the partner firms. Several studies in this vein have emphasized in-depth case analyses (Hamel, 1991; Doz, 1996; Arino and de la Torre, 1998). Inspired by the resource-based view of the firm, many of these studies have insisted on the importance of learning and skill acquisition that tend to occur between the allied firms, especially in alliances among competitors (Doz, 1988; Hamel et al., 1989; Hamel, 1991; Kanter, 1994). A few larger sample studies have also explored the impact of alliance activity on the ongoing financial performance and survival of the parent businesses (Berg et al., 1982; Hagedoorn and Schakenraad, 1994; Mitchell and Singh, 1996; Singh and Mitchell, 1996). The studies report that parents often benefit from alliances, but that alliance activity also carries the risk of becoming dependent on a partner's capabilities. Khanna et al. (1998) stressed the impact of learning on the dynamics of alliances, linking the relative competitive or cooperative nature of the relationship to the extent to which the partners could exploit the skills they acquire in the alliance within the context of their own activities.

Overall, the research on alliance outcomes which has attempted to go beyond examining the fate of the alliance itself to evaluate the performance implications of the alliance for the partner firms has focused primarily on interpartner learning and capability acquisition as a measure of success. In doing so, this research has in fact assumed that alliance partners have an incentive to learn from each other, which in turn suggests that they have different capabilities. In addition, for alliances to lead to interpartner learning, they must create a context in which each partner has access to attractive capabilities possessed by the other. This in turn is made possible if the partner firms make different contributions to the joint activity, that is, have formed a link alliance. It thus appears that research on alliance outcomes and performance has primarily focused either on the fate of the alliance itself, without discriminating between types of alliances, or on the impact of collaboration on the involved firms in terms of learning and capability acquisition, focusing implicitly on link alliances. In contrast, very little research has explored the drivers of performance in scale alliances.

Toward a Resource-Based View of Scale Alliances

The classical resource-based approach (Penrose, 1959) suggests that a firm's resource endowment determines its growth. Indeed, according to Penrose (1959), most resources are fungible, that is, they can be redeployed to additional uses, other than the current one. The same argument has been applied to more intangible competences (Teece et al., 1997).

Because its main focus is on the growth of the firm, the resource-based view has primarily considered the use that firms can make of their excess resources. Pursuing this line of reasoning, subsequent work has examined how firms can leverage these excess resources by combining them with complementary resources possessed by other firms, when these complementary resources are not easily tradable (Teece, 1986). This view thus explains the formation of link alliances. In this perspective, link alliances are formed to pursue expansion opportunities at the frontiers of the partner firms' current businesses. As a consequence, firms engaged in link alliances have an incentive to reduce their dependence on their partner and to acquire or replicate, whenever possible, the resources they lack to carry out the new business on their own. Hence the above-mentioned focus on interpartner learning and capability acquisition as a determinant of alliance outcome and even as a criterion of success for the partner firms.

While the resource-based view has theorized the use of excess resources as a driver of firm growth, it has paid less attention to the implications of a firm's lack of resources. Indeed, existing firms in any business are assumed to possess a resource endowment which allows them to operate at an adequate level of performance. However, industry evolution and competitive dynamics may raise the minimum level of resources required to continue competing in the industry. The additional resources required may be different in nature, which then takes us back to the case examined above, or similar to those already possessed, but in greater quantities. When confronted with the latter challenge, firms must increase their stock of existing resources or disappear. They can acquire such additional resources on the market for resources (through hiring, investing in additional assets) or on the market for corporate control (through mergers and acquisitions). An alternative option is to pool their existing resources with those of other industry incumbents facing the same issue. Building on this logic, we propose that scale alliances are formed primarily by firms lacking sufficient quantities of similar resources within their core business. The main purpose of scale alliances is therefore survival, while the main purpose of link alliances is growth.

Indeed, combining different resources in link alliances often creates innovation opportunities (Brown and Eisenhardt, 1995) that allow the partner firms to extend the limits of their existing business, either by entering adjacent product-market areas or by substituting existing products and technologies with innovative ones. On the contrary, pooling greater quantities of similar resources in scale alliances enhances performance within the boundaries of the core business by improving efficiency on current product lines or by mobilizing sufficient resources to fuel the ongoing renewal of product lines. Innovation in scale alliances is not radically different from what each partner would have achieved on its own, had it had sufficient resources; innovation in link alliances stems from the combination of different resources contributed respectively by each partner and could not be achieved by any partner on its own. Most empirical research on alliances, which we argued focused on link alliances, viewed these alliances as mechanisms to take advantage of business opportunities that would have been outside the reach of each partner on its own: Mitchell and Singh (1992) examined how alliances between incumbents and innovators allow entry into new technical sub-fields of the industry; Shan (1990), as well as Eisenhardt and Schoonhoven (1996), studied how start-ups and established competitors collaborate in order to market new technologies. The few studies that explicitly considered scale alliances and contrasted them with link alliances (Nohria and Garcia-Pont, 1991; Dussauge and Garrette, 1995; Dussauge et al., 2000, 2004) showed that scale alliances are formed by direct competitors exhibiting similar features (size, geographic origin, etc.), all facing similar issues, which choose to collaborate in order to maintain or enhance their position in their core business.

The Formation of Scale Alliances

Because of the distinctive resource features of scale and link alliances, the decision to form one or the other type of alliance is an alternative to radically different baseline strategies. Scale alliances are essentially an alternative to autonomous production in the firm's core business. Link alliances in contrast are formed primarily to pursue new business developments that would be left aside if no partnering opportunities were available. In other words, in scale alliances, partnering firms face the choice of collaborating or going it alone; in link alliances, partnering firms face the choice of collaborating or forgoing a new business opportunity. In a context where it might consider forming a scale alliance, a firm possessing resources in sufficient quantities is more likely to choose autonomous production over collaboration because of the financial, organizational and strategic cost of cooperating with a competitor (e.g. Hamel, 1991). If in turn, the considered firm lacks sufficient resources and rejects collaboration, it will be forced to give up the considered investment altogether and therefore compromise its ongoing presence in entire areas of its core business, unless it is willing to consider merging with other incumbents. In a position where it might consider forming a link alliance, most firms will not have the option of pursuing the same new business opportunity on their own, at least in the short run. In such a context, a firm can choose not to form the alliance and not to implement the considered project, without jeopardizing its position in its core business. In this case, taking advantage of such a business opportunity alone will require the acquisition of different resources, and therefore lead to either long-term investments to develop such resources internally or to the acquisition of an existing firm that possesses the needed resources. Overall, scale alliances are primarily defensive in nature while link alliances support more offensive strategies. It can be noted here that scale and link alliances are not substitutes for one another. In other words, a firm is almost never confronted with the choice of

Table 2.1   Scale versus link alliances

	Link alliances	Scale alliances
Initial conditions	Partners possess complementary resources	Both partners lack resources
Partners' contributions	Complementary assets and skills	Similar assets and skills
Partners' relative size	Unbalanced	Balanced
Partners' competitive positions	Strong competitors with some resource gaps	Weaker incumbents
Motivation, expected benefits	Access to new skills and capability appropriation	Scale economies in current business
Main purpose	Expansion into adjacent businesses	Survival in existing business
Dominant logic	Offensive	Defensive
Alternative option	Forgo the expansion opportunity	Go it alone
Dynamics	Race to learn	Mutual specialization
Outcome	Internalization by one partner	Stability/renewal
Managerial recommendation	Take over joint activity or maximize price of exit	Optimize efficiency

forming either a scale or a link alliance. Instead, firms face one of the following two choices: (1) forming a scale alliance or producing autonomously, or (2) forming a link alliance or not engaging in the considered project.

Given the differences between scale and link alliances outlined above (see also Table 2.1), it is unlikely that those factors leading firms to form link alliances will also motivate the formation of scale alliances. As most past research on alliance formation has implicitly focused on link alliances, their conclusions may not be generalizable to all alliance types. Research focusing specifically on the formation of scale alliances would contribute to a broader understanding of collaboration as an alternative to other strategic and organizational choices. In addition, most existing research has examined the propensity of firms to collaborate, and has thus compared collaboration to non-collaboration, which implicitly includes both producing alone and not engaging in the considered project. Our focus on scale alliances leads us to contrast firms choosing to collaborate with firms choosing to produce autonomously.

Contrary to complementary alliances where reciprocal strengths and weaknesses drive alliance formation, scale alliances are built on similar weaknesses in all partners. The very co-existence of similar needs in multiple industry incumbents creates the opportunity for collaboration. Indeed, if several firms are simultaneously hindered by a constrained stock of resources, they have a mutual incentive to pool their resources in order to undertake activities jointly. While the benefits of scale advantages can theoretically accrue to all industry incumbents, the costs of collaboration create a disincentive to collaborate. Collaboration costs include transaction costs, coordination costs, the risks associated with mutual dependence as well as a competitive risk (Hamel, 1991; White and Lui, 2005). Only those firms that most need additional stocks of given resources contributed by other partners will engage in scale alliances. Stronger competitors have the option to produce on their own while weaker competitors may often be faced with the alternative of either forming an alliance or giving up the considered activity. Moreover, stronger firms will be reluctant to enter into scale alliances because the costs and risks involved will more than outweigh the expected benefits. Hence the following proposition:

> P1: Scale alliances are predominantly formed by weaker competitors seeking to maintain or enhance their position in their core business.

The Performance and Outcomes of Scale Alliances

Because scale alliances are formed to compensate for a resource weakness of all partner firms in their core business, their performance must be benchmarked against the performance of similar activities undertaken by single firms. If the performance of activities undertaken in the context of scale alliances were systematically greater than the performance of single-firm activities, we would expect scale alliances to become the predominant form of organization. Therefore we propose that scale alliances, while allowing firms to undertake an activity that they could not undertake alone, will tend to exhibit lower performance than similar activities undertaken on a single-firm basis. More specifically, we argue that, provided the partner firms have pooled together the required resources, an activity undertaken as a scale alliance has a similar likelihood of commercial success as an activity undertaken by a single firm. Indeed, all products or services that reach the market compete on similar grounds irrespective of the fact that they originate in a scale alliance or in a single firm. As, in scale alliances, we assume out any resource complementarity between the partners, alliances create no greater opportunities for generating superior products than single firms and vice versa. However, as mentioned above, collaboration creates specific costs: negotiation costs, monitoring costs, and coordination costs. We therefore expect scale alliances to incur specific costs not supported by single-firm activities. On this basis, we formulate the two following propositions:

> P2a: Activities undertaken in the context of scale alliances are equally likely to meet with commercial success as activities undertaken on a single-firm basis.
>
> P2b: Activities undertaken in the context of scale alliances entail higher costs than single-firm activities.

In sum, the commercial performance of scale alliances being similar to that of single-firm activities while their costs are higher, the overall performance of scale alliances is likely to be lower than that of single-firm activities. This is consistent with our prediction concerning the formation of scale alliances: scale alliances are only attractive for those firms that lack the resources required to carry out the activity on their own. Moreover, our predictions on scale alliance performance differ from existing views on the performance of link alliances. Indeed, because of the complementarity in the resources that they leverage, link alliances make it possible to pursue new business opportunities without making a commensurate investment. Therefore the performance of activities carried out in the context of link alliances is likely to exceed that of single-firm activities.

Evidence from Aircraft Production

To provide empirical support for the above propositions, we examined new aircraft launches in the global aerospace industry between 1949 and 2000. We studied 334 new aircraft projects undertaken either through alliances or on a single-firm basis by all 130 major aircraft manufacturers in the Western hemisphere. In this industry, we considered as horizontal alliances those projects that were carried out by several firms sharing the prime contracting responsibility. In contrast to collaborative projects, we defined as autonomous projects those projects that were implemented under the authority of a single prime contractor. This definition of autonomous production does not preclude outsourcing large parts of the project to suppliers, including through vertical partnerships.

Sharing the prime contracting responsibility in aircraft production results in the formation of scale alliances since all prime contracting partners contribute resources in all major functional areas: R&D, manufacturing, marketing, and sales. Because the industry is characterized by considerable and ever increasing economies of scale, new aircraft projects require the mobilization of huge resources that may be beyond the reach of any individual company even when the company in question has produced similar products in the past. The resources required to launch a new project include both tangible and intangible resources such as R&D facilities and capabilities, manufacturing assets, and access to large enough markets.

As expected in proposition P1, we found that aircraft manufacturers are more likely to form scale alliances rather than to autonomously undertake a new aircraft project when:

- They are small relative to their industry peers.
- They have access to a smaller market base.
- Their experience in the considered product category is more limited.

These results support the idea according to which scale alliances are primarily formed by weaker competitors.

As expected in propositions P2a and P2b, and using production runs as an indicator of commercial success and development time as an indicator of project costs, we found that:

- aircraft produced through a scale alliance achieve similar production runs as comparable aircraft produced by a single prime contractor;
- aircraft produced through a scale alliance have longer development times than comparable aircraft produced by a single prime contractor.

These results support the idea according to which scale alliances make it possible for weaker firms to close the gap on commercial performance with larger competitors, but entail additional costs specific to collaboration. In sum, scale alliances appear as a second best option for weaker firms to survive and maintain a viable position in the industry despite their unfavorable resource endowment.

Conclusion

Overall, while interpartner learning and capability appropriation are critical issues in many alliances, it is risky to generalize these concerns to all types of cooperation. We believe our argument and our results support the idea according to which these issues are primarily associated with link alliances which are formed when partner firms contribute complementary skills and assets to their joint endeavor. Interestingly, most of the research on alliances and networks has focused on such link alliances. This has led many authors to consider that value was created in alliances by combining and transferring knowledge across firm boundaries while particular positions in a network of alliances made it possible to capture more value by controlling a greater flow of knowledge (Burt, 1992; 2004). Conversely, the main risk associated with link alliances rests in the potential appropriation of a firm's valuable skills by its partners. In contrast, we suggest that scale alliances, which co-exist with link alliances in many industries and are the dominant form of collaboration in some sectors (Dussauge and Garrette, 1999), correspond to a radically different logic: value in scale alliances is created through the pooling of similar resources. These alliances allow weaker competitors to maintain a position in their core business. Learning in such alliances is only a marginal phenomenon, and is more akin to fine-tuning existing capabilities through benchmarking with similar partners than to gaining access to entirely new areas of expertise. The challenge in scale alliances is not to protect proprietary know-how but to limit the costs of collaboration in such a way that the efficiency gap with larger competitors is bridged.

Acknowledgement

The authors are members of the GREGHEC – CNRS – UMR 2959 research center and acknowledge the research support of the Atos-Origin Chair on Growth Strategies and Integration Management.

References

Ahuja, G. (2000) The duality of collaboration: Inducements and opportunities in the formation of interfirm linkages. *Strategic Management Journal*, 21(3), 317–43.

Arino, A. & de la Torre, J. (1998) Learning from failure: Towards an evolutionary model of collaborative ventures. *Organization Science*, 9(3), 306–25.

Beamish, P. W. (1984) Joint venture performance in developing countries. Doctoral dissertation, University of Western Ontario.

Beamish, P. W. (1985) The characteristics of joint ventures in developed and developing countries. *Columbia Journal of World Business*, 20, 13–19.

Beamish, P. W. & Banks, J. C. (1987) Equity joint ventures and the theory of the multinational enterprise. *Journal of International Business Studies*, 18, 1–16.

Berg, S. V., Duncan, J. & Friedman, P.(1982) *Joint Venture Strategies and Corporate Innovation.* Cambridge, MA: Oelgeschlager.

Berg, S. & Friedman, P. (1978) Technological complementarities and industrial patterns of joint venture activity, 1964–1975. *Industrial Organization Review*, 6, 110–16.

Berg, S. & Friedman, P. (1981) Impacts of domestic joint ventures on industrial rates of return: A pooled cross-section analysis. *Review of Economics and Statistics*, 63, 293–8.

Blodgett, L. L. (1992) Factors in the instability of international joint ventures: An event history analysis. *Strategic Management Journal*, 13, 475–81.

Brown, S. & Eisenhardt, K. (1995) Product development: Past research, present findings, and future prospects. *Academy of Management Review*, 20, 343–79.

Burgers, W. P., Hill, C. W. L., Kim, W. C. (1993) A theory of global strategic alliances: The case of the global auto industry. *Strategic Management Journal*, 14(6), 419–32.

Burt, R. S. (1992) *Structural Holes: The Social Structure of Competition.* Cambridge, MA: Harvard University Press.

Burt, R. S. (2004) Structural holes and good ideas. *American Journal of Sociology*, 110, 349–99.

Contractor, F. J. & Lorange, P. (1988) Why should firms cooperate? The strategy and economics basis for cooperative ventures. In F. J. Contractor and P. Lorange (Eds.) *Cooperative Strategies in International Business*, 3–31. Lexington, MA: Lexington Books.

Doz, Y. L. (1988) Technology partnerships between larger and smaller firms: Some critical issues. In F. J. Contractor and P. Lorange (Eds.) *Cooperative Strategies in International Business*, 317–38. Lexington, MA: Lexington Books.

Doz, Y. L. (1996) The evolution of cooperation in strategic alliances: Initial conditions, or learning processes? *Strategic Management Journal*, 17, 55–83.

Dussauge, P. & Garrette, B. (1995) Determinants of success in international strategic alliances: Evidence from the global aerospace industry. *Journal of International Business Studies*, 26(3), 505–30.

Dussauge, P. & Garrette, B. (1999) *Cooperative Strategy.* Chichester, UK: Wiley.

Dussauge, P., Garrette, B. & Mitchell, W. (2000) Learning from competing partners: Outcomes and durations of scale and link alliances in Europe, North America and Asia. *Strategic Management Journal*, 21(2), 99–126.

Dussauge, P., Garrette, B. & Mitchell, W. (2004) Asymmetric performance: The market share impact of scale and link alliances in the global auto industry. *Strategic Management Journal*, 25(7), 701–11.

Eisenhardt, K. M. & Schoonhoven, C. B. (1996) Resource-based view of strategic alliance formation: Strategic and social effects in entrepreneurial firms. *Organization Science*, 7(2), 136–50.

Geringer, J. M. & Hebert, L. (1989) Control and performance of international joint ventures. *Journal of International Business Studies*, 20, 235–54.

Ghemawat, P., Porter, M. E. & Rawlinson, M. E. (1986) Patterns of international coalition activity. In M. E. Porter (Ed.) *Competition in Global Industries*, 345–66. Boston, MA: Harvard Business School Press.

Gulati, R. (1998) Alliances and networks. *Strategic Management Journal*, 19(4) (Special Issue: Editor's Choice), 293–317.

Hagedoorn, J. & Schakenraad, J. (1994) The effect of strategic technology alliances on company performance.*Strategic Management Journal*, 15, 291–310.

Hamel, G. (1991) Competition for competence and inter-partner learning within international strategic alliances. *Strategic Management Journal*, 12 (Special Issue: Global Strategy), 83–103.

Hamel, G., Doz, Y. L. & Prahalad, C. K. (1989) Collaborate with your competitors – and win. *Harvard Business Review*, 67(1), 133–9.

Harrigan, K. R. (1985) *Strategies for Joint Ventures*. Lexington, MA: Lexington Books.

Harrigan, K. R. (1988) Joint ventures and competitive strategy. *Strategic Management Journal*, 9(2), 141–58.

Hennart, J.-F. (1988) A transaction costs theory of equity joint ventures. *Strategic Management Journal*, 9(4), 361–74.

Hergert, M. & Morris, D. (1987) Trends in international collaborative agreements. *Columbia Journal of World Business*, 22, 15–21.

Janger, A. H. (1980) *Organizations of International Joint Ventures*. New York: Conference Board.

Kanter, R. M. (1994) Collaborative advantage: The art of alliances. *Harvard Business Review*, 72, 96–108.

Khanna, T., Gulati, R. & Noria, N. (1998) The dynamics of learning alliances: Competition, cooperation and relative scope. *Strategic Management Journal*, 19, 193–210.

Killing, J. P. (1982) How to make a global joint venture work. *Harvard Business Review*, 60, 120–7.

Killing, J. P. (1983) *Strategies for Joint Venture Success*, New York: Praeger.

Kogut, B. (1988) Joint ventures: Theoretical and empirical perspectives. *Strategic Management Journal*, 9(4), 319–32.

Kogut, B. (1989) The stability of joint ventures: Reciprocity and competitive rivalry. *The Journal of Industrial Economics*, 38(2), 183–98.

Mariti, P. & Smiley, R. H. (1983) Cooperative agreements and the organization of industry. *Journal of Industrial Economics*, 31(4), 437–51.

Mitchell, W. & Singh, K. (1992) Incumbents' use of pre-entry alliances before expansion into new technical subfields of an industry. *Journal of Economic Behavior and Organization*, 18, 347–72.

Mitchell, W. & Singh, K. (1996) Survival of businesses using collaborative relationships to commercialize complex goods. *Strategic Management Journal*, 17, 169–95.

Mitchell, W., Shaver, J. M. & Yeung, B. (1992) Getting there in a global industry: Impacts on performance of changing international presence. *Strategic Management Journal*, 13(6), 419–32.

Nohria, N. & Garcia-Pont, C. (1991) Global strategic linkages and industry structure. *Strategic Management Journal*, 12 (Special Issue: Global Strategy), 105–24.

Park, S. H. & Russo, M. V. (1996) When competition eclipses cooperation: An event history analysis of joint venture failure. *Management Science*, 42, 875–90.

Park, S. H. & Ungson, G. R. (1997) The effect of national culture, organizational complementarity, and economic motivation on joint venture dissolution. *Academy of Management Journal*, 40, 279–307.

Penrose, E. T. (1959) *The Theory of Growth of the Firm*, London: Basil Blackwell.

Porter, M. E. & Fuller, M. B. (1986) Coalitions and global strategies. In M. E. Porter (Ed.) *Competition in Global Industries*, 315–43. Boston, MA: Harvard Business School Press.

Prahalad, C. K. & Hamel, G. (1990) The core competence of the corporation. *Harvard Business Review*, 68(3), 79–92.

Sakakibara, M. (1997) Heterogeneity of firm capabilities and cooperative research and development: An empirical examination of motives. *Strategic Management Journal*, 18 (Summer 1997 Special Issue: Organizational and Competitive Interactions), 143–64.

Shan, W. (1990) An empirical analysis of organizational strategies by entrepreneurial high-technology firms. *Strategic Management Journal*, 11(2), 129–39.

Singh, K. & Mitchell, W. (1996) Precarious collaboration: Business survival after partners shut down or form new partnerships. *Strategic Management Journal*, 17 (Special Issue on Evolutionary Perspectives on Strategy), 95–115.

Teece, D. J. (1986) Profiting from technological innovation. *Research Policy*, 15, 285–305.

Teece, D. J., Pisano, G. & Shuen, A. (1997) Dynamic capabilities and strategic management. *Strategic Management Journal*, 18, 509–33.

Uzzi, B. (1996) The sources and consequences of embeddedness for the economic performance of organizations: The network effect. *American Sociological Review*, 61, 674–98.

White, S. & Lui, S. S. Y. (2005) Distinguishing costs of cooperation and control in alliances. *Strategic Management Journal*, 26(10), 913–32.

CHAPTER THREE

Teaching in Supplier Networks

Lars-Erik Gadde and Håkan Håkansson

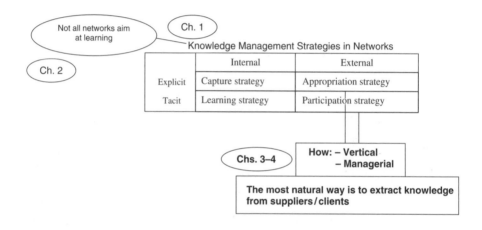

Abstract

Knowledge exchange and purchasing are two management issues that are strongly inter-twined. It is only recently, however, that they have come to be regarded as interrelated, in turn leading to enhanced emphasis on learning and teaching. In this chapter two mini-cases – about IKEA and Volvo Cars – are used to illustrate learning and teaching in supply networks as a complement to a more general discussion of these issues in individual sup-plier relationships. The main conclusions is that a buying firm may benefit considerably from encouraging learning and teaching processes both in single relationships and in the total supply network.

Introduction

"The essence of the firm is its ability to create, transfer, assemble, integrate, and exploit knowledge assets" (Teece, 1998: 75). This quotation is representative of a general view, developed during recent decades, of the enhanced importance of the knowledge dimension in business. Contemporary management issues relate to organizational learning, strategies for knowledge intensive companies, and marketing of high tech products, particularly in terms of software. Handling these complex issues requires a multitude of technologies, of which the individual company can have expertise in only a few. Technical developments in other areas of importance are therefore exploited through alliances and relationships with other firms, making knowledge exchange among firms a crucial issue. However, most companies strive to be more than passive recipients of knowledge. To be able to make the best use of technology they also aim to influence and control the technical development efforts of other firms. Therefore, the individual company needs to be involved in a number of important knowledge issues and knowledge processes.

A great deal of management attention has also been paid in recent years to the supply side of the company. The enhanced focus on core competence is accompanied by massive outsourcing of activities and partnering with suppliers, putting purchasing at the top of the management agenda. Critical issues in this respect are development and management of appropriate relationships with individual suppliers and coordination of these relationships into supply networks (Gadde and Håkansson, 2001).

These two management issues – knowledge exchange and purchasing – are obviously strongly intertwined. For example, the potential contribution of purchasing to the knowledge expansion of the firm might be formulated as increasing utilization of suppliers' technical competence and abilities in order to improve process and product development in the buying firm. However, only recently have purchasing and knowledge acquisition come to be regarded as interrelated (e.g. Hult et al., 2003; Wynstra et al., 2003), with a consequent emphasis on learning and teaching.

Learning and teaching in supplier networks

One reason for the increasing attention paid to the interplay between purchasing and knowledge exchange has to do with changes in the division of labor between supplier and customer. Suppliers have become increasingly involved in their customers' product development. Contributions based on the technical capabilities of vendors have become crucial to buying companies, as technical issues have become increasingly important in purchasing (see e.g. Ghingold and Johnson, 1997). Learning from suppliers is thus a main concern for buying firms in this respect. In the UK motor industry it has been found that no less than 93 percent of the car assemblers and component manufacturers used their suppliers as technology providers (Beecham and Cordey-Hayes, 1998).

Albino et al. (1998) illustrate the crucial role of knowledge exchange between firms in what has been identified as "industrial districts." The performance of the companies in such districts was shown to be strongly dependent on efficacious knowledge transfer. The "leader firm" of the district needs technical input from small and specialized companies. In order to obtain this information the central firm must stimulate knowledge transfer from suppliers by "teaching" them what is important in this respect. Ernst and Kim (2002) arrive at the same conclusion from a different perspective, showing how the development of "global production networks" increases the need for knowledge transfer to suppliers. Large multinational corporations tend to "break down the value chain into a variety of discrete functions and locate them wherever they can be carried out most effectively, where they improve the firm's access to resources and capabilities and where they are needed to facilitate the penetration of important growth markets" (Ernst and Kim, 2002: 1420). These characteristics imply a dispersed production structure and greater dependence on local suppliers in different geographical areas. Efficiency in these global production networks requires transfer of technical and managerial knowledge to local suppliers to upgrade their skills to meet the technical specifications of the large customer. Assisting these suppliers' development in various respects is thus a prerequisite for the performance of the buying firm. Helping suppliers to learn by actively teaching them has therefore become important to customers.

Aim and scope of the chapter

The purpose of this chapter is to explore the role of teaching in supply networks. We begin by discussing knowledge exchange in three types of purchasing situations with different characteristics. In this part of the chapter we conclude that the reason for the limited attention to the interplay between purchasing and knowledge exchange has to do with buyers' approaches to suppliers in two of these situations.

The remaining part of the chapter deals with the third approach, where buyer and supplier are actively involved in stimulating knowledge exchange and capability development across the boundaries of the two companies. These efforts include the ambitions of the buying firm to influence suppliers to work in areas of common interest as well as the buying firm's adaptations in relation to how suppliers change and develop. In order to get the best out of this collaboration, suppliers and buyers have to influence one another actively. We continue the chapter by delving into these processes by first examining the needs and benefits related to teaching individual suppliers. In the final part of the chapter, building on two case studies, we deal with teaching in networks of suppliers.

Knowledge Exchange in Three Purchasing Situations

In order to illustrate how knowledge issues have been related to purchasing we identify three "theoretical" purchasing approaches. The first is the buying situation, which can be defined as the "classical" one, as it is represented by the approach utilized when something is purchased from a market. This approach has also been used for normative recommendations – something buying companies should strive for. The second approach is when a manufacturing company uses a supplier as an external production unit, that is, outsourcing part of its own operations. This situation can be regarded as almost the opposite of the first one, because the relationship between buyer and supplier is almost hierarchical, since in many of these situations the buyer prescribes the features of the product that is exchanged. The third approach builds on the assumption that buyer and supplier, through close interaction, strive to utilize their joint capabilities in order to find efficient solutions.

Purchasing from a market

Purchasing from a market means that buying companies search for what they need among the products and services available on the market. The products and services are thus perceived as "givens" and the buyer compares these potential solutions and selects one. This is the prescription for "rational" behavior that purchasers have historically been recommended to follow – to specify exactly what they want and then put out a call for tenders. The bids are then compared and the best offer – normally the least expensive – is chosen.

In this situation there is little need for knowledge exchange between buyer and supplier, which is the reason the market is assumed to be efficient. The buying side adapts its requirements to its internal conditions and to what is available on the market. Suppliers develop their offerings on the basis of their internal capabilities in the direction of some general idea about demand. Knowledge development basically takes place within each company and there is no reason for extensive information or knowledge exchange. Such exchange situations are normally restricted to sending and receiving price signals.

These conditions lead to arm's-length relationships between buyer and supplier, which has long been regarded as the most efficient type of interaction. Consequently, the interplay between knowledge development and purchasing has not been a major issue, in a situation where knowledge of use is perceived as more or less unrelated to knowledge of production. The market mechanism is assumed to direct the division of labor which, in turn, determines the process of knowledge exchange. The outcome of these processes is that the supplier and the buyer are characterized by very clear knowledge boundaries.

Purchasing as outsourcing production

The second approach is completely different from the first. In this case the buying company makes use of a supplier as part of its own production structure – that is, choosing the strategy of "buy" rather than "make" – but retaining the decision about what is to be made. The buyer specifies the design of the product and asks for someone to produce the item specified. These conditions are typical in traditional subcontracting, where large buying companies specify exactly what smaller specialized suppliers are supposed to manufacture. This, too, is quite a simple process concerning knowledge exchange. The buyer has all the knowledge about the solution needed, the supplier knows about the production process required, and the specification connects the two. Therefore, it is basically a question of buying production capacity and there is only a limited need for knowledge exchange between the two companies, primarily scheduling and delivery information.

In these buyer-supplier relationships, the buying company handles knowledge issues and is responsible for knowledge-related problems. In this situation, too, the knowledge boundary between buyer and supplier is clear, and is the outcome of a managerial process.

Purchasing involving extensive knowledge exchange

In both the above cases the need for interaction and exchange of knowledge between the two parties is limited. Accordingly, the knowledge residing within the boundaries of buyer and supplier is quite different, and complementary. When these conditions are at hand business exchange is very efficient because few, if any, dedicated investments are required for the interaction and transactions, as long as the current division of knowledge is maintained.

However, there are situations when increasing interaction and knowledge exchange will pay off. For example, buyer and supplier may jointly develop the specification of the solution required. In this case the user needs to be aware of the opportunities on the production side, and the producer needs to know more about the context on the user side. In these situations both parties benefit, because the value of the interaction increases. Buyer and supplier will need to become involved in knowledge exchange, knowledge sharing and knowledge creation. This requires that both sides develop the relationship in order to make the knowledge process function – arm's-length conditions are not appropriate in these situations.

In this type of exchange, the knowledge boundary is much more diffuse and the two parties must have overlapping knowledge. What is even more important is the fact that the value of this knowledge is relative – the value of the knowledge of one of the firms is dependent on the knowledge developed by the business partner.

Purchasing and Knowledge Exchange

Historically, there is no question that purchasing has been regarded as belonging to the first of the three types of exchange (see e.g. Gadde and Håkansson, 2001). Buying companies have been recommended to avoid becoming dependent on individual sources. Moreover, they have been encouraged to stimulate competition among multiple suppliers through various tendering procedures. Purchasing was generally considered mainly a commercial process and purchasers thus more of businessmen than technicians. This way of perceiving purchasing is still very common and is justified when the costs of developing a relationship in the direction of enhanced knowledge exchange exceed the potential benefits.

The second type of exchange involves more knowledge-related issues than the first. However, as discussed above, there is little need for exchange of knowledge because the buyer decides about the specifications for the solution. An alternative approach related to this situation is when the buyer specifies the functionality of the solution rather than its detailed characteristics. In this case the directions from the buyer leave a great deal of freedom for the supplier to develop the solution (Araujo et al., 1999). The responsibility of the supplier is enhanced in this situation, but can be accomplished without major efforts in terms of knowledge exchange.

As described in the beginning of the chapter our main interest is in the third type of exchange – where the parties are involved in extensive interaction and knowledge exchange. This situation is more difficult for the buying company to handle than the two others but it also involves greater potential, because suppliers may contribute considerably to both productivity and innovation for a customer (e.g. Carlisle and Parker, 1989; Lamming, 1993; Nishiguchi, 1994; Gadde and Håkansson, 2001). These benefits, however, do not follow automatically, because suppliers are often only as good as they have to be and buying firms often "deserve what they get" from suppliers because they have not asked for more (Leenders and Blenkhorn, 1988). In order to realize the potential of supplier contributions, buying firms have to influence suppliers through teaching – particularly if prevailing purchasing behavior has been characterized by arm's-length relationships and specifications from the buyer's side.

Teaching Suppliers

As long as the main mission of purchasing was to avoid too much involvement with vendors, the development of suppliers was not a big issue. The term "supplier development" first appeared almost forty years ago, but the meaning of supplier development in that article was identification of new sources (Leenders, 1966). Once the view of efficiency in purchasing was reinterpreted (see e.g. Gadde and Persson, 2004) the perception of suppliers and their potential contributions changed. "Supplier development" has more recently been defined as "any effort of a buying firm with its suppliers to increase the performance and/or capabilities of the supplier and meet the buying firm's short- and/or long-term supply needs" (Krause and Ellram, 1996: 21). Various examples of supplier development were presented in studies in the 1990s, for example short-term improvement of product features (e.g. Watts and Hahn, 1993) and more long-term oriented attempts to increase the capability of suppliers (e.g. Hahn et al., 1989).

The actions required for successful supplier development programs has been described in different ways (see, for example, Krause and Ellram, 1996; De Toni and Nassimbeni, 2000). For our discussion we use the following dimensions to illustrate how buyers can be involved in teaching suppliers:

- supplier monitoring and evaluation;
- supplier assistance and training;
- effective two-way communication;
- cross-functional teams;
- supplier incentives and motivation.

Successful implementation of these supplier development efforts calls for a long-term orientation and a total cost perspective on both sides. Motivation and incentives are important because supplier development represents investments not only for the buyer but also for suppliers.

Monitoring and evaluation

Lamming et al. (1996) discuss supplier monitoring and evaluation in terms of "vendor assessment programs." The basic idea underpinning such programs is that information obtained in supplier assessments can be used to help the supplier improve performance. The customer conducts the assessments and then interprets and communicates the findings to the supplier and takes a leading role in the development process. A relevant illustration of the dimensions evaluated in such assessments is the list of criteria developed by Kodak for the monitoring of their supplier partnerships (see Box 3.1).

> **Box 3.1**   Kodak's supplier evaluation criteria
>
> - Amount of technical support
> - Number of innovative ideas
> - Supplier's ability to communicate effectively on important issues
> - Flexibility shown by the supplier
> - Cycle time, responsiveness and improvements shown
> - Supplier identification with Kodak goals
> - Level of trust
> - Strength of the relationship at each plant
>
> *Source*: Ellram and Edis (1996: 25).

When the performance level of the supplier does not meet expectations and standards at Kodak, various measures are taken to improve conditions. Similar arrangements are established by other large firms. For example, Harley Davidson reports that the company has ongoing continuous improvement activities where teams are sent out to suppliers to review their processes. When a supplier is not doing well HD makes suggestions for improvements, and allocates resources for their achievement, for example calling in consultants (Gadde and Håkansson, 2001). These responses stand in contrast to traditional buying behavior where, in similar situations, the customer tended to switch to another supplier. One common implication of supplier evaluation and assessment is that training is required for performance improvements.

Assistance and training

Supplier training programs have been shown to be one of the most important means of enhancing supplier capabilities. For example, De Toni and Nassimbeni (2000) found that supplier assistance and training was the only element of the supplier development program that supported all three capability improvements analyzed in their study. One typical illustration of these activities is the supplier training programs put in place by Motorola in the early 1990s. This company had reorganized its own internal production structure to gain from advancements in manufacturing techniques and factory layout, in particular related to total quality management. To get the most out of this reorganization Motorola had to involve its suppliers because, according to company representatives, suppliers "affect quality more than any other factor in the equation" (Gadde and Håkansson, 1993: 112). Therefore, the performance of suppliers needed to be improved in terms of quality, technological capability, and just-in-time (JIT) supply. Formalized training and education were important tools in this supplier development program based on the internal courses Motorola had implemented in its own organization. The most important training involved statistical process control, design for manufacturability, and short-cycle management (including JIT). Initially, this training was not compulsory but later Motorola required suppliers to take these courses if they wanted to remain suppliers. The results achieved from the training programs were perceived by Motorola representatives to be considerable – within a few weeks of basic training suppliers had made dramatic strides towards improved quality.

However, there are possible problems related to the perception of supplier assessment and training. Lamming et al. (1996) found that what the customer regarded as developmental cooperation was sometimes perceived by suppliers as an element of a coercive strategy on the part of the buying firm. Customer ambitions in this respect therefore need to be accompanied by incentives of various types, particularly if the buyer's behavior was previously characterized by an adversarial approach.

Effective two-way communication

Vendor assessments and training programs are formalized, direct means of stimulating knowledge exchange. Such efforts are often supplemented with less formalized and more indirect means of strengthening supplier capabilities. Examples of such activities were included in the Motorola development program described above, and they seem to be representative of what many buying firms do in relation to their suppliers. One means of improving two-way communication was to establish a "supplier advisory board," where a core of selected suppliers were given the opportunity to respond to the Motorola requirements and come up with ideas of their own. The annual supplier conferences, involving top managers from Motorola as speakers, provide a forum for exchange of information and insights into various business activities. Technical symposia and seminars have similar functions with regard to exchange of technical information. At these seminars representatives of both the buyer and the suppliers present new tools and equipment.

IBM uses seminars similarly to make their own technology converge with the technology of their suppliers (see e.g. Gadde and Håkansson, 2001). This process takes the form of two-day seminars where technicians from suppliers and purchasers and designers from IBM meet to keep each other informed about ongoing development projects. Other companies' informal arrangements include supplier and customer visits at the business partners' plants. For example, Okada (2004) describes such joint activities with people representing Suzuki in Japan and the suppliers of their Indian automotive plants. Sometimes these arrangements gradually become formalized and long term and buyer representatives stay with suppliers for extensive time periods. Similar expatriate arrangements are reported from the footwear industry, for example, involving Nike and its Korean operations (Donaghu and Barff, 1990).

Cross-functional teams

Cross-functional teams in the buying organization have been identified as important contributors to supplier development (e.g. Krause and Ellram, 1996), because of the wide range of activities involved in these programs, requiring expertise from various specialties. Over time the need for interaction among the various functions in the buying company has increased. The purchasing task has become more complex, calling for interaction between purchasing and the technical functions of the company, particularly in product development projects. By involving supplier representatives in these teams lead times and costs in product development processes have been reduced, resulting in short-term improvements. The interaction between these functional teams crossing the boundaries of firms may result in substantial capability enhancement as well. One important contribution is that these arrangements bring in issues of relevance from different perspectives in the design phase. The issues highlighted are sometimes conflicting, because the various functions tend to reflect diverse opinions concerning both what the appropriate features of the product should be and in what ways they are best created (Sobek et al., 1998).

Cross-functional teams are a way of integrating buyer and supplier operations directly. An indirect organizational arrangement with the same objective is the establishment of a "Key account management" function with responsibility for coordinating the buying company's involvement with the supplier by integrating the supplier into the buying organization. Key account functions have previously been more common on the selling side, but are now increasingly observed on the purchasing side. This type of organizational solution has been shown to impact on knowledge exchange and learning, particularly in global settings (Harvey et al., 2003).

Incentives and motivation

Supplier development programs impose costs on buying firms, which are assumed to be outweighed by future benefits owing to performance improvements from suppliers. However, development programs also lead to increasing costs for suppliers. High involvement with buyers is a matter of investment, and suppliers cannot be expected to engage in these activities unless they see the benefits for themselves associated with closer cooperation. Therefore, suppliers must be motivated and encouraged to become involved in learning experiences. A study of pitfalls in supplier development identified insufficient inducements to suppliers as one of the main problems (Handfield et al., 2000).

Supplier advisory boards, supplier conferences, and seminars are examples of instruments for motivation. However, the most important incentive for a supplier is the prospect of more business in the future. Learning from a customer how to improve performance is obviously one way of strengthening the relationship and fostering future business with this actual "teacher." But there are additional benefits to be gained from these activities. Enhanced understanding of the directions and needs of a demanding buyer gives the supplier insights that may be useful for developing business with other buying firms with similar requirements. Other incentive arrangements proposed in the literature include, for example, contractual forms including extended duration and financial conditions that take suppliers' increasing costs into account (De Toni and Nassimbeni, 2000). Krause and Ellram (1997) argue that supplier recognition in terms of "certification" or "preferred supplier status" can serve as important motivational factors.

Discussion

The analysis above shows that buying firms have obvious reasons to be involved in the teaching of their suppliers. These teaching activities concern modification and improvements of day-to-day activities, as well as more long-term capability enhancement including operations in manufacturing, logistics, product design, and development. Krause and Ellram (1997) investigated the occurrence and effects of supplier development programs in a study of 527 US firms. The study shows that buying firms demonstrating greater willingness to cooperate with suppliers and to invest more time and more resources in development programs achieved superior results compared with buying firms that interacted less intensively with their suppliers. The main differences between the two groups concerned the likelihood of visits at suppliers' plants, inviting suppliers to the buyer's site, supplier recognition through awards, investments in the supplier operations, and the existence of formal training programs. The better performing buyers were also more likely to provide feedback to suppliers on the basis of vendor assessments, and to offer programs for certification of suppliers.

As regards the efforts with teaching suppliers, three issues appear significant for the buying firm. The first is to identify: (1) what knowledge areas are crucial for the buying company to relate to; (2) what role a supplier can play in these areas and what the supplier needs to know about the buyer's unique features; and (3) what development activities are required in order to best utilize the supplier. This issue is particularly important concerning emerging technologies, and when established technologies are to be used in new applications. In both cases they have to be "adapted" to the buying firm's own technical features. The second issue relates to the learning processes at the supplier company. To be able to teach the supplier, the buyer must know how its counterparts learn. Powell (1998) argues that learning from collaboration requires insights into *how* to collaborate. The teaching activities of the buyer must take into consideration what other development processes the supplier is involved in and the other parties who are cooperating in these efforts. Thirdly, to gain as much as possible from specific teaching and training programs, the supplier needs to be familiar with the whole context of the buyer. The supplier must be aware of the internal capabilities of the buying firm, the development projects being conducted in the buying organization and those going on in other relationships of the buying firm. Once these conditions are at hand it would be possible for other buying firms to reap similar benefits from their suppliers, as Fuji Xerox has. This company gains a great deal from collaborating with suppliers who "learn to bring in precisely what we are looking for, even if we only show them a rough sketch" (Nonaka and Takeuchi, 1995: 31).

Teaching in Networks

So far we have dealt mainly with the benefits a buying company may attain from developing and teaching individual suppliers. The cumulative effect of teaching the whole network of suppliers consists not only of the aggregated effects of the enhanced knowledge of the individual supplier companies – there are also network effects to be gained. In a multi-project study of a construction company it was shown that "there is a much greater probability for a supplier to learn in a business relationship when it is connected to a number of the buyer's other relationships" (Håkansson et al., 1999: 450). This implies that the more connected a relationship is to others, the greater the potential (and the demands) for learning. Therefore, a buying company aiming at teaching suppliers should systematically encourage suppliers to teach one another. These factors form the background for both "supplier associations" and the efforts of individual companies to develop their supply networks, as discussed below.

Supplier associations

A supplier association is a group of companies who regularly share knowledge and experience in an open and cooperative manner (Hines et al., 1998). Such associations are increasingly being established by European and US firms inspired by the "kyoryoku kai" organizations developed in Japan. The three most important objectives of these organizations are related to supplier development (Hines, 1996):

- To improve the abilities and skills of suppliers in terms of various tools and techniques (such as just-in-time, total quality management, statistical process control, value analysis, etc.);
- To design a uniform supply system using the same types of techniques;
- To facilitate the flow of information and strategy formulation to and from and within supply networks.

Hines et al. (1998) describe the findings from a study of a supplier association. They show how the buying firm evolved, in a little more than one year, from a situation where it had only a very limited supplier integration process to a strong system with a well-charted future development plan. The program greatly improved communication with suppliers and raised the presence of the customer in the minds of the suppliers. Once the program had been established, many initiatives were proposed by suppliers. One unexpected benefit for the buyer was that the performance of suppliers not involved in the supplier association program also improved. This finding may be explained either as attempts by these companies to put extra effort into the relationship in order to become members at a later date or as a network effect when members of the program began to implement similar improvements with non-member firms.

In supplier associations, the member companies are treated as a homogeneous group. Another approach to developing suppliers is to handle each vendor in a special way to get the most out of each partner. Below we present two examples of supply networks described in recent research studies dealing with IKEA and Volvo Cars.

IKEA

The supply network of the Swedish furniture retailer IKEA involves about 2,000 vendors. IKEA's efforts in stimulating teaching and learning among these suppliers have been one of the main determinants of the success of the company. Our illustration of these efforts is taken from a study by Baraldi (2003) dealing with the continuous development of a table. Twenty-two years ago IKEA launched the "Lack" table as a low price item. This product has been a major success and more than 2.5 million a year are sold today. One of the main reasons is the low price. The price was set at SEK 99 (approximately €10) when the product was launched and it has been kept at the same level ever since. The outer appearance of the table has been exactly the same for the whole period. However, over the years the "internal" features of the product have changed completely. In order to keep the outer appearance and the price the same during the period a huge number of development projects have been conducted, involving more than 20 different business units within and external to IKEA. Suppliers involved represent engineering firms, chemical firms, furniture producers, and logistics units.

The sole producer of the table today is an IKEA owned Polish based company, Swedwood, operating three plants. The basic technology used is "board-on-frame," involving a thin board put on ultra-resistant honeycombed paper yielding a very resistant surface and low-weight piece of furniture. This technology dramatically reduces material costs for the tables "since they are almost empty inside" (Baraldi, 2003: 126). The main inputs into the production process are HDF (high density fibreboard), honeycomb filling, lacquers, chipboard, and veneers. Some of the main suppliers involved are Wicoma – an engineering company in Poland, KronoPol a producer of HDF chipboard, Becker-Acroma and Akzo-Nobel – producers of lacquers, and Sorbini (Italy) and Bürkle (Germany) – producers of coating lines. Several IKEA business units were also involved, including GBA2 at IKEA of Sweden (product responsibility), IKEA TSO (Poland) purchasing, IKEA Sales, Retail Operations, and Distribution Centres. All these units have been more or less active during the different projects and all the projects have been based on very lively interplay among the participants in the projects.

One of these development projects – the "printed veneer project" – involved various actors and triggered a number of problems that had to be solved in the interfaces between these units (Baraldi, 2003: 169ff.). Veneers represent costly input – accounting for 30 percent of material costs – and require extra operations in a tight production flow. Eliminating veneers could thus provide a number of advantages, but veneer is a key material, as it is central both from the aesthetic and durability points of view. It was consequently important to keep the "veneer feel" when the real veneer was to be eliminated as input. In cooperation with Akzo-Nobel and the coating line producers Sorbini and Bürkle, the project was directed towards a production technology that allowed for printing an artificial veneer profile directly on HDF surfaces. This change required Swedwood to install new equipment at its three Polish plants, and each of the companies involved had to adapt its own operations in relation to the others. These modifications required reciprocal teaching and learning among suppliers. For example, Swedwood had to conduct hundreds of tests at their plants to be able to implement the new technology. In these efforts: "Akzo supervised the tests and instructed Swedwood on how to use its new lacquers together with the printing line" (Baraldi, 2003: 169). However, the IKEA sales organization was also affected by the change of technology. For example, the new "print-on-wood" technology made it possible to produce "customized tables" where customers could select any image they wished to be printed on their own table.

In this way IKEA has been systematically involved in interrelating the different suppliers in the development of the Lack table. The whole process can be seen as a combined teaching/learning process where the different actors have learnt from each other, and also taught each other extensively about opportunities and restrictions related to their own capabilities. The resulting production structure is unique and extremely specialized, in spite of the fact that the product, as it appears, is both mundane and highly mature. The outcome of the development processes is thus an interactive structure where the business units involved are closely related but still maintain their uniqueness.

Volvo Cars

In 2003 Volvo Cars launched the last of four passenger car models based on a joint platform. This platform was developed in the late 1990s and the development process was the subject of a doctoral thesis (Corswant, 2003). Inspired by efforts of other car manufacturers to shorten lead times and reduce costs, Volvo decided to change its working procedures in design and development. The main change in this respect was increasing reliance on supplier capabilities, in turn requiring organizational modifications in order to make the best use of the joint resource constellations of Volvo and the suppliers. In organizing this process, Volvo applied the principle of modularity, dividing the car into 20 separate modules with one main supplier for each. The main supplier of each module was then made responsible for product development and production, as well as the organization of the network of sub-suppliers.

Coordinating the whole development project involving four different car models was a complex matter. In order to handle these issues, Volvo organized 13 cross-functional teams. The teams involved representatives from different functional areas at Volvo (product development, pre-production, production, after-sales, purchasing, and design, etc.) and suppliers. The teams varied in size from 50 to 250 (including 80 people representing 35 suppliers).

Two aspects of teaching and learning in networks proved to be important in the development process. One concerned teaching within the various teams, and the other teaching among the teams. The first was seen, for example, in the relationship between Volvo and Delphi, the supplier of the electrical system. The mutual teaching and learning in this relationship is illustrated in the following quotation:

> Volvo's representatives had knowledge regarding the interaction between the electrical system and other components in the car, and requirements concerning the complete car. They also had experience from developing electrical systems for previous car models. Delphi's representatives contributed with knowledge and experience regarding various technologies used in the components for the electrical system and the production of these components. (Corswant, 2003: 171)

The knowledge gained from this reciprocal teaching and learning process was then shared with the whole module team.

The second issue concerned teaching across the module teams. One of the key problems in the development work was how to inform the module teams about what was going on in the other teams. Owing to interdependencies between modules, changes and delays of one team could have serious implications for the others. Furthermore, it was impossible to plan the whole process in detail from the beginning, which meant that it was necessary to make adjustments in line with the actual progress of the project.

The case clearly shows how the companies involved have to influence each other actively – both learning and teaching – in order to develop solutions that are efficient from several perspectives. The complexity of these influencing efforts is illustrated in Figure 3.1, describing some of the most important firms involved in the development of the electrical system, which was one of the 20 modules.

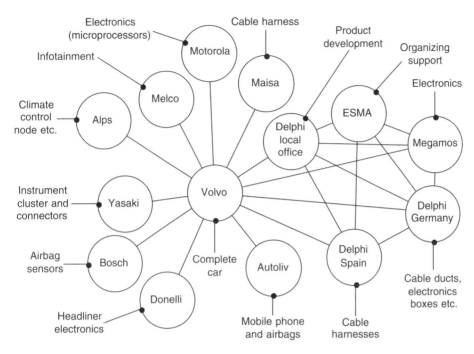

Figure 3.1 Suppliers involved in the development of the electrical system

Discussion

These two cases demonstrate the importance and the benefits of knowledge develop-ment in supply networks. They also clearly show the effects of active involvement in terms of teaching and learning for both buyers and suppliers. The two cases presented are complementary in the sense that they represent teaching in different contexts in spite of the fact that they both deal with product development.

Both buyers are large customers in absolute terms. However, in relative terms Volvo, in most situations, represents a minor part of the turnover of the vendors who also supply to other car manufacturers (e.g. Motorola and Bosch in Figure 3.1). IKEA, on the other hand, is often the dominant customer of its suppliers, as is the case in relation to KronoPol, Swedwood, and Wicoma. The Volvo Platform consists of a huge number of interrelated components and systems, while the Lack table contains only a few parts. However, in another sense the table is the more complex item of the two. When it comes to cars, there are established product architectures as well as a recognized production set-up shared by most car producers. For the manufacturing of tables, neither of these conditions is at hand.

These features make the product development processes in the two cases different, which impacts on the role and the task of teaching. For Volvo, product development activities take place within the boundaries of a fairly predetermined framework in terms of product architecture and manufacturing configuration. Within this struc-ture, however, there is quite a high level of complexity involved in adjusting the various components and systems from suppliers to fit the features of Volvo's particular platform. As described in the case, these development activities required substantial teaching directed towards a huge number of people both within and among the module teams. As development projects in the car industry tend to follow a formal process, teaching may be formalized to some extent. In such projects teaching is primarily about coordinating the development efforts of the various actors.

The IKEA case is characterized more by "experimentation" in order to find new and innovative ways for cutting the costs of the table while retaining its external features. These changes required completely new solutions in terms of materials and processes, which made formalized procedures less suitable. As described in the case, Swedwood had to conduct "hundreds of tests" in order to implement the new technology because there was no predetermined framework to follow. In such projects knowledge exchange takes other forms, turning the buyer's teaching activities in the direction of experimentation. This condition seems to be a general characteristic in projects featuring radical changes. Particularly in the early stages of development "experimentation is a much more important concern than co-ordination" (Langlois and Robertson, 1992: 311).

Teaching in the form of experimentation is sometimes required, owing to the complexity of the contexts in which joint knowledge development takes place. The word "experimentation" emphasizes the importance of analyzing the supplier's reactions to attempts to teach them. Sometimes it may be more important to reflect on and adjust to the outcome of experimentation than to try to prescribe the form of the teaching beforehand. Experimentation is not just an activity where opportunities and restrictions are tested. It is also a type of signaling in the network where the teacher indicates issues of importance as well as what actors are crucial. Thus, teaching through experimentation has a political dimension because it contributes to forming the identity of the buying firm (Gadde and Håkansson, 2001).

Concluding Remarks

The IKEA and Volvo cases are also good examples of the thoughts emphasized in the previous section, where teaching and active involvement in individual relationships were discussed. One of the main conclusions to draw from this discussion is that a buying firm may benefit considerably from encouraging learning and teaching processes both in single relationships and in the total supply network. These joint processes may lead to both cost rationalization and innovation through improvements of production technologies, product design, logistics systems and so on. It is always possible to improve performance in these respects, provided that existing or potential resources are better utilized or further developed. Teaching plays an important role in the efforts of a buying firm to increase the performance and/or capabilities of suppliers in order to enhance short and/or long-term supply operations. Along with these benefits, however, we need to raise the question of what drawbacks might be associated with teaching.

The main issue in this respect is whether a buying firm can be overly ambitious in its teaching efforts. Potential problems in this respect are indicated in the Volvo case where one supplier "remarked that Volvo interfered too much in the detailed product design" and argued that other types of specifications would improve conditions for product development activities (Corswant, 2003: 106). The supplier's opportunities were thus restricted through Volvo's teaching efforts, implying that there might be some danger associated with pushing teaching too far – particularly in relation to long-term development. For example, Quinn (1998: 19) argues that too much direction might "kill innovation and vitiate the supplier's real advantage." This problem arises when the view of potential enhancement of the operations of a supplier is too focused on the internal conditions of the buying firm. Detailed directions in this respect can make it difficult for the supplier to use its internal capabilities in the best way. These instructions may also prevent the supplier from utilizing learning gained through other relationships in the network and thus preventing the supplier from exploiting knowledge gained from business exchanges with other customers (Araujo et al., 1999).

These problems do not arise in truly interactive relationships. In such relationships supplier and buyer are well aware not only of the capabilities of the business partner, but also of those in the network surrounding each party. Through joint projects the two parties learn a great deal over time about the operations on the other side. In these processes the interactive experimentation may also shift the roles of teaching and learning, as illustrated by the knowledge exchange between Volvo and Delphi. Such teaching and learning processes in networks are self-reinforcing. In general, more exchange of knowledge breeds knowledge creation, as new knowledge is often developed in the interface between established bodies of knowledge. These conditions have significant implications for teaching and learning, as indicated in the study by Ernst and Kim (2002) mentioned above. They conclude that once a big customer had upgraded the technical and managerial skills of the local suppliers this condition "creates an incentive to transfer more sophisticated knowledge, including engineering, product and process development" (Ernst and Kim, 2002: 1422). The problem of knowledge transfer is therefore seldom that there is too little knowledge or that the knowledge to be transferred is hidden. The main problem for the buying company is to select what knowledge to transfer or, in other words, what and how much to teach their suppliers.

The network context increases the complexity of the teaching/learning processes. The buyer's relationships with the companies in the supply network become interconnected. Moreover, all these suppliers are simultaneously involved in multiple relationships with other buyers who also strive to influence them. The various buying firms perceive the actual and potential value of a particular supplier differently and make their own demands regarding capability development. Consequently they tend to encourage different learning objectives. Therefore, teaching and learning processes where two companies' bodies of knowledge are brought together are never smooth or easy (Håkansson and Waluszewski, 2002). The more the companies learn about one another, the more they will understand not only about opportunities, but also about limitations. Therefore, the more companies learn about their respective approaches and the more they strive to teach each other in order to better combine their resources, the more likely it is that they will confront restrictions that may require considerable changes in their current way of working. Thus, the intertwined processes of teaching and learning are a truly never-ending story.

References

Albino, V., Garavelli, C. & Schiuma, G. (1998) Knowledge transfer and inter-firm relationships in industrial districts: The role of the leader firm. *Technovation*, 19, 53–63.

Araujo, L., Dubois, A. & Gadde, L.-E. (1999) Managing interfaces with suppliers. *Industrial Marketing Management*, 28, 497–506.

Baraldi, E. (2003) When information technology faces resource interaction: Using IT tools to handle products at IKEA and Edsbyn. Doctoral thesis No. 105, Department of Business Studies, Uppsala University.

Beecham, M. & Cordey-Hayes, M. (1998) Partnering and knowledge transfer in the U.K. motor industry, *Technovation*, 18(3), 191–205.

Carlisle, J. & Parker, R. (1989) *Beyond Negotiation: Redeeming Customer–Supplier Relationships*. Chichester: Wiley.

Corswant, F. von (2003) Organizing interactive product development. Dissertation, Chalmers University of Technology, Department of Operations Management and Work Organization, Gothenburg.

De Toni, A. & Nassimbeni, G. (2000) Just-in-time purchasing: An empirical study of operational practices, supplier development and performance. *Omega*, 28, 631–51.

Donaghu, M. & Barff, R. (1990) Nike just did it: International subcontracting and flexibility in athletic footwear production. *Regional Studies*, 24(6), 537–52.

Ellram, L. & Edis, O. (1996) A case study of successful partnering implementation. *International Journal of Purchasing and Materials Management*, Fall, 20–8.

Ernst, D. & Kim, L. (2002) Global production networks, knowledge diffusion, and local capability formation. *Research Policy*, 31, 1417–29.

Gadde, L.-E. & Håkansson, H. (1993) *Professional Purchasing*. London: Routledge.

Gadde, L.-E. & Håkansson, H. (2001) *Supply Network Strategies*. Chichester: Wiley.

Gadde, L.-E. & Persson, G. (2004) Developments on the supply side of companies. In H. Håkansson, D. Harrison & A. Waluszewski (Eds.) *Rethinking Marketing*, 161–86. Chichester: Wiley.

Ghingold, M. & Johnson, B. (1997) Technical knowledge as value added in business markets: Implications for procurement and marketing. *Industrial Marketing Management*, 26, 271–80.

Hahn, C., Watts, C. & Kim, K. (1989) The supplier development program: A conceptual model. *International Journal of Purchasing and Materials Management*, 26(2), 2–7.

Håkansson, H., Havila, V. & Pedersen, A.-C. (1999) Learning in networks. *Industrial Marketing Management*, 28, 443–52.

Håkansson, H. & Waluszewski, A. (2002) *Managing Technological Development: IKEA, the Environment and Technology*. London: Routledge.

Handfield, R., Krause, D., Scannel, T. & Monczka, R. (2000) Avoid the pitfalls in supplier development. *Sloan Management Review*, 41(2), 37–49.

Harvey, M., Novisevic, M., Hench, T. & Myers, M. (2003) Global account management: A supply-side managerial view. *Industrial Marketing Management*, 32, 563–71.

Hines, P. (1996) Network sourcing: A discussion of causality within the buyer-supplier relationship. *European Journal of Purchasing and Supply Management*, 2(1), 7–20.

Hines, P., Rich, N. & Esain, A. (1998) Creating a lean supplier network: A distribution industry case. *European Journal of Purchasing and Supply Management*, 4, 235–46.

Hult, T., Ketchen, D. & Nichols, E. (2003) Organizational learning as a strategic resource in supply management. *Journal of Operations Management*, 21, 541–56.

Krause, D. & Ellram, L. (1996) Success factors in supplier development. *International Journal of Physical Distribution and Logistics*, 27(1), 39–52.

Krause, D. & Ellram, L. (1997) Critical elements of supplier development: The buying firm perspective. *European Journal of Purchasing and Supply Management*, 3(1), 21–32.

Lamming, R. (1993) *Beyond Partnership: Strategies for Innovation and Lean Supply*. Hemel Hempstead: Prentice Hall.

Lamming, R., Cousins, P. & Notman, D.M. (1996) Beyond vendor assessment: Relationship assessment programmes. *European Journal of Purchasing and Supply Management*, 2(4), 173–81.

Langlois, R. & Robertson, P. (1992) Networks and innovation in a modular system: Lessons from the microcomputer and stereo computer industries. *Research Policy*, 21, 297–313.

Leenders, M. (1966) Supplier development. *Journal of Purchasing*, 2(4), 47–62.

Leenders, M. & Blenkhorn, D. (1988) *Reverse Marketing: The New Buyer-Supplier Relationship*. New York: The Free Press.

Nishiguchi, T. (1994) *Strategic Industrial Sourcing: The Japanese Advantage*. New York: Oxford University Press.

Nonaka, I. & Takeuchi, H. (1995) *The Knowledge-creating Company*. New York: Oxford University Press.

Okada, A. (2004) Skills development and interfirm learning linkages under globalization: Lessons from the Indian automobile industry. *World Development*, 32(7), 1265–88.

Powell, W. (1998) Learning from collaboration: Knowledge and networks in the biotechnology and pharmaceutical industries. *California Management Review*, 30(1), 67–87.

Quinn, J. (1998) Strategic outsourcing. *Sloan Management Review*, Summer, 9–21.

Sobek, D., Liker, J. & Ward, A. (1998) Another look at how Toyota integrates product development. *Harvard Business Review*, July–August, 36–49.

Teece, D. (1998) Capturing value from knowledge assets: The new economy, markets for know-how and intangible assets. *California Management Review*, 40(3), 55–79.

Watts, C. & Hahn, C. (1993) Supplier development programs: An empirical analysis. *International Journal of Purchasing and Materials Management*, 29(2), 11–17.

Wynstra, F., Weggeman, M. & van Weele, A. (2003) Exploring purchasing integration in product development. *Industrial Marketing Management*, 32, 69–83.

CHAPTER FOUR

On the Challenges of Buyer–Supplier Collaboration in Product Development Projects

Stephan M. Wagner and Martin Hoegl

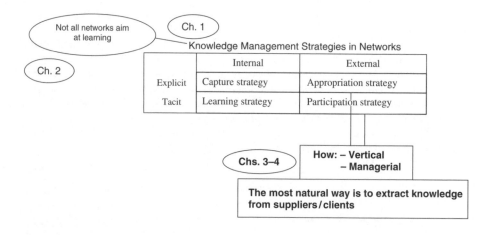

Abstract

Integrating key suppliers with superior technological knowledge into a buyer's product development projects has long been discussed as a mutually value-creating strategy. However, empirical evidence shows that such supplier involvement often impedes project performance in terms of quality, budget, and time. This chapter focuses on the difficulties faced by companies engaged in interorganizational collaborative product development projects. Our analysis highlights issues at the organizational level (e.g., each partner aiming to maximize transaction value) and the project level (e.g., collaborating on a project staffed by members of different organizations with different identities, cultures, goal structures, etc.). We conclude by offering suggestions on how to deal with these challenges and pointing to necessary further research in this area.

Introduction

It is widely accepted that firms' boundary decisions and the alignment between the firms' governance structures and exchange characteristics have far-reaching implications on firm performance (Leiblein et al., 2002; Teece, 1996). Firms may particularly benefit from the utilization of specialized competencies residing outside their boundaries (Dyer and Nobeoka, 2000; Dyer and Ouchi, 1993; Mowery et al., 1996). Therefore, firms no longer limit their outsourcing approaches to manufacturing and service tasks (Quinn, 2000; Quinn and Hilmer, 1994; Venkatesan, 1992), but increasingly extend new product development (NPD) activities and integrate internal company resources with those of other supply chain members: customers and, increasingly, suppliers (Fritsch and Lukas, 2001; Rogers et al., 2004; Roy et al., 2004; see also Box 4.1, executive interview question 1). The so-called early supplier involvement strategy aims at capitalizing on the specific expertise of advanced suppliers by soliciting their services not only for production of parts and components, but also for their design and development (Clark and Fujimoto, 1991; O'Neal, 1993; Wagner, 2003).

Corporate practitioners and numerous scholars have argued that buyers can benefit from involving suppliers in the development process rather than working independently when it comes to time-to-market of new products, product quality, development cost, and product cost, and that such a strategy can also help firms conserve resources, share risks, gain new competencies, and move faster into new markets (Birou and Fawcett, 1994; Bonaccorsi and Lipparini, 1994; Bozdogan et al., 1998; Clark, 1989; Dröge et al., 2000; Handfield et al., 1999; Ragatz et al., 1997; Wagner and Johnson, 2004; see also Box 4.1, executive interview question 2).

Box 4.1 Executive interview with Professor Dr.-Ing. Raimund Klinkner

Profile: GILDEMEISTER AG
GILDEMEISTER is one of the major manufacturers of metal cutting machine tools worldwide. Its range of products includes turning and milling technologies along with trend-setting "ultrasonic" and "laser" technologies. Its customers can rely on top quality, proficient technical services and state-of-the-art software products all from a single producer. GILDEMEISTER has its headquarters in Bielefeld, Germany.

Profile: Professor Dr.-Ing. Raimund Klinkner
Professor Dr.-Ing. Raimund Klinkner is Deputy Chairman of the Executive Board. His area of responsibility includes production and logistics. Furthermore, he is Honorary Professor of Production Logistics at Berlin Technical University. Before he joined GILDEMEISTER, Professor Dr.-Ing. Klinkner worked in the car industry.

Question 1: Professor Klinkner, over the past decade many industrial firms have outsourced assembly, production and increasingly R&D responsibilities to their suppliers. Did this occur at GILDEMEISTER as well? And if so, what urged you to outsource?

Continued.

Box 4.1 Continued.

Answer: Indeed, at GILDEMEISTER the degree of outsourcing has increased considerably in recent years – in the same way it did in the automotive industry a few years ago. The major drivers behind this development include more demanding global customers, a shorter time-to-market, and the fast technological developments in our industry, coupled with our goal to remain a global market leader. This encouraged us to focus even more on our core competencies and to align our supply chains with our specialist and competent suppliers.

As a consequence, our supplier base had to take over more and more assembly and manufacturing capacity and responsibility for components and modules. For example, the production of control cabinets and chip conveyors was no longer considered a core area of expertise of GILDEMEISTER, therefore, we decided to buy these modules from suppliers specializing in the development and production of control cabinets and chip conveyors. Furthermore, our "modular logistics concept" urges suppliers to take over logistical responsibilities, such as setting up, planning, and running transshipment points in our plants for the components and modules they deliver to us.

We carefully evaluate what we outsource and where we outsource. For example, we successfully assemble most of the standard machines in low-cost countries with local content from local suppliers. Because of the high degree of engineering required for customer-specific machines, we prefer to manufacture these customer-specific machines in Germany. We also pay close attention to our suppliers' capabilities. While we try to partner only with the best suppliers in each technology, we still follow a dual-sourcing strategy, that is, if a supplier fails to satisfy our requirements, we have a backup source. A professional supplier management is vital.

Question 2: Your company is renowned for offering trend-setting solutions, for example three-dimensional laser beam machining. Also, over 90 percent of GILDEMEISTER's current delivery programme consists of machines that were developed during the past three years. How important are suppliers if GILDEMEISTER wants to remain an innovation leader?

Answer: We can only be an innovation leader if our entire supply chain supports our efforts in this direction. If our suppliers were not innovation leaders, we couldn't be either. For example, laser head is key for the functioning of our three-dimensional leaser beam machines. This high technology we buy from a specialized supplier. At GILDEMEISTER we encourage our suppliers to come up with innovative products, share their latest developments with us, and engage in joint R&D projects. In return we offer them the opportunity to participate in the success of our machines in the market.

Question 3: Many industrial firms have had positive but also negative experiences with selecting and integrating suppliers in product development in terms of product functionality, product quality, development time and development cost, for example. What are the key issues GILDEMEISTER pays close attention to when suppliers are involved in the development of new products?

Answer: As a consequence of a reduced manufacturing penetration we increasingly have to integrate suppliers into our product development activities. For example, GILDEMEISTER and

Box 4.1   Continued.

its suppliers strive to develop standardized components that can be integrated into a large number of machine types. This helps to reduce material and manufacturing costs.

At GILDEMEISTER we have learned that integrating suppliers is inherently difficult due to the uncertainty, risk, and necessary investments associated with new joint developments. This is where a professional and reliable supplier management comes in again: Firstly, our supplier portal "coSupply" (www.cosupply.de) helps us with everyday communication with suppliers and to transfer information to suppliers in a coordinated manner. Suppliers can also obtain general information and can call up their specific and evaluated performance ratios. With coSupply GILDEMEISTER coaches and coordinates its suppliers in order to develop highly efficient supply partnerships. The supplier portal is characterized by the three performance features: communication, cooperation, and competence. The adoption of these will lead, over a process of constant review and change, to the further optimization of our higher aim, that of competitiveness. All processes serve to improve the competitiveness of our products and thus safeguard our business and the businesses of our suppliers. Secondly, the implementation of long-term "win-win" partnerships and cooperation is crucial.

Question 4: Supplier involvement must be managed at a "strategic level" as well as at a "human level," that is, people from two different organizations work together on highly complex and often sensitive tasks. How important are "soft facts" for a successful outcome when your engineers work with supplier engineers in joint R&D projects?

Answer: GILDEMEISTER has a hybrid R&D organization, that is, there are centralized R&D resources at headquarters and decentralized R&D resources in the manufacturing plants. Central R&D manages the strategic level and is responsible for R&D strategy, standardization, and coordination of all R&D activities. The decentralized units are responsible for the operative implementation of the strategy. They also work with suppliers. When our engineers work with engineers from supplier firms, we are careful that the suppliers have the same working philosophy as GILDEMEISTER and if possible the same CAD system. We also encourage a culture of open discussion and the use of compatible working methods.

Question 5: How do you see the future for working with suppliers in product development at the GILDEMEISTER group?

Answer: We intend to further streamline our supplier base, reduce the number of suppliers we work with, and access the most innovative suppliers' know-how. At the same time we are aware that we have to intensify our R&D partnerships with suppliers. Selected suppliers will be given access to GILDEMEISTER's CAD system. Some suppliers will be given defined work packages and we will evaluate the progress of the supplier's development in joint "design reviews." In contrast, with other suppliers we will work in an integrative manner, that is, we will work with them in the concept phase of a new machine and jointly develop new technical solutions with them.

Professor Klinkner, I thank you for this short interview on such a contemporary topic.

(The interview was conducted by Stephan M. Wagner)

Other studies, however, repeatedly found no positive relationships or even showed negative effects, that is, more supplier involvement leading to increased product and development cost, worse product performance, and longer development times (Eisenhardt and Tabrizi, 1995; Hartley et al., 1997; Littler et al., 1998; Tukel and Wasti, 2001; von Corswant and Tunälv, 2002; Wynstra et al., 2001).

As a consequence, it seems that supplier involvement in NPD requires that the customer firm is able to cope with such a strategy's inherent challenges on the organizational and the project level (see also Box 4.1, executive interview question 3). Previous research has mainly focused on the organizational level and resulted in the aforementioned mixed results. For better results, successful industrial firms have tried to optimize not only on the organizational level, but to reinforce the "soft facts" and the "human level" as well (see also Box 4.1, executive interview question 4). Correspondingly, a few publications have pointed out that the positive effects of supplier involvement are not easily achieved in product development processes on the project level, where human beings from both organizations interact (Ragatz et al., 1997; von Corswant and Tunälv, 2002; Wynstra et al., 2001). Three recent publications have specifically taken a project level perspective and highlighted the quality of buyer–supplier collaboration as a key success factor to the successful implementation of supplier involvement in product development projects (Gerwin, 2004; Gerwin and Ferris, 2004; Hoegl and Wagner, 2005). In Gerwin and Ferris's (2004) conceptual investigation of various project organizational options the authors suggest that the preferred option of firms working either independently or with partners in NPD projects depends on the newness of the NPD alliance, the cooperativeness of the alliance in the past, and the distribution of skills among the partners. Gerwin's (2004) theoretical model emphasizes the importance of reducing the coordination gap in joint NPD projects. Mismatches between the required and actual coordination of tasks negatively influence the performance of a NPD project. In their empirical study of product development projects, Hoegl and Wagner (2005) point out that it is important to conceptualize the quality of buyer–supplier collaboration on the project level of analysis, as project members from both organizations are living the relationship between the buyer and the supplier and that the interactions within the project shape the interorganizational exchange and thus are critical in determining its outcomes. The quality of buyer–supplier collaboration is characterized by an open sharing of information, mutual support and accommodation, and high project commitment. The study revealed that an increase in the supplier's share of the project was in itself not significantly related to project success. Rather, the quality of the collaborative working between the buyer's and the supplier's project members was key in explaining project success (Hoegl and Wagner, 2005).

We take this state of the literature and research on supplier involvement in product development as our point of departure and further investigate the challenges companies are facing when suppliers are involved in NPD projects.

It should be noted that the supplier involvement strategy, as defined here, differs from the strategy of creating a modular product architecture with clearly defined technical interfaces between product modules, followed by the external sourcing of modules (Sanchez and Mahoney, 1996; Worren et al., 2002). This strategy, while also ultimately including suppliers for both development and production of modules, is aimed at reducing the amount of coordination required between the supplier(s) and the buyer. Rather, this chapter pertains to integrative product development with supplier involvement, where the aim is to create value by combining the expertise of the buyer and the supplier firm to develop an integrated and comprehensive, rather than modular, product (Boutellier and Wagner, 2003; see also Box 4.1, executive interview question 5).

As this chapter investigates project-level collaboration nested in interorganizational relationships, the challenges of buyer–supplier collaboration in product development projects will be related to both levels of analysis, that is, the organizational and the project level. As such, in the remainder of this chapter, we first ground the challenges of supplier involvement in NPD theoretically by establishing a link to transaction cost economics. Second, we specifically address value appropriation as a key issue in the successful implementation of supplier involvement in NPD projects. Third, we highlight a number of project-level barriers to collaboration between buyer and supplier members of product development teams. The chapter concludes by outlining possible avenues for necessary further research.

Maximizing Transaction Value

The importance of effective interorganizational governance structures has been addressed in economic theories, most notably transaction cost economics (TCE). This theory recommends structuring an institutional arrangement (e.g., the relationship between a buyer and a supplier who is involved in the buyer's product development activities) in a transaction cost economizing way (Williamson, 1985). Transaction costs can be broken down into search costs, contracting costs, monitoring costs, and enforcement costs. They are supposed to increase with an increasing level of relationship-specific investments, because such investments have to be protected against the hazards of opportunism; and the employment of safeguards against opportunistic behavior is associated with transaction costs. A safeguard suggested by TCE is strong formal commitment which is enforceable through legal institutions (Williamson, 1985). Informal commitment and social institutions, on the other hand, have essentially been neglected in the Western economies (Dyer, 1997). However, the prerequisites for the enforceability of formal commitments, in particular the ability to properly specify the buyer's and supplier's mutual obligations (Casson, 1997), are not given in complex R&D environments with intensive buyer–supplier collaboration. Specifying all contingencies of a R&D project, such as the required resources, the outcome in terms of technical solutions, quality or the cost of the product or service to be developed, at an early stage of supplier involvement is nearly impossible. Therefore, collaborative R&D projects ought to rely more heavily on informal commitment and appropriate self-enforcing mechanisms, such as trust (Choi, 1994; Morgan and Hunt, 1994).

As product development activities are concerned with creating value for customers in the form of new or enhanced products and services, buyers and suppliers working together in collaborative product development should not only be concerned with minimizing transaction costs, but also with maximizing transaction value (Dyer, 1997;

Zajac and Olsen, 1993). The level of relationship-specific investments and the degree and type of safeguard largely determine the incentive of the buyer and supplier to provide solutions, and put effort into the project beyond the contractual agreement (Dyer, 1997). Again, informal commitment seems to benefit the firm more than formal commitment.

Issues of Value Appropriation

To satisfy their shareholders, firms have to extract the maximum value from buyer–supplier relationships (Porter, 1980) and protect themselves from supplier opportunism (Provan and Skinner, 1989; Stump and Heide, 1996). Despite recent developments in collaborative buyer–supplier relationships and supply chain integration, with profit maximization being a major goal of the individual firm, each firm linked with other firms in a relationship or supply chain has to strive for extracting the maximum value for itself. Therefore, in every buyer–supplier relationship where "pie expansion" (Jap, 1999) occurs through collaborative processes, such as joint product development, the appropriate sharing of the pie is an issue of major concern (Cox, 2001; Jap, 2001; Jeuland and Shugan, 1983). The notion of value appropriation in buyer–supplier relationships implies that (additional) value is created through inter-firm linkages and assumes that one or both parties seek advantage over the other by maximizing transaction value.

A comparison of two opposite supplier management approaches shows how tricky supplier involvement can be with respect to value appropriation issues. In *traditional production outsourcing*, the buyer company developed a new product largely in-house. Toward the end of the development process, detailed technical specifications for parts and components to be sourced from outside are the basis for a competitive bidding process, with the supplier offering the lowest price taking the contract (Bingham, 1989; Boutellier and Wagner, 2003; Clark and Fujimoto, 1991). By contrast, companies pursuing *supplier involvement* typically commit earlier in the development process to a specific supplier, however, regularly still after a competitive and negotiated price-finding process. Given the earlier stage in the development process, suppliers compete or negotiate for this collaboration under increased uncertainty. The result is a series of changes in cost/price of the supplier's component as the development project unfolds, so-called engineering change orders (Frey and Schlosser, 1993). This, in effect, creates a situation where pricing negotiations carry on for the duration of the product development project.

The "close but adversarial" model of buyer–supplier relationships, which could be observed in the US automotive industry, also underscores how the buying firm can take advantage of the supplier to reap short-term benefits and despite close relations strives to maximize period-by-period profit (Mudambi and Helper, 1998). Hence, this model underscores the contradiction between the cooperativeness that joint NPD projects require on the one hand and the firms' adversarial behavior on the other hand.

So far, only a few investigations have touched upon antecedents and outcomes of value appropriation issues and sharing processes in an NPD setting. Riordan and

Sappington (1989) investigated contradictions and effects of buyers' rent maximizing behavior in multistage defense procurement processes encompassing concept design, development, initial production, and full production. The buyer, that is, the Department of Defense (DoD), usually awards a development contract to one supplier, who also undertakes the initial production, and has the option to transfer the technology to a second source prior to the full production stage. Based on numerical simulation results the authors show that second sourcing has two negative consequences because second sourcing takes away rents from the developer (i.e., the first source supplier); the developer can anticipate lower rents in the production stage. First, the developer is less inclined to offer low R&D costs (negative R&D incentive effect). For the buyer, lower costs in the production stage through second source arrangement are offset by higher R&D costs in earlier stages. Second, the developer's R&D efforts will be reduced, resulting in longer development times and lower-quality products (Riordan and Sappington, 1989). In order to circumvent such negative influences, the authors' fundamental conclusion is that rent appropriation should be determined ex ante, that is, should be clarified at the development stage.

The focus of Jap's (2001) recent survey was on the impact of sharing principles (equity and equality principle) on the quality of buyer–supplier relationships in R&D settings. Although only a few proposed hypotheses could be supported, the findings nevertheless indicate that the sharing principle in complex collaboration contexts such as collaborative R&D has an impact on relationship quality. For example, the use of the equity principle has a negative impact on relationship quality when buyers and suppliers understand each other's transformation processes, that is, understand how the other party converts its resources to outputs. As a result, this research underscores the practical relevance of the contradiction between rent sharing (i.e., value appropriation) and relational interfirm processes, calling for a more fine-grained investigation and potential solutions for such contradictions.

Given that the "right" treatment of value appropriation issues seems to be a major challenge when NPD projects are carried out together with suppliers and that prior research (Jap, 2001; Riordan and Sappington, 1989) in this area is limited to the organizational level, the impact of value appropriation issues on collaborative processes on the project level deserves much more research attention.

Issues of Project-level Collaboration

On the project level, successful supplier involvement requires collaboration between the buyer and the supplier members involved in the project. However, interorganizational product development projects are distinctly different from development projects without supplier involvement (so-called in-house projects). Below, we outline such principal differences and identify how these characteristics can set substantial barriers to collaboration in product development projects with supplier involvement.

First, the buyer and supplier members operate in at least two relevant capacities in the project, as members of the project (with its objectives) and as members of their respective organizations (with their objectives). This may result in role conflicts for the project participants from both firms (Levine and Moreland, 1990). For instance, as their role as project members emphasizes open exchange of relevant information (Hoegl and Wagner, 2005), the role as members of their organizations may emphasize their respective organizations' desire to maximize their value appropriation from this business relationship. Hence, for example, the above-described process of "engineering change orders" and related price adjustments. Moreover, relevant elements of the two firms' organizational designs such as the goal and reward systems are likely to be oriented toward focusing all its members on organizational goals (e.g., rent appropriation) rather than supporting interorganizational collaboration.

Second, the project participants are also likely to differ with regard to their social identities based on their membership in two distinct organizations, the buyer and the supplier firm (Ashforth and Mael, 1989). Such differing social identities of project members, however, are likely to make project commitment and project collaboration more difficult to achieve (Hoegl et al., 2004). Also here, relevant elements of firms' organizational designs, such as its corporate culture, generally support the formation of individuals' social identities based on organizational membership in an effort to foster organizational integration (Lawrence and Lorsch, 1967). This, too, can pose barriers to collaboration in interorganizational NPD projects.

Third, in NPD projects with supplier involvement, sentiments of superiority of either partner may hamper strong buyer–supplier collaboration. For instance, buyer members may assume to have "the final say" as the "customer is king," or the members of a highly specialized and critical supplier may perceive themselves as "technically superior." Both cases provide barriers to collaboration similar to the well-known obstacles to cross-functional collaboration in in-house projects resulting from departmental rivalries, for example, between R&D and marketing (Brown and Eisenhardt, 1995; Denison et al., 1996; Keller, 2001), including the "not-invented-here syndrome" (Katz and Allen, 1988; Ragatz et al., 1997). Following social exchange theory (Homans, 1958), buyer and/or supplier members under the impression of superiority (technical or economic) may be taking less initiative in engaging in collaborative interaction with each other.

Fourth, the inclusion of supplier members in the buyer's NPD project is likely to inflate the project team in terms of head count. Team size, however, has been considered an important structural variable determining team processes – for example, team collaboration, social loafing, etc. – and subsequently team performance (Gladstein, 1984; Hackman, 1987; Steiner, 1966; Ziller, 1957). Research suggests that smaller teams provide for more direct and efficient intra-team communication (Bray et al., 1978), greater effort by all team members (i.e., reduced social loafing; Latané et al., 1979), and hence a better utilization of all team members' potential.

Fifth, supplier involvement is also likely to introduce a higher level of geographical dispersion relative to in-house projects. The geographical dispersion of team members, however, has potentially important implications for the collaborative working of teams (Brown and Eisenhardt, 1995). While evidence from a laboratory study (Schmidt et al., 2001) suggests that virtual teams may even produce superior performance on innovative tasks (e.g., new product development decision-making) when compared to teams with high geographical proximity, research by Hoegl and Proserpio (2004) suggests that geographical dispersion hinders important elements of teamwork such as communication, coordination, mutual support, and cohesion.

Taken together, these characteristics of NPD projects with supplier involvement highlight the challenges of creating high quality buyer–supplier collaboration and thus obtaining the intended benefits of an early supplier involvement strategy.

Conclusions and Outlook

This chapter aimed at highlighting some critical difficulties at the organizational and the project level with regard to the involvement of supplier firms in buyers' product development. While such early supplier involvement has long been advocated to provide strategic advantages, this chapter aimed at offering possible reasons for why companies have found it difficult to reap the desired strategic potential.

However, the question of "What can be done?" remains, for both management scholars and practitioners. This chapter describes a decidedly unsatisfactory state of affairs, where we can offer explanations for why early supplier involvement in innovation can fail, even though it may make "strategic sense," but at present we can provide little on how to make it work. Nonetheless, we would like to give this much advice to practitioners.

First, this chapter should create awareness of the seriousness of issues in early supplier involvement, both at the organizational level and the project level. Hence, managers should take these discussions into consideration before moving forward with crafting and implementing early supplier involvement strategies. It would certainly make little sense abandoning a well-functioning system of in-house development and production outsourcing for an early involvement strategy that does not offer good answers to the issues raised in this chapter.

Second, if pursuing an early supplier involvement strategy, this chapter does point to a number of project-level considerations that may offer advice. For instance, as with in-house development projects, the teams should be kept small (even though we are now adding supplier members), providing for (at least at times) physical proximity of all team members, creating a distinct project identity that can help integrate members from different organizations, and keeping questions of value appropriation outside the project team, but dealing with these issues perhaps at an elevated managerial level.

Third, value appropriation should be dealt with and settled ex ante. This last point, however, is where we see the greatest work ahead for management research.

Our discussions in this chapter underscore that, at present, management theory and research does not seem to offer pointed advice on this issue. Transaction cost economics tends to suggest *not* engaging in early supplier involvement, due to the inherent risks of opportunism and the high transaction costs associated with it. At the same time, the case for early supplier involvement in integrative product development is also convincing and has been around for a while. Moreover, companies are increasingly pursuing such avenues in search of competitive advantage.

This present state strongly emphasizes the pressing need for further research, and we see the following elements as important.

First, such further research would ideally address the cross-level nature of this phenomenon, where elements at the interorganizational relationship level, the organizational level, the project level, and the individual level likely interact to affect the success of interorganizational innovation endeavors.

Second, future inquiries should also build on and expand the related work on product modularity. Rarely are product development projects "fully modular" or "fully integrative," with most projects ranging somewhere in between. Moreover, the process of defining a modular product architecture may well also be an interorganizational endeavor, likely posing similar issues.

Third, research on issues of value appropriation in interorganizational innovation will likely need to move beyond transaction cost considerations in explaining such aspects as value creation and trust.

Finally, future research should build on related work from various literatures on such topics as relationship marketing, interorganizational relationships, supplier management, product development, team management, and dispersed collaboration.

References

Ashforth, B.E. & Mael, F. (1989) Social identity theory and the organization. *Academy of Management Review*, 14(1), 20–39.

Bingham, F.G. (1989) When, how, and why suppliers consider price moves. *Journal of Purchasing and Materials Management*, 25(3), 2–8.

Birou, L.M. & Fawcett, S.E. (1994) Supplier involvement in integrated product development: A comparison of US and European practices. *International Journal of Physical Distribution & Logistics Management*, 24(5), 4–14.

Bonaccorsi, A.J. & Lipparini, A. (1994) Strategic partnerships in new product development: An Italian case study. *Journal of Product Innovation Management*, 11(2), 134–44.

Boutellier, R. & Wagner, S.M. (2003) Sourcing concepts: Matching product architecture, task interface, supplier competence and supplier relationship. In H. Österle & R. Winter (Eds.) *Business Engineering*, 2nd edn, 223–48. Berlin: Springer.

Bozdogan, K., Deyst, J., Hoult, D. & Lucas, M. (1998) Architectural innovation in product development through early supplier integration. *R&D Management*, 28(3), 163–73.

Bray, R.M., Kerr, N.L. & Atkin, R.S. (1978) Effects of group size, problem difficulty, and sex on group performance and member reactions. *Journal of Personality and Social Psychology*, 36(11), 24–40.

Brown, S.L. & Eisenhardt, K.M. (1995) Product development: Past research, present findings and future directions. *Academy of Management Review*, 20(2), 343–78.

Casson, M. (1997) *Information and Organization*. Oxford: Clarendon Press.

Choi, C.J. (1994) Contract enforcement across cultures. *Organization Studies*, 15(5), 673–82.

Clark, K.B. (1989) Project scope and project performance: The effect of parts strategy and supplier involvement on product development. *Management Science*, 35(10), 1247–63.

Clark, K.B. & Fujimoto, T. (1991) *Product Development Performance: Strategy, Organization, and Management in the World Auto Industry*. Boston: Harvard Business School Press.

Cox, A. (2001) Managing with power: Strategies for improving value appropriation from supply relationships. *Journal of Supply Chain Management*, 37(2), 42–7.

Denison, D.R., Hart, S.L. & Kahn, J.A. (1996) From chimneys to cross-functional teams: Developing and validating a diagnostic model. *Academy of Management Journal*, 39(4), 1005–23.

Dröge, C.L., Jayaram, J. & Vickery, S.K. (2000) The ability to minimize the timing of new product development and introduction: An examination of antecedent factors in the North American automobile supplier industry. *Journal of Product Innovation Management,* 17(1), 24–40.

Dyer, J.H. (1997) Effective interfirm collaboration: How firms minimize transaction costs and maximize transaction value. *Strategic Management Journal,* 18(7), 535–56.

Dyer, J.H. & Nobeoka, K. (2000) Creating and managing a high-performance knowledge-sharing network: The Toyota case. *Strategic Management Journal,* 21(3), 345–67.

Dyer, J.H. & Ouchi, W.G. (1993) Japanese style business partnerships: Giving companies a competitive edge. *Sloan Management Review,* 35(1), 51–63.

Eisenhardt, K.M. & Tabrizi, B.N. (1995) Accelerating adaptive processes: Product innovation in the global computer industry. *Administrative Science Quarterly,* 40(1), 84–110.

Frey, S.C. Jr. & Schlosser, M.M. (1993) ABB and Ford: Creating value through cooperation. *Sloan Management Review,* 35(1), 65–72.

Fritsch, M. & Lukas, R. (2001) Who cooperates on R&D? *Research Policy,* 30(2), 297–312.

Gerwin, D. (2004) Coordinating new product development in strategic alliances. *Academy of Management Review,* 29(2), 241–57.

Gerwin, D. & Ferris, J.S. (2004) Organizing new product development projects in strategic alliances. *Organization Science,* 15(1), 22–37.

Gladstein, D.L. (1984) Groups in context: A model of task group effectiveness. *Administrative Science Quarterly,* 29(4), 499–517.

Hackman, J.R. (1987) The design of work teams. In J.W. Lorsch (Ed.) *Handbook of Organizational Behavior,* 315–42. Englewood Cliffs, NJ: Prentice-Hall.

Handfield, R.B., Ragatz, G.L., Peterson, K.J. & Monczka, R.M. (1999) Involving suppliers in new product development. *California Management Review,* 42(1), 59–82.

Hartley, J.L., Zirger, B.J. & Kamath, R.R. (1997) Managing the buyer-supplier interface for on-time performance in product development. *Journal of Operations Management,* 15(1), 57–70.

Hoegl, M. & Proserpio, L. (2004) Team member proximity and teamwork in innovative projects. *Research Policy,* 33(8), 1153–65.

Hoegl, M. & Wagner, S.M. (2005) Buyer–supplier collaboration in product development projects. *Journal of Management,* 31(4), 530–48.

Hoegl, M., Weinkauf, K. & Gemuenden, H.G. (2004) Interteam coordination, project commitment, and teamwork in multiteam R&D projects: A longitudinal study. *Organization Science,* 15(1), 38–55.

Homans, G.C. (1958) Social behavior as exchange. *American Journal of Sociology,* 63(6), 597–606.

Jap, S.D. (1999) Pie-expansion efforts: Collaboration processes in buyer–supplier relationships. *Journal of Marketing Research,* 26(4), 461–75.

Jap, S.D. (2001) "Pie sharing" in complex collaboration contexts. *Journal of Marketing Research,* 38(1), 86–99.

Jeuland, A.P. & Shugan, S.M. (1983) Managing channel profits. *Marketing Science,* 2(3), 239–72.

Katz, R. & Allen, T.J. (1988) Investigating the Not Invented Here (NIH) syndrome: A look at the performance, tenure, and communication patterns of 50 R&D project groups. In M.L. Tushman & W.L. Moore (Eds.) *Readings in the management of innovations,* 293–309. Cambridge: Ballinger Publishing Company.

Keller, R.T. (2001) Cross-functional project groups in research and new product development: Diversity, communications, job stress, and outcomes. *Academy of Management Journal,* 44(3), 547–55.

Latané, B., Williams, K. & Harkins, S. (1979) Many hands make light the work: The causes and consequences of social loafing. *Journal of Personality and Social Psychology*, 37(6), 822–32.

Lawrence, P.R. & Lorsch, J.W. (1967) Differentiation and integration in complex organizations. *Administrative Science Quarterly*, 12(1), 1–47.

Leiblein, M.J., Reuer, J.J. & Dalsace, F. (2002) Do make or buy decisions matter? The influence of organizational governance on technological performance. *Strategic Management Journal*, 23(9), 817–33.

Levine, J.M. & Moreland, R.L. (1990) Progress in small group research. In L.W. Porter & M.R. Rosenzweig (Eds.) *Annual Review of Psychology*, 41, 585–634. Palo Alto: Annual Reviews.

Littler, D., Leverick, F. & Wilson, D. (1998) Collaboration in new technology based markets. *International Journal of Technology Management*, 15(1/2), 139–59.

Morgan, R.M. & Hunt, S.D. (1994) The commitment-trust theory of relationship marketing. *Journal of Marketing*, 58(3), 20–38.

Mowery, D.C., Oxley, J.E. & Silverman, B.S. (1996) Strategic alliances and interfirm knowledge transfer. *Strategic Management Journal*, 17 (Special Issue "Knowledge and the Firm"), 77–91.

Mudambi, R. & Helper, S.R. (1998) The "close but adversarial" model of supplier relations in the U.S. auto industry. *Strategic Management Journal*, 19(8), 775–92.

O'Neal, C. (1993) Concurrent engineering with early supplier involvement: A cross functional challenge. *International Journal of Purchasing and Materials Management*, 29(2), 3–9.

Porter, M.E. (1980) *Competitive Strategy: Techniques for Analyzing Industries and Competitors.* New York: The Free Press.

Provan, K.G. & Skinner, S.J. (1989) Interorganizational dependence and control as predictors of opportunism in dealer-supplier relations. *Academy of Management Journal*, 32(1), 202–12.

Quinn, J.B. (2000) Outsourcing innovation: The new engine of growth. *Sloan Management Review*, 41(4), 13–28.

Quinn, J.B. & Hilmer, F.G. (1994) Strategic outsourcing. *Sloan Management Review*, 35(4), 43–55.

Ragatz, G.L., Handfield, R.B. & Scannell, T.V. (1997) Success factors for integrating suppliers into new product development. *Journal of Product Innovation Management*, 14(3), 190–202.

Riordan, M.H. & Sappington, D.E.M. (1989) Second sourcing. *The Rand Journal of Economics*, 20(1), 41–58.

Rogers, D.S., Lambert, D.M. & Knemeyer, A.M. (2004) The product development and commercialization process. *International Journal of Logistics Management*, 15(1), 43–56.

Roy, S., Sivakumar, K. & Wilkinson, I.F. (2004) Innovation generation in supply chain relationships: A conceptual model and research propositions. *Journal of the Academy of Marketing Science*, 32(1), 61–79.

Sanchez, R. & Mahoney, J.T. (1996) Modularity, flexibility, and knowledge management in product and organization design. *Strategic Management Journal*, 17 (Special Issue "Knowledge and the Firm"), 63–76.

Schmidt, J.B., Montoya-Weiss, M.M. & Massey, A.P. (2001) New product development decision-making effectiveness: Comparing individuals, face-to-face teams, and virtual teams. *Decision Sciences*, 32(4), 575–600.

Steiner, I.D. (1966) Models for inferring relationships between group size and potential group productivity. *Behavioral Science*, 11(4), 273–83.

Stump, R.L. & Heide, J.B. (1996) Controlling supplier opportunism. *Journal of Marketing Research*, 23(4), 431–41.

Teece, D.J. (1996) Firm organization, industrial structure, and technological innovation. *Journal of Economic Behavior and Organization*, 31(2), 193–224.

Tukel, O.I. & Wasti, S.N. (2001) Analysis of supplier buyer relationships using resource constrained project scheduling strategies. *European Journal of Operational Research*, 129(2), 271–76.

Venkatesan, R. (1992) Strategic sourcing: To make or not to make. *Harvard Business Review*, 70(6), 98–107.

Von Corswant, F. & Tunälv, C. (2002) Coordinating customers and proactive suppliers: A case study of supplier collaboration in product development. *Journal of Engineering and Technology Management*, 19(3–4), 249–61.

Wagner, S.M. (2003) Intensity and managerial scope of supplier integration. *Journal of Supply Chain Management*, 39(4), 4–15.

Wagner, S.M. & Johnson, J.L. (2004) Configuring and managing strategic supplier portfolios. *Industrial Marketing Management*, 33(8), 717–30.

Williamson, O.E. (1985) *The Economic Institutions of Capitalism*. New York: The Free Press.

Worren, N., Moore, K. & Cardona, P. (2002) Modularity, strategic flexibility, and firm performance: A study of the home appliance industry. *Strategic Management Journal*, 23(12), 1123–40.

Wynstra, F., Van Weele, A.J. & Weggemann, M. (2001) Managing supplier involvement in product development: Three critical issues. *European Management Journal*, 19(2), 157–67.

Zajac, E.J. & Olsen, C.P. (1993) From transaction cost to transactional value analysis: Implications for the study of interorganizational strategies. *Journal of Management Studies*, 30(1), 131–45.

Ziller, R.C. (1957) Group size: A determinant of the quality and stability of group decisions. *Sociometry*, 20, 165–73.

CHAPTER FIVE

Observing the Learning Process in an Interfirm Team

Thomas Durand

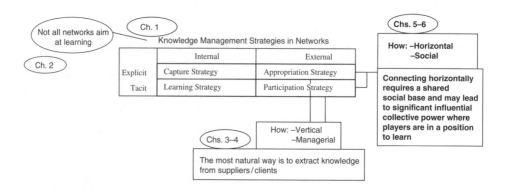

Abstract

This chapter is an attempt to describe empirically the process of learning in a specific, rather heterogeneous, group setting. The author studied an interfirm project team in charge of building a business plan for a potential new venture, e-business based, involving world players from the chemical industry. The team comprising 20 participants representing 8 different firms met about 12 times for 2–3 day sessions in the USA and Europe, over a 12-month period, while working on a virtual mode in between meetings.

The chapter adopts the perspective of constructivism to address the issue of reconciling individual and collective learning. The chapter presents four stages of the learning process: (1) participants share objectives, leading to a cognitive agreement to cooperate; (2) each team member contributes its competence, bringing in complementarities; (3) routines, shared vocabulary and concepts, and interpersonal links emerge, helping to save time and facilitating efficient work and the production of deliverables; (4) negotiation for the venture's future governance – that is, struggle for power – starts, based on the intimate cognitive, behavioral, and social knowledge which emerged within the team, thus reshaping the team itself. Each of the stages is documented with concrete illustrations drawn from the case study.

The chapter further analyzes how each step builds upon the previous stages and in particular why step 4 above could not start before the necessary learning (steps 1–3) took place within the group, in turn constructing the team. Several attempts to start negotiation earlier were made but failed. This suggests that the group, which did not exist as a team beforehand, operated as a learning community, in a way generating "competence *for* governance." All in all, the chapter discusses the role of business plans as a process of jointly exploring and consolidating knowledge within and among organizations. It argues that "business plan" project teams represent interesting cases to study organizational learning within networks, at the level of an interfirm work group.

Introduction

The process of learning in organizations has been studied extensively in the management literature over the last two decades. Yet, much remains to be done to describe in detail how the various forms of organizational knowledge are actually constructed.

One of the main difficulties encountered throughout the literature has to do with the level of analysis (individual, group, organization, interorganizations) and the interactions between these levels of learning. More specifically, relating individual learning to the construction of knowledge at group and organizational level remains a major theoretical challenge for management research. One of the promising perspectives to address this challenge may be found in constructivism and interactionism.

Interactionism as the foundation of our theoretical framework

We choose to advocate for this theoretical approach. We call upon the concepts of social representations, adopting the perspective of interactionism *à la* Moscovici (1976, 1988) together with the dual role of structuring (Giddens, 1987). The overall model stems from de la Ville's work (1996) and operates in three layers, similar to Russian dolls. The first layer calls upon social interactions as the founding mechanism of representations and knowledge (Vygotsky, 1978 and Moscovici, 1988). This suggests that individual learning takes place as actors interact in their social context. The second layer borrows from Goffman's (1991) interpretive frames which we metaphorically transform and extend into "competence leaves" (Durand, 2006) which, in our view, constitute elements of organizational knowledge. The competence leaves both support and channel subsequent learning taking place among actors throughout their joint activities. Learning is in turn increasingly constrained and structured, thus becoming shared, at least to a certain extent. Obviously, along the way, competence leaves evolve as they are adapted and reshaped. The third layer deals with the process of "memorizing." Indeed competence leaves cannot constitute the basis of knowledge if they are volatile. Some form of permanence is needed. This is what the concept of routinization (Nelson and Winter, 1982) has to offer, together with Giddens' (1987) idea of the duality of structuring which suggests that competence leaves tend to reinforce themselves in time as they channel, structure, and thus constrain subsequent learning.

In other words, competence leaves emerge and develop over time through learning while at the same time they structure and condition the learning taking place, thus building some form of permanence.

In our metaphor, organizational knowledge is similar to the overall foliage of a tree. The competence leaves actually combine, overlap, interfere with, and contradict one another. They are not neatly organized building blocks but look more like the leafy and fuzzy foliage which give the volume, the texture, and the shape to the tree.

All in all, social interaction among actors, interpretive frames or competence leaves and institutionalization through routines and dual structuring constitute the architecture of our theoretical framework. This is in line with a paradigmatic shift which was proposed by Durand et al. (1996).

This is the theoretical representation of organizational knowledge which we want to use as a conceptual background for our discussion of learning in groups.

Learning at group level

Several authors have studied the way groups cooperate and build some form of shared understanding. For a literature review on this theme, see Dameron (2000). Zajac and Olsen (1993) identify three phases in such cooperation within groups (clarification of objectives and contributions, work process with concrete learning including trust building, and reconfiguration when objectives are reformulated and strategy is revisited). Along similar lines, Doz (1996) suggests an iterative process where initial conditions (mostly defining task allocation) may facilitate or hinder learning, making it possible to reassess the work design and allocation of tasks among the group members (efficiency, fairness, adaptability). In turn this leads to redefining the work arrangements in the group, thus looping back to earlier stages. Ring and Van de Ven (1992) and Ring (1997) also present a three-step iterative process: a preliminary negotiation on objectives and contributions leads to commitments for action (with a contract as well as informal promises and/or psychological expectations); real work then follows, before feeding back into a renegotiation, in a way revisiting expectations. As the loop unfolds, group members assess the other members' contribution on the basis of efficiency and fairness. Dameron (2000) observed learning processes in groups within firms. She argues that groups are operating simultaneously on two different modes: "complementary mode" (when each member trades in its competence as a way to gain power or obtain some form of compensation) and a "pro-social" or "community mode" (when the players thrive to be recognized as members of the group, sharing a common identity). Dameron systematically codified events in the life of the groups she studied. This codification helps assess when the group is cooperating on a "complementary" mode or a "pro-social or community" mode. Her findings show that groups cooperate on both modes at the same time, while each of the two modes turns out to be dominant in sequence. More specifically, groups seem to first adopt a community mode as a way to get together as a team, then switch to a complementary mode to do whatever tasks need to be done jointly, then come back to a dominant community mode when the participants have the feeling that the work accomplished legitimated membership. See Figure 5.1.

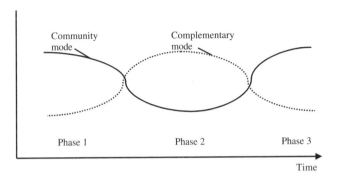

Figure 5.1 Community and complementary modes of cooperation. *Source:* Dameron (2000)

The present contribution aims at presenting a model of learning at group level, based on the results of an empirical, longitudinal study of one year with an interfirm team. The research is primarily interpretive.

The EHS NewCo Case Study

The author studied an interfirm project team in charge of building a business plan for a potential new venture, e-business based, involving world players from the chemical industry. The team comprised 20 participants representing 8 different firms. The team met about 12 times for 2–3 day sessions in the USA and Europe, over a 12-month period, while working on a virtual mode in between meetings. The case study made it possible to observe the group build into a team through a sequence of learning stages. This section is devoted to the overall description of the work as it took place. The next section presents the four stages of learning which emerged from the observation of the team work. Each of the stages is documented using the case study.

The context of EHS in the chemical industry

World chemical companies are struggling with the issue of protecting consumers and the environment from chemical hazards, ensuring that their products are properly handled, utilized, and transformed, avoiding any misuse which could cause health, safety, or environmental damage. Many laws and regulations have been passed in most countries on this matter which is now known as EHS (Environment, Health and Safety).

We focus here on the part of EHS which deals with products. Indeed, there is another EHS issue dealing with manufacturing plants and the corresponding chemical processes. This is a different, though related, matter.

The pressure from governments, citizens, and the media is steadily increasing. Industrial customers live under the same pressure and pass it on to their suppliers of basic chemical substances, upstream in the value chain. Any incident could seriously damage the reputation of the supplying company. EHS matters may thus be seen to be critical.

While these EHS concerns are quite legitimate, they turn out to be nightmares for managers in charge of EHS in large chemical companies. In practice, these managers have to continuously follow the evolution of the regulations in more than 130 countries where they ship their products. They have to produce (write, edit, and print) "safety data sheets" and labels describing the products, their toxicity and characteristics, and the recommendations to properly transport and handle the products. The labels must conform to the regulatory specifications of each of the countries where the products travel. Thus, among other requirements, the product documentation has to be edited in more than 30 different languages.

In other words, complying with the law in each country where the products are shipped is a difficult and extremely costly task.

The initial trigger

In this context, the EHS manager of a large French-based chemical manufacturer decides to approach one of his colleagues in charge of information systems for EHS at a large German competitor. He offers to jointly develop an internet-based solution to deal with EHS matters. He envisions a system which will store and retrieve on demand the relevant pieces of information regarding the products (overall formula, toxicity, recommendations for transportation and utilization, etc.). Databases for product and substance characteristics as well as legal phrases to be used in certain countries are to be created and updated, together with a system to automatically edit and print safety data sheets, labels and transportation documents where needed, in real time. The main idea for such a system is threefold. First, the system will help share the burden of keeping track of the constraints and regulations worldwide, country by country, while sharing the cost of updating the databases. Second, services from the system may be offered and sold to other chemical companies as well as customers down the value chain (transformers, e.g. paint producers, as well as industrial users, e.g. car manufacturers or pharmaceuticals). The system may thus become a "one stop shopping" for users downstream in the value chain. Third, this platform may in fact be incorporated into a profit center for which a business model should be designed, with a business plan to evaluate the financial attractiveness of a venture.

The building of an interfirm group

Although the context of the time when this thinking takes place is already that of the decline of the e-business wave, the two Franco-German EHS "colleagues" decide to start exploring the idea further. They subsequently invite some of their service providers on board, first a US consulting firm specialized in regulatory intelligence on EHS matters, and then a large ERP-software European company with extensive experience in the chemical industry. At this stage the author is invited on board to help facilitate the work process among the four early participants. At the same time, one more player is invited to join: this is a small German software implementer specializing in EHS.

A meeting is organized, showing a strong interest from the participants, and even some form of enthusiasm, while at the same time each participant remains extremely cautious regarding any resource commitment. At that stage, the French EHS manager starts expressing concerns about the purely European profile of the five participants represented so far in the project. He feels that the geographical scope of the venture is the world, thus requiring that at least the American continent be represented. A list of several US-based large chemical companies which could be interested in the venture is built. The potential candidates are approached. Two of them decide to join. Within two months, several telephone conferences are organized to finalize their participation. This makes seven players on the team.

At the last minute, an eighth player is invited on board. This is a French e-based start-up company specializing on the environment, heavily funded by venture capitalists to develop a vertical market place. They are to bring in an e-marketing dimension to the project.

All in all, eight different companies participated in the project: four large chemical companies (two European and two American), one large European ERP-software company, and three small players, a US legal company, a German software implementer and a French Internet start-up. An interesting cultural melting pot.

Timing and work process

The first discussion between the French manager and his German colleague from IS took place in June 2000. In October 2000, the five first participants had met twice. In December 2000, the two US companies had agreed to be part of the project and two telephone conferences had taken place. The group then decided to meet physically every 2 weeks, at first for 3 months, starting mid-January 2001. This was then extended to 3 more months until July 2001. The objective of the team was to build a business plan to be submitted to their respective management for approval. The project was named EHS NewCo, a new company for EHS services in the chemical industry and beyond.

From September 2000 onwards, the author was invited to participate in the project as a third party in charge of animating the work process. This meant that the researcher contributed to the project on a mode close to "action-research," with an ethnology flavor.

A steering committee was created comprising eight senior members, one from each participating company. The author animated the steering committee. A project team was also created, with a project leader from one of the companies plus various members, equivalent to one person full time per partner, plus some additional temporary help called upon from the partners whenever needed. These additional contributors brought in specific pieces of knowledge on a case-by-case basis. The steering committee (SC) was to set up the objectives for the project, build the strategy, monitor the progress of the project team, negotiate the governance and equity in the future venture. The project team (PT) was to build the business plan. It turned out that this distinction between the steering committee and the project team tended to blur on various occasions, as the physical meetings of both SC and PT took place at the same time, while members of the steering committee got increasingly involved in direct production of deliverables at the project team level. In a way, one could view both the steering committee and the project team as one overall group which prepared the business plan for the venture.

The aim of this chapter is to describe the learning process which took place within both the steering committee and the project team. Before entering into the description of the learning stages which emerged from the observation, several additional contextual traits of the work process on the project are worth mentioning.

- Throughout the entire work, there was persistent disagreement about the objective of the project. Was NewCo about making money out of a business idea, namely offering efficient solutions to deal with EHS matters, or was the project primarily about sharing cost among large players of the chemical industry to ensure that each participating company would be in a better position to comply with EHS regulations throughout the world, thus improving the overall image of the industry as such?

  While some of the representatives of the participating companies were EHS managers, other participants happened to work for the e-business Venture Capital unit, at corporate level. This was the main cause of a difference in perspective. The former viewed EHS as a cost issue for their company thriving to comply with existing regulations, thus contributing to address societal concerns ("We've got to share the burden and we have to improve the image of our industry which is wrongly seen as a source of pollution.") The latter viewed EHS as a mere source of revenues, a business opportunity, in turn paying much less attention to the image of the industry and its reputation. ("How much should we invest, for what return?")

  This created an ideological conflict which prevailed during all the interactions. Making money, growing a new business thanks to environmental concerns (!), or promoting sustainable development for the whole chemical sector while decreasing the cost of complying with regulations for its own company – the debate at times turned bitter. This also illustrated the cultural gap between a liberal economy advocated for by US representatives and a typical European perspective on cooperative action at industry level for the benefit of all.

- The whole business idea behind the project may be translated mechanistically into an externalization issue. Indeed several chemical companies were considering externalizing their EHS departments. This obviously strongly influenced the perception of some of the participants to the team. These clearly feared that their whole activity might be jeopardized as a result of the creation of NewCo. (One may actually question whether this would be the way to go. Indeed EHS matters may actually become so critical in the event of significant incidents that it may be risky for companies to rely on external services to deal with an issue which may be so strategic.) Nevertheless, this concern for potential externalization indirectly affected the work on the project as some of the team members explicitly wondered what would happen to them and their people next.

- Building a business plan may be seen as an attempt to reduce subjectivity. It consists of documenting a business model through data and rational analyses, presenting the business case in an orderly and logical way, leading to a set of concrete recommendations for decision makers. However, it should be stressed that the whole exercise is in fact usually more about building a convincing argument, shared among the proponents and sellable to their respective boss.

Sharing subjectivity and making it sound logical is not necessarily equivalent to reducing subjectivity. This exercise was no exception. The heart of the matter was to build a PowerPoint presentation, together with detailed and intricate Excel spreadsheets as a way to convince higher management, those emphatically called "my board" by the senior members on the team. In a way, building a business plan is not about testing the relevance of the ideology behind a business idea, it is about re-composing and sharing an ideology which makes sense to all stakeholders, including those mysteriously designated under the mythical label "my board." Should the business plan be as rational and documented as possible, or should it be primarily convincing? This exercise suggested once more that it is not so important that the plan be "accurate" as long as everyone is candidly convinced that it is as close to accuracy as it can be, given the resources allocated to do the job.

A Four-stage Model of the Learning Process

In observing the EHS NewCo group work, four stages of the learning process emerged: (1) First, participants shared objectives, leading to a cognitive agreement to cooperate; (2) then each team member contributed its competence, bringing in complementarities; (3) subsequently, as the work unfolded, routines, shared vocabulary and concepts, interpersonal links and emotions emerged, helping to save time and facilitating efficient work and the production of deliverables; (4) finally, negotiation for the venture's future governance, that is, struggle for power, could start based on the intimate cognitive, behavioral, and social knowledge which emerged within the team, thus reshaping the team itself.

The objective of this section is to discuss and document each of these phases with concrete illustrations drawn from the case study.

Stage 1: Re-cognition of objectives and need to cooperate

Each participant first wants to understand whether the other potential team members share the same overall objectives. They pay attention to the motives behind the involvement of other partners. They check the fit among objectives claimed and potential hidden agendas. In addition, they try to assess the capabilities and knowledge of each contributor and the complementarities of the capabilities at hand.

This is done through formal and informal discussions whereby each partner is to declare its strategic intent, experience, and project-related competence base. Other partners listen, ask questions, get a feel for the potential of the partners and thus the team.

Throughout this process, everyone builds or confirms the belief that the team is strong enough to meet the expectations and produce the deliverables.

At this stage, this is primarily a cognitive assessment, based on declarations, reputation, and consistency check (Are the presentations of their objectives consistent over time? Do their objectives and motives fit to what we know about their strategy? Can they really bring in what they promise and will it be useful? etc.). In a way, this is also a sniffing out process, but primarily cognitive.

Typically, in the case of NewCo, this first stage took off a few weeks before the formal process of meeting started. It went on during the first full meeting in January 2001. Each participant made a formal presentation in front of the others, explaining why they were interested, what their past experience had been and how they planned to contribute to the project. Every participant was keen to behave positively, showing both respect and interest in the presentations from their partners-to-be in the team. Only during the breaks and in between sessions was it possible to observe some bilateral discussions where more skeptical questions could be debated, but that remained marginal. This led to some minor comments on the side about what could be really expected from one or two partners, but that was all. Obviously, participants were doing their best to look at the bright side of the team.

In a way, this first phase was a bit like a set of sales presentations, in a context where there would be no or very few really challenging questions. Everyone behaved nicely. This was particularly so as the cultural mix around the table was so diverse. Most participants were keen not to hurt anyone.

It should, however, be clearly mentioned that these preliminary interactions in fact subsequently strongly influenced the emotional perceptions in the group. Suspicion, mistrust, or positive perceptions and behaviors emerged later but were partly formed very early on.

This resulted in the lengthy negotiation of a "Memorandum of Understanding" (MOU). The drafting became even more difficult when each party started calling up their lawyers to have the successive drafts validated. Finally the MOU was signed. This was the first deliverable from the group. This indicated the end of a first phase.

Stage 2: Complementary competence at work

A work plan is built. Tasks are split among the group members. This is helping the participants feel better as they can now really show what they can contribute to the project. Intense work interaction starts among group members. The first misunderstandings appear and need to be overcome. At first, this is done rather smoothly. More fundamental issues also emerge and turn out to be more difficult to deal with. More interactions are needed and some tension may appear. This requires revisiting the project objectives to reassure every participant in their belief that this is a winning team, with converging objectives. In other words, the second stage requires to build upon the output of stage 1, including through revisiting and confirming some of its content to reassure participants.

Preliminary results are obtained and galvanize the group. There is still plenty to do but progress is being made. Progressively basic technical vocabulary around the project is shared among participants. Yet, persistent misunderstandings reappear about key concepts, who is in charge of what, or how to collect or process data, and even more so regarding fundamental issues about the whole project. This may generate difficulties and delay in obtaining additional results, in turn leading to the first real complaints about misbehaviors or hidden agenda. Some tension emerges. This may require adapting the work plan, modifying the tasks split or respecifying the tasks and assignment. The minor conflicts are thus resolved at this stage but will be remembered later and may cause some irritation.

Work appears to be more difficult than anticipated, especially in an interfirm, multicultural context. The team faces the challenge of both leveraging the existing competence base brought in by each partner and building joint knowledge through ad hoc learning. This is challenging and stimulating. Despite the difficulties, group members enjoy the challenge and appreciate working in the group, with the feeling of building a real team. They still believe that the team has the capabilities to solve most project issues.

Typically, in the case of NewCo, after what was seen as a rather lengthy presentation, negotiation, and planning process, the start of real work was seen as a relief. Team members started collecting data and producing analyses very aggressively. This had to do with competition, market data, potential service offerings, pricing the services and evaluating potential sales.

If the review of competition was done extensively with little difficulty, the lack of market data turned out to be a major problem, especially for downstream industries where none of the participants had enough experience. Segmentation was difficult and generated hot discussions and several iterations. But this was solved rather smoothly. However, given time constraints, there was no other choice but to go for rough estimates for some of the market segments. This created some tension and uneasiness, if not frustration for some of the participants who would have preferred to conduct extensive market surveys while others were explaining that this was not worth the expense and the time needed.

A key issue soon appeared with the priority among the services which EHS NewCo should offer. For some, the offerings had to fit first the need of the large chemical companies. For others, the priority offerings should go for where the most significant and profitable markets could be found. This obviously worsened the fundamental difference in objectives among some of the key participants (solving the nightmare of managing EHS at large chemical companies or making money with EHS). The discussions turned sour on several occasions. This difficulty remained a controversial topic until the end of the project and was never fully resolved.

Yet, along the way, participants were satisfied to show what they brought in. Positive comments were made about the technical competence of most participants. The complementary capabilities were clearly demonstrated (e.g., ability to work with an elaborate template for financial spreadsheets in sophisticated ways, in-depth under-standing of where EHS needs may be encountered in some downstream industrial processes using chemical substances, concrete knowledge of price acceptability for certain service offerings according to quantities and context, etc.).

In other words, on one hand the team building process was on track, with growing respect for the competence demonstrated. On the other hand, significant divergence in the overall strategic intent of the project plus various minor misunderstandings paved the way for more difficulties down the road.

Stage 3: Routines, rituals, and interpersonal links become essential

As the group builds itself into a team, non-purely cognitive elements become dom-inant. The team creates work routines, adopts shared symbols, and sets up rituals. This helps to save time, work more efficiently, facilitate coordination while promoting team membership. New entrants joining the team at this time find it harder as the team shares much in common that cannot be easily explained. Participants know each other. They know what to expect, they anticipate biases and tacit preferences, they adopt attitudes to fit the group.

At this stage, both trust and suspicion have emerged, although being kept mostly tacit. Subgroups and coalitions also emerge and are recognized and felt throughout the group.

This is no longer a purely cognitive arrangement of rational players having coldly decided to cooperate, working together with no emotions. This is more of a living team, where feelings, perception, and behavior count; where past reactions and attitudes matter a great deal; where cultural fit or misfit plays a key role. Along similar lines, McAllister (1995) proposed a useful distinction: trust based on cognition and trust based on affect and emotions. In that sense, stages 1 and 2 rely on cognition-based trust while stage 3 operates more in a context of affect-based trust.

Rituals, collective habits, and symbols, if not shared values – at least to a certain extent – have developed: a collection of individuals coming from different horizons in a network built into a team.

Typically, in the case of NewCo, rituals soon emerged. In order to keep some balance between the three main countries represented in the group, it was decided that meetings would take place in turn in Germany, France, and the USA. Each of the main participating companies was thus hosting the meeting. In addition, for the meetings to start on time on the first morning, it was decided that those traveling from abroad would arrive the day before and participate in an informal dinner. In the event, in each successive meeting, the host made a particular effort to take better care of the participants, leading to an escalation in the way participants were treated over time. This went from a simple buffet on the first evening and sandwiches at lunch the next day on the first meeting, to wine tasting in a winery, a dinner at a crab place near Washington DC, a post dinner visit to a casino to gamble, dinner at the Lido in Paris, etc. Each host increasingly tried to mobilize the best local resources available to treat his guests. While some of the discussions during the sessions were at times tense and difficult, all these informal socializing activities helped keep the group together.

Routines emerged about starting hours for meetings, duration of breaks, items on the agenda, use of Excel sheets for minutes of meetings, same template for PowerPoint presentations, acceptance that participants would connect to the Internet to check their email several times a day, principles to control mobile phones, etc. All of that contributed to create not only a certain style, an atmosphere, but also made it possible to save time, to smooth work, to facilitate interactions and collective work, and to share meaning.

National cultures played a significant role. One of the German participants was of an Italian origin and openly conveyed a Latin flavor in his behavior, contrasting sharply with another German participant. One of the US representatives was from Brazil while one of the French participants had spent several years in this country and spoke fluent Portuguese as well. Another participant from a US company was originally from Eastern Europe, etc. All in all, the informal socialization process did gravitate around this mix of cultures which obviously meant a lot to most of the group members. English was the working language used on most occasions but bilateral discussions took place in other languages as well. After some discussion, it was decided to use the US dollar as the currency unit for the financial evaluations in the business plan. Yet the European participants had seemed to unite around a proposal to use the euro instead.

This should not be regarded as anecdotal. Tacit coalitions indeed emerged, which in many instances overlapped national or continental clusters (e.g., EHS technicians clearly understood one another and got along very well). These coalitions obviously varied according to topics and issues, but the cultural proximity remained always present.

One of the participants kindly offered to write minutes for the meetings, real time. (He obviously aimed at keeping some form of a control on the way things would be recorded.) The notes were taken on the spot, as the discussion took place. Everyone soon got used to his writing style and wording, thus saving a lot of time and energy for all participants.

An extranet platform was set up to facilitate the collective work for distant members, interacting on a virtual mode, both electronically and asynchronically. This was to store all outputs from the team and permit exchange through a forum for both the steering committee and the project team. This platform was not really used in practice. The interactions in between meetings were made by emails. Even large files were sent by email. In addition a few phone conferences were organized to keep enough momentum to the work when needed. It should be stressed that email dialog in a team may become more aggressive than discussion in a physical meeting. When frustration is expressed through an email, there is no body language nor the presence of other participants to smooth the message or act as a buffer. Regular telephone contacts and even more so physical meetings were thus very important.

All in all, the group learnt how to best operate, given the knowledge and skills available, and given the personalities involved. Each group member became part of a complex set of cognitive and interpersonal work linkages with other participants. Accordingly, everyone was thus in a position to learn from the others.

Stage 4: Negotiation – "competence for governance"

At this point, the collection of individuals has become a team. The group has converged around the same objectives, leveraged complementary knowledge and skills, built shared concepts and vocabulary, adopted common routines, rituals and attitudes. The group has developed some competence of its own. In so doing, the group is more than the sum of individuals, it has evolved into a team.

At this point, real negotiation (or re-negotiation) can take place. At stages 1 and 2, a preliminary negotiation about objectives, priorities, deliverables, work tasks and split among partners has taken place. But at that time participants did not know enough of the other group members. This is no longer the case.

Now it is possible to discuss sensitive topics, based on the intimate knowledge that participants have of other members, plus the ability to work and interact in efficient ways. In addition, a cold and formal agreement on objectives has been complemented by some form of affect-based trust (and obviously some distrust as well).

Among the sensitive topics, the issue of power for the next steps of the project is essential. Discussions about governance can really start, based on the emerging collective competence of the team. This is what may be called "competence *for* governance."

In the case of NewCo, all attempts made earlier to start negotiations about governance issues failed. Participants did not wish to discuss critical issues such as future power and control of the venture. They claimed they could not do it before having seen the "business plan." Another interpretation would be that they did not feel like doing it before having taken the time to learn about the other participants.

After several unsuccessful attempts, discussions could finally start when everyone felt about ready for it. Although there was no clear signal for it, it happened. The discussion took place around concrete scenarios which were constructed and presented by participants. To start the process, two rather obvious scenarios were put on the table by the author operating as a facilitator. The others then followed. Each scenario was sketched and illustrated using a set of variables and criteria which emerged along the way.

Some participants advocated for the large chemical companies taking the leadership, while others would suggest that smaller service organizations would be better fit to deliver quality service offerings.

Some of the coalitions which had tacitly appeared through the previous stages became more visible. At the same time, suspicion and distrust could also be felt throughout the discussions. The point is not that these were good or bad. The point is that both affect-based trust and distrust as well as coalitions which were built before, that is, during stages 1–3, played a major role in the negotiation process. In addition, this emotional basis was clearly needed to conduct the discussion about governance and power as none of that could start beforehand. Stage 4 required stages 1–3 to have taken place.

This idea may actually be extended to the other stages as well.

The model operates in successive layers

Before real work can start, members need to have discussed and agreed cognitively about the project objectives. Are the others really interested? Are the knowledge bases of the partners complementary? Can the group deliver what is expected? No cognitive commitment can be reached without positive answers to these questions. Collective action at stage 2 needs cognition at stage 1.

Common language and shared concepts, routines and rituals can emerge only through interaction and common work within the group. Leveraging complementary knowledge and skills to produce the project deliverables means building additional competence, this time at group level. Group competence creation, including emotional trust at stage 3 needs action and interaction at stage 2.

Real negotiation on sensitive matters, mostly power and governance requires maturity and intimacy within the working group. This may not be done on a purely cognitive and cold basis. Some form of trust and a feel for emotions within the team are needed. A fully-fledged competence base for the group (knowledge, know-how, and attitudes) is a prerequisite for meaningful negotiations. This is the "competence *for* governance" idea.

Figure 5.2 summarizes the four-stage model for the learning process in an interfirm setting which emerged from our case study. In a way the four stages operate

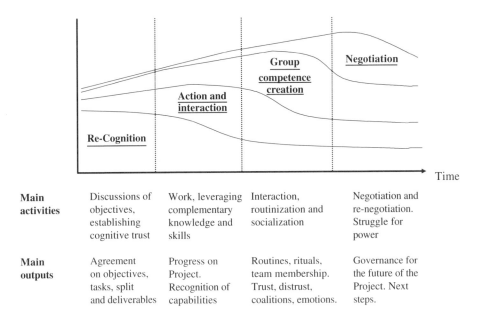

Figure 5.2 A four-stage model of group learning

more as layers building up over time: cognition paving the way for action and inter-action, permitting in turn group competence creation, thus opening the door for (re-)negotiation.

Conclusions

The chapter presented a case study, describing empirically the process of learning in a specific, interfirm project team in charge of building a business plan for a potential new venture.

The chapter adopted the perspective of constructivism to address the issue of recon-ciling individual and collective learning. As a result, a four-stage model of the learning process was presented and discussed: (1) *cognition*: participants share objectives, lead-ing to a cognitive agreement to cooperate; (2) *action and interaction*: each team member contributes its competence, bringing in complementarities; (3) *group com-petence creation*: routines, shared vocabulary and concepts, interpersonal links emerge, helping save time and facilitating efficient work and the production of deliverables; (4) *negotiation*: discussions for the venture's future governance, that is, struggle for power, start based on the intimate cognitive, behavioral and social knowledge which emerged within the team, thus re-shaping the team itself.

The model operates in layers as each step builds upon the previous stages. In particu-lar, negotiation (step 4 above) could not start before the necessary learning (steps 1–3) took place within the group, in turn constructing the team. This led to the idea that the group, which did not exist as a team beforehand, operated as a learning community, in a way generating "competence *for* governance." This takes time. All in all, the chapter discussed the role of business plans as a process of jointly exploring and consolidating knowledge within and among organizations. It may be worth pointing out that "business plan" project teams represent interesting cases to study organizational learning within networks, at the level of an interfirm work group.

References

Dameron, S. (2000) Génération de la Coopération dans l'Organisation', Thèse, Paris IX Dauphine.

Doz, Y. (1996) The evolution of cooperation in strategic alliance: Initial conditions or learning process', *Strategic Management Journal*, 17, 55–83.

Durand, T. (1998) The alchemy of competence. In G. Hamel, C. K. Prahalad, H. Thomas & D. O'Neal (Eds.) *Strategic Flexibility: Managing in a Turbulent Environment*. Chichester: John Wiley & Sons.

Durand, T. (2001) 'La compétence organisationnelle au macroscope: accéder aux cadres de compétence pour explorer la formation de la stratégie', in *Le management stratégique en représentations*. Drisse, Ellipses.

Durand, T. (2006) The making of a metaphor: Developing a theoretical framework. In J. Löwstedt & T. Sternberg (Eds.) *Producing Management Knowledge*, ch. 11. Routledge (in press).

Durand, T. Mounoud, E. & Ramanantsoa, B. (1996) Uncovering strategic assumptions: Understanding managers' ability to build representations. *European Management Journal*, 14(4), 389–98.

Giddens, A. (1987) *La constitution de la société: éléments de la théorie de la structuration*. Paris: PUF, Collection Sociologies.

Goffman, E. (1991) *Les cadres d'expérience*. Paris: Editions de Minuit.

La Ville, V. de (1996) Apprentissages collectives et structuration de la stratégie dans la jeune entreprise de haute technologie: Etude de cas et éléments de modélisation procédurale. Thèse de doctorat, Université Lyon III, Juillet.

McAllister, D. J. (1995) Affect- and cognition-based trust as foundations for interpersonal cooperation in organizations. *Academy of Management Journal*, 38(1), 24–59.

Moscovici, S. (1976) Psychologie des representations sociales. *Cahiers Vilfredo Pareto*, 14, 409–16.

Moscovici, S. (1988) Notes towards a description of social representations. *European Journal of Social Psychology*, 18, 211–50.

Nelson, R. & Winter, S. (1982) *An Evolutionary Theory of Economic Change*. Cambridge, MA: Harvard University Press.

Piaget, J. (1948) *La naissance de l'intelligence chez l'enfant*. Geneva: Delachaux et Niestlé.

Prahalad, C. K. & Hamel, G. (1990) The core competence of the corporation. *Harvard Business Review*, 68, 79–91.

Ring, P. S. (1997) Patterns of process in cooperative interorganizational relationships. In P. Beamish & P. Killing (Eds.) *Cooperative Strategies: A North American Perspective*, 286–307. San Francisco: New Lexington Press.

Ring, P. S. & Van de Ven, A. (1992) Structuring cooperative relationships between organizations. *Strategic Management Journal*, 13, 483–98.

Strategor (1988, 1993) Stratégie, Structure, Décision, Identité: Politique Générale d'Entreprises. Paris: Ouvrage collectif, InterEditions.

Vygotsky, L. (1978) *Mind in Society: The Development of Higher Psychological Processes.* Cambridge, MA: Harvard University Press.

Weick, K. (1979) *The Social Psychology of Organizing.* Reading, MA: Addison-Wesley.

Zajac, E. J. & Olsen, C. P. (1993) From transactional cost to transactional value: Implications for the study of interorganizational strategies. *Journal of Management Studies*, 30(1), 131–45.

CHAPTER SIX

Consocia et impera: How French and Italian Fabric Producers Cooperate to Conquer the "Dominant Design" in the Fashion Industry

Diego Rinallo, Francesca Golfetto, and Michael Gibbert

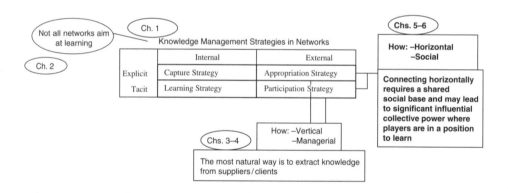

Abstract

Concertation is a process used by French and Italian producers of high quality fabrics to build and sustain – season after season – their position as world leaders in the fine fashion industry, despite strong competition from emerging countries. In this chapter, we employ ethnographic methods to make sense of the concertation process. Concertation is an interpretive enterprise, where a favorable business environment is socially constructed through the interaction of key actors. An outcome of the concertation mechanism is a social stratification of the marketplace, that is, leaders versus followers and innovators versus imitators, which has implications in terms of marketplace status and premium prices. Our ethnographic interpretation of the concertation process has managerial implications, as it suggests guidelines along which to manage interorganizational collaboration among competitors.

The mills have surpassed the designers.
The weavers are so advanced that they give ideas to the designers.
The pupils have become more astute than their teachers.
            (Angelo Uslenghi, head of Moda In's style commission)

Access is restricted . . . and based on criteria of product quality, creativity (with
an obligation of renewing collections bi-annually) as well as the enterprise's
financial health.[1]
            (Hélène Pichenot, Première Vision's PR manager)

Introduction

Consider the competitive dynamics in the fine fashion industry: there are up to four cycles of disruptive innovation every year, incumbents (the Italian and French fashion houses such as Armani, Gucci, Chanel, Dior, etc.) fight for market share in an increasingly differentiated global market place, and their suppliers – in particular the European weavers supplying fine fabrics – are struggling with greater-than-ever competition from the Far East. In an industry as old as mankind, but more dynamic even than, say, the software industry, how do firms maintain a competitive edge?

In this chapter, we discuss a sophisticated process that industry members call concertation. French and Italian weavers in the fine fashion apparel industry use this process to maintain season after season their position as world leaders in their industry, despite strong competition from competitors from emerging countries. Essentially, these companies forecast future evolutions in social and consumer values, in order to guide their style innovation in a way that does not disperse individual efforts. As a consequence, the network of members can affirm standards in ways not dissimilar to those found in high tech industries. Concertation is thus able to: (1) provide a competitive advantage to the group of companies which with individual innovation accept and support what will be the winning standard; (2) unite competitors to create a "critical mass" so as to accelerate the adoption of the concerted standard; (3) construct a favorable competitive environment, since each season's "previsions" become true in the manner of a self-fulfilling prophecy; and (4) publicly broadcast the new trend.

We describe the concertation process by reference to two cases: the *Première Vision* trade fair in Paris and *Moda In* in Milan. These two trade fairs establish common ground for cooperation and provide visibility to the innovations that the collaboration between the companies affirms as the "dominant design" in the season's fabrics. In its initial phases, when common paths of innovation are imagined and shared, concertation ensures collective value creation for network members – even though these members are competitors. In later phases of concertation, each member competes against the others in a strategic game to gain individual value.

How can rival companies cooperate to achieve a common good? To make sense of these insights conceptually, we draw on Daft and Weick's (1984) model of organizations as interpretive systems and on ritual theory to suggest that concertation meetings and the resulting trade fairs are instrumental in the creation of what anthropologists would term *communitas*, that is, a sense of belonging to a community that, particularly in contexts of increasing competitive pressure from emerging countries, permits overcoming rivalries. Our interpretive model suggests implications for other organizations, particularly when collaborating with competitors is required to create value.

The structure of this chapter is as follows. In the section that follows, we provide some industry background, looking into issues such as innovation and modularity in order to illustrate the supply chain in the fine-fashion apparel industry. Next, we give full details about the ethnographic method we employed. We then describe *Première Vision* and *Moda In* and provide a description of the concertation process from the point of view of industry insiders. In the discussion section, we propose an interpretation of concertation as an enactment of the competitive environment, and we employ ritual theory to make sense of the apparent paradox of cooperating with one's own rivals. We conclude by offering managerial implications valid beyond the field we observed.

Background: Innovation in Fabric for Fine Fashion Apparel

In the fashion apparel industry, innovation mostly regards style rather than technical features, that is, creativity in cut, colors and relative combinations, patterns, fabrics and their processing and finishing, which when embodied in clothing will satisfy symbolic functions (allowing consumers to express individual identity and signal social status). Contrary to the widespread belief that innovation in fashion style is mainly created by a limited set of celebrity designers (e.g., Armani, Dolce & Gabbana, etc.) working in the isolation of the genius, in the fashion pipeline the fabric sector is a central locus of innovation. Designers, in most cases, could not provide clothes with an aspect that consumers associate with dominant trends in fashion (e.g., attention to natural environment) if their suppliers did not have the technical ability and end-market knowledge to produce the yarns and fabrics that incorporate creative solutions aligned with those trends. Only under these conditions will it be possible to exploit such yarns/fabrics to produce garments with, say, a raw and "natural" aspect in line with current fashion. In other words, designers are inspired by upstream creativity which is aligned with what consumers value and with what they want to express with their clothes. This means that fabric producers have to anticipate consumer needs to develop solutions that complement the core competence of designers and apparel companies in creating fashionable end products (Golfetto et al., 2004).

Fabric collections present both technical and creative content. Technical content is mostly provided by upstream actors (e.g., textile machinery producers, chemical component companies) and is equally available to most competitors. Consequently, it cannot be a source of competitive advantage. To differentiate their goods, fabric producers therefore vary their bi-annual collections in terms of color (e.g., ruby or clay furrow), structure (e.g., jacquard, satin, chiffon), aspect (e.g., structured, light, washed-out, opaque), touch (e.g., soft, warm, fluid, compact), decoration (e.g., arabesque, cashmere, irregular stripes), treatment (e.g., burnt-out, washed, gummy coating). These highly differentiated elements are deliberately designed to be invested in finished goods with symbolic and expressive properties that will be valued by consumers. However, in the development of their new collections, fabric companies have to face severe problems of modularity tied to consumer behavior (clothes and accessories are jointly bought and used by consumers) and the fragmentation and non-integrated nature of the fashion industry supply chain. Innovation in the high fashion industry cannot occur in a vacuum.

To avoid the risk of deviant innovations that do not fit with the prevailing trends at a given moment, companies have to consider both consumers' future tastes and the innovation efforts of upstream and downstream partners and producers of complementary products when preparing their own collections. For example, a fabric firm will have to decide whether its range of colors will correspond with that realized by knitwear, velvet, and other semi-finished textile manufacturers, as well as by its competitors. Furthermore, all semi-finished textile products will have to fit with the style and cut that will be prevalent in apparel. Finally, compatibility from the purchaser's point of view has to be taken into account, since consumers will combine apparel with accessories (e.g., shoes, bags) to express their identity and, at the same time, signal membership of specific reference groups. This means that standards are needed to reduce uncertainty in innovation to the benefit of all firms in the system.[2]

Although modularity/compatibility problems are not unique to this setting, fabric companies have to face additional, and rather unique, challenges that have to be solved if they want to thrive or even survive. First, the fabric industry is fragmented and not integrated, that is, it includes numerous companies within each of the specialized phases of a very articulated value chain (see Figure 6.1 for an illustration).[3] Moreover, most of these companies are small and medium-sized enterprises (SMEs), and even the market leaders lack the resources and skills needed to establish their own innovative solutions as the "dominant design." Secondly, because it is linked to the fashion system, the innovation cycle for fabrics is very rapid with seasonal collections launched (at least) once every six months. Thirdly, the new products have to be presented far in advance of consumer purchase. For example, in September 2003 fabric producers have to present to their customers (apparel producers) their proposals for the spring/summer 2005 apparel collections, that is, 18 months before the end products will be available in the shops. Thus, since consumer tastes are ever-changing, new product development activities are unavoidably risky and require some form of fashion forecast.

Methods

The data and interpretations presented in this paper derive from an extensive field investigation of *Première Vision*, *Moda In* and the European fabric industry at large, conducted in the period 2002–2005. To capture the complexities of the concertation process, we employed an ethnographic approach, mostly based on participant observation and both directive and nondirective interviews. Ethnographic research (Arnould & Wallendorf, 1994): (1) is characterized by systematic data collection and recording of human action in natural settings; (2) involves extended, experiential participation by researchers into the contexts to be studied; (3) produces interpretations

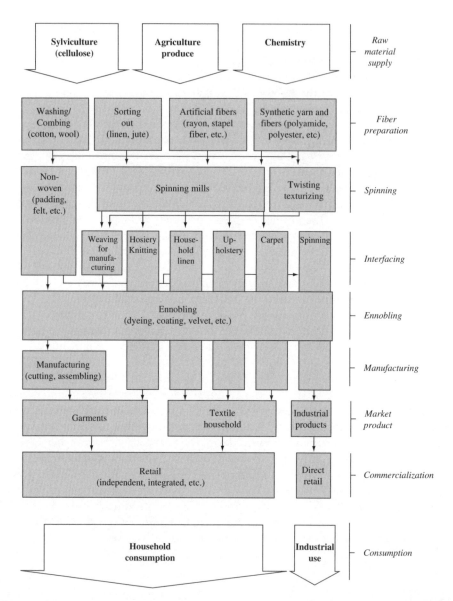

Figure 6.1 The textile-apparel supply chain. *Source*: Adapted from Bellon and Chevallier (1983).

of behaviors that the subjects investigated find plausible; (4) incorporates multiple sources of data to generate varying perspectives on the phenomena studied.

In the course of the present study, data gathering activities included interviews with the trade associations involved in the concertation mechanism, coupled with participant observation of the many backstage events that take place to coordinate activities before the two trade fairs are held, such as meetings of different natures and the workshops employed to explain the new trends to exhibitors. The bulk of the field activities consisted, however, in the participant observation of the trade fairs themselves in several editions, during which field notes, photographs, and videos were employed to document the interactions between and among visitors and exhibitors. Directive and nondirective interviews with informants took place during *Première Vision* and *Moda In*. Additional interviews were carried out at other trade fairs of the fabric industry in order to include in our analysis the perceptions of those companies that do not participate in the concertation process, and to avoid biases in our research findings. Overall, 95 interviews were conducted with informants, ranging from 10 to 90 minutes in length. Data gathering also included the collection of secondary data and artifacts, including trend documentation, *Première Vision* and *Moda In* press releases and official pictures, exhibitor brochures, fabric samples, etc.

Overall, verbatim interview transcripts and field notes of our observations were over 350 pages long, and included rich narratives and anecdotes from informants, together with visual material (hundreds of pictures of trade show booths and trend areas; hours of videos of visitor behavior in trend areas, etc.). Such data were separately analyzed by the first and second authors, through the logical operations and phases typical of qualitative analysis (Spiggle, 1994), when previous readings of texts inform later readings, and at the same time later readings permit the researcher to identify patterns in the data not identified in the initial analysis. The result of these analyses is a proposition of the concertation mechanism as it is seen by the participating actors, that is, an "insider" view. In ethnography, this first-level typology of research findings would be defined as an *emic account* which reflects informants' viewpoints.[4] Our second-level research findings, reported in the discussion section, consist of an *etic account* of concertation, which reflects our viewpoint as management scholars. The distinction between emic and etic accounts of cultural systems, first proposed by Pike (1967), is related to the difference proposed by methodologists of qualitative data between analysis and interpretation (Spiggle, 1994). By relying on these two activities of inference, which are related but distinct, it was possible to achieve a theoretical generalization of emic research findings beyond their local significance.

Première Vision and *Moda In*: Key Events in Concertation

The tough environmental challenges previously described provide Italian and French producers with formidable inducements to cooperate in order to reduce the risks in innovation. In both countries, concertation mechanisms are centered on bi-annual, international trade fairs managed by private organizers owned and supported by the national producers' associations. These fairs are *Première Vision*, held in Paris, and *Moda In*, held in Milan[5] (see Table 6.1 for details). The two exhibitions are held in the same period: in February (spring/summer collections) and September (fall/winter collection).

Première Vision

Première Vision's origins date back to 1973 with a joint promotion undertaken by 15 Lyon weavers who decided to present their fabric collections at the International

Table 6.1   *Première Vision* and *Moda In*: key facts

	Première Vision, Paris	*Moda In*, Milan
Organizer	Première Vision Le Salon s.a. (supported by French textile trade association)	Si.Tex s.r.l. (supported by Italian textile trade associations)
Dates (2004)	Spring/Summer collections: Feb. 12–15 Fall/Winter collections: Sept. 21–24	Spring/Summer collections: Feb. 9–11 Fall/Winter collections: Sept. 7–11
Space hired (2002)	41,016 sq. m.	18,350 sq. m.
Exhibitors (2002)	775 (77% foreign)	513 (26% foreign)
Visitors (2002)	32,634 (77% foreign)	18,820 (20% foreign)
Trade show positioning	Trade fair for innovation	Trade fair for innovation

Source: Elaborations on organizer data.

Textile Centre in Paris. It was only in 1976 that the idea of a "trend concertation" was established. The "weavers decided to meet together before the Salon to propose a synthesis of seasonal color and fabric trends, paving the way for a coherence in the textile offer, and market structure" (*Première Vision*, 2003). In following years, the cooperative effort was extended to other types of fabric producers both from France and other European countries. More recently, there has been some opening to rigorously selected non-European exhibitors. In 1997, *Première Vision* established an International Observatory which acts as a socio-cultural surveillance unit on a global scale and aims to identify the emerging trends likely to have an impact on the textile and fashion industries. The Observatory's analyses in Europe, North and South America, and Asia are carried out by a broad network of specialists including architects, designers, trend forecasters, experts in new technologies, sociologists, and anthropologists.

In terms of both "objective" data (i.e., space hired, number of exhibitors, and number of visitors) and "subjective" rank attributed by operators in the field, *Première Vision* is the top event in the industry. Being highly internationalized from both exhibitor and visitor side, it is an event primarily dedicated to international exchanges (Cermes-Bocconi, 2004a). Visiting companies attribute to *Première Vision* an "informative," rather than "commercial," function, considering participation as a "learning expedition," the value of which resides in inspiration and awareness of fashion trends. In contrast, most of the other trade fairs around the world (e.g., in Hong Kong, China; New York, USA; Düsseldorf, Germany) fulfill a "commercial" function, providing information of a more operational nature linked to specific purchasing processes. This means that those companies admitted as exhibitors at *Première Vision* are usually considered the innovators in the industry, with the consequent implications in terms of reputation and, frequently, premium price.

Moda In

Moda In was launched in 1984 by the Italian trade associations with the aim of promoting the national textile industry. The organizer soon established a concertation formula centered around trend forecasting by a Style Committee composed of a small group of collaborating professionals, each focusing on a specific area (i.e., colors, accessories, etc.). Similar to *Première Vision*'s International Observatory, the Style Committee analyzes macro-changes in terms of style, taste, habits, society, and new materials. The results of this research merge into themes ("directions") presented during the trade fair to guide exhibitors' new collection development. Although larger and much more internationalized than most textile trade fairs, *Moda In* ranks second to *Première Vision* on basically all parameters (see again Table 6.1). It has, however, traditionally secured a market by hosting the Italian fabric producers which are generally smaller but much more numerous than their French rivals. As a consequence, *Moda In* provides international customers (mostly apparel companies and fashion designers) with more information on product variety than that available by visiting *Première Vision* only.

An Emic Account of the Concertation Process

The concertation process comprises several phases, each of which involves a differentiated set of actors (see Figure 6.2 for a stylized model of the overall process). *Trend forecasting*, that is, the identification of future trends in consumer society, is realized by each trade fair's set of experts (i.e., the International Observatory in the case of *Première Vision*, and the Style Committee in the case of *Moda In*) several months before the actual events.

Trend forecasting may appear a rather esoteric activity, but it is nowadays a fairly institutionalized process. The creative experts engaged in trend forecasting usually spend a considerable amount of time in the observation of street style and often travel around the world in an activity often defined as "cool hunting," that is, identifying consumption patterns in specific subcultures which in the experts' opinion anticipate the directions in which society as a whole will move. From these patterns, implications in terms of new fashion products and fabrics are then derived. In other words, emerging trends in society are "translated" into new ideas in fabrics and clothing.

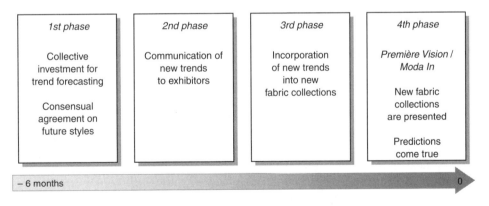

Figure 6.2 The concertation process. *Source*: Adapted from CERMES-Bocconi University (2004b).

For example, as a result of the affirmation of social values taking into account the world's ecological problems, products, colors, and designs that respect or recall such principles are increasingly appreciated by consumers, for example raw materials that do not harm the environment, natural colors, simpler clothing styles, and so on. Similarly, in the aftermath of the Twin Towers terrorist attack of September 11, 2001, the world for many consumers was a less secure place and conspicuous consumption was no longer considered appropriate. Consequently, apparel (and fabrics) had to fit with a consumer desire for safety, which meant less blatantly luxurious products.

The trends forecast by the Observatory and Style Committee are validated by concertation meetings, which are a way to bring together in the same place and at the same time representatives of all phases of the fragmented and not integrated textile-apparel value chain. At the "concertation tables," representatives and members of trade associations in the fabric industry, in upstream and downstream markets (e.g., fiber and yarn producers, textile finishing and printing companies, fashion designers, apparel producers, etc.) and in complementary products (accessory producers) all have a seat and the right to express their opinion on the future trends that will be pursued collectively. In addition, the leading companies (those that are able to launch their own trends) are involved for the specific contribution that they may provide to the concertation process. In this phase, an important role is also played by the *bureaux de style*, that is, companies specializing in trend forecasting.[6] For these organizations, being part of the set of experts that set trends is considered prestigious, and they often mention this in their promotional activities.

During concertation meetings, the trends identified by the trade fair organizers are communicated and compared with those forecast individually by the invited parties. These meetings, then, serve to create a *consensual agreement* among all relevant actors of what will become the common trends. Extreme ideas that most members cannot share are abandoned. As nicely put by one of our informants:

> Often, there isn't agreement ... Individual positions are radical, but all those who are present are interested in reaching an agreement, and individual positions are eventually mediated. (CEO of an Italian fabric company that has long participated in *Première Vision*'s concertation mechanism)

Thus, these meetings *reduce variety* in new collections, increasing compatibility on the purchaser side. Although noteworthy differences do exist between the two groups, the trends identified by *Première Vision* and *Moda In* share some commonalities and are mostly compatible, as the majority of the interested parties sit at both concertation tables and so provide a similar input.

In a subsequent phase, the agreed trends are communicated to exhibiting companies during *ad hoc* workshops. Documents synthesizing the directions for innovation (e.g., color cards, trend books, CD-ROM) are distributed for reference during the development of new collections in the following months. Color tones are specified very precisely by means of the Pantone color system with which a color can be selected and specified by assembling creative palettes and conceptual color schemes. The concepts underlying the trends are communicated with the use of metaphors and suggestive pictures whose aim is to inspire rather than communicate in a precise way. One of the *Moda In*'s Style Commission experts commented on this way of presenting trends by saying "we make a lot of poetry, here". For example, the "directions" for fashion innovation developed by *Moda In* for the Fall/Winter 2005/2006 collection included "Nesting," verbally described as "from nature, protection and intimacy with a techno touch," and "Excessive," a "delirium of creativity in a mix of culture and imagination." Visual descriptions are similarly suggestive and evocative.

During the two trade fairs, exhibitors present their collection to visitors (potential buyers) from all over the world. Now, "forecasts have become true." Generally speaking, an exhibitor's products are aligned with the concerted trends and, more importantly, with end consumers' emerging sensibilities. Generally, smaller companies tend to follow the trends in a very precise way, while bigger companies adapt their offer to the trends with greater degrees of freedom, as suggested by the quotes that follow.

> Our style director goes to the workshop [where trends are presented], takes notes, and when she comes back to the factory, she discusses with the production and marketing guys. It's very useful for us to have the trend books and the color cards, it would be tough otherwise..." (Italian Exhibitor at *Moda In*, 16 employees)
>
> We follow the trends, but not always. We have our own brand image, and sometimes we propose new fabrics that aren't entirely compatible with the trends. But customers won't care, they'll follow us. (Italian Exhibitor at *Première Vision*, 120 employees)

Both *Première Vision* and *Moda In* organizers present forecast trends in specially equipped areas, created with the help of experts in visual communication who arrange samples of exhibitors' new fabrics in particularly creative ways. Visitors greatly appreciate these areas, which give a comprehensive idea of trends in a limited period of time.

> I'm here to find new yarns for the next collection, and I can see them all in one time. In New York, it would take two weeks... (American clothing designer, interviewed at *Moda In*'s trend area)
>
> This morning, the first thing I did when I arrived was to come here... It's great, in just one look you have a comprehensive idea of what's new this season... I have a look at each of the samples, I touch them, I compare them, and in this way I can select the producers that have the kind of fabrics I'm interested in... (Italian fabric buyer, at *Première Vision*'s trend area)

There are many benefits from spending long hours in the trend area instead of visiting individual exhibitors. Apparel companies' buyers and designers seek inspiration for their new product development activities, new potential suppliers and confirmation of the creativeness and competence of their present business partners:

> Sometimes, you know, when you design new collections...you have to get inspired...perhaps I see a collar here and suddenly I have an idea for something I'll include in my new collection (Italian clothing designer, at *Moda In*'s trend area)
>
> This trade show is a starting point where you go to find the idea, the new fabrics, the colors...to find the inspiration...Then everybody will make his own the ideas that are nearest to his products, and will take them as a starting point. (Italian clothing entrepreneur, *Moda In*)
>
> I'm not here to look for new suppliers: If a supplier is ok, there's no reason to change it, new suppliers are risky, I prefer to rely on somebody I can trust. But, you know, it's nice to see that my old suppliers are still updated, to see that they are at the forefront of fashion. (Italian fabric buyer, *Première Vision*)

Figure 6.3 The trend area at *Moda In*, February 2004. *Source*: The authors.

As shown in Figure 6.3, the information search process in trend areas has a physical, embodied nature, that is, it involves handling and inspecting fabric samples with attention, in order to imagine new apparel products that could be realized with these fabrics. At present, "virtual" searches (based on online catalogs and pictures of fabrics) do not provide the same depth of information, because of the often tacit nature of what the buyer is seeking. For most, then, the actual visit is considered irreplaceable: visitors need to actually touch and feel the fabrics to make sense of them.

It should be noted that together with buyers and product designers from apparel companies, *Première Vision* and *Moda In* also attract numerous "atypical" visitors (Borghini et al., 2004) whose presence contributes to make the establishment of a concerted trend more rapid and effective. With respect to exhibitors, "atypical" visitors are:

- *Competitors*: these companies are fabric producers not admitted to the concertation process (both from Western and emerging countries). In general, they seek competitive intelligence and "inspiration" for their own new product developments.[7]
- *Suppliers and producers of collateral products*: these companies visit the trend areas of the two trade fairs to learn about future fashion trends and to align their own innovative efforts correspondingly. In the case of suppliers (e.g. yarn or textile machinery producers), this means understanding how their customers use the products they are providing. Collateral producers (e.g. shoe and bag producers) look to increase the compatibility of their new products in terms of color, pattern, etc. with those in the apparel industry.[8]

- *Experts and journalists*: for many professionals and service providers, visiting the two trade fairs is a routine but valuable activity to discover in advance "what is going on in the industry" and in society as a whole. Journalists working for specialized media, in particular, tend to provide great visibility in their articles to the trends identified by *Première Vision* and *Moda In*. As a result, the innovations are spread to those people in the field that were not able to visit the events in person.

The presence of large numbers of these "atypical" visitors is primarily due to the high level of information externalities provided by the two trade fairs to upstream, downstream, and collateral industries (Borghini et al., 2004). In this sense, the two events are occasions when the usually fragmented textile-apparel value chain is unified and the various dispersed actors aligned. From the exhibitors' point of view, the presence of atypical targets means that the concerted trends receive worldwide visibility and recognition, and that their collections are immediately imitated. Attitudes towards imitation are heterogeneous, however, and range from anger and bitterness to serene acceptation.

> It doesn't matter that taking pictures is forbidden here, people are continuously doing that and there's no way to stop them. They don't even need digital cameras, a cell phone will suffice. There are a lot of people from Asia here, we don't give samples to them, but they go in the trend areas and they can see our samples there: before the end of *Première Vision*, they can start producing their low-cost imitation . . . They steal our creativity . . . And there are customers that can't see (or don't want to see) the difference in quality between our fabric and their fabric . . . So it's a neat damage for us . . . But what do you do? It's globalization . . . (Italian fabric producer, exhibitor at *Moda In*)
>
> All this fuss about imitation . . . It's much ado for nothing . . . Being imitated is in the order of things . . . Leaders are always imitated; it's the price for glory. (French fabric producer, exhibitor at *Moda In*)

Some exhibitors also try to hinder imitation of their new collections. Tactics employed include the decision not to show products in the stand's window displays (Rinallo and Borghini, 2003) and a careful selection of the fabrics shown in the trend areas. Other exhibitors are more creative in their attempt to slow down imitators.

> We select people that enter in our booth; we have a white list of companies that we invited through our salesmen. The problem is not just China . . . Also big retailers come to us, want samples, but then they give them to their third-world suppliers and ask them to produce precise imitations of our fabrics. This year, before coming here, I checked in our archives all retailers that have asked for our samples in the past five years but never made an order . . . I put them in a black list, they can't enter in the booth this year . . . And there are big names in this list . . . (Italian fabric producer, exhibitor at *Première Vision*)
>
> Oh, the samples in our window display are not from our real collection . . . They are false innovation . . . We put them there to divert our competitors." (French fabric producer, exhibitor at *Moda In*)

By means of concertation, and through an able exploitation of their reputation as trend-setters, French and Italian fabric producers together with carefully selected foreign firms can rapidly establish the style innovation they collectively identified as the dominant designs in fashion. Hence, by belonging to these networks of innovators, companies are able to affirm themselves as creators of the fashion prevalent in a given moment. In this way, local-level cooperation yields advantages in terms of global competition. Or, as suggested by one of our informants:

> [Concertation] is a great marketing and communication enterprise that, as a matter of fact, puts Italian and French producers in a high position in front of the rest of the world. (Italian fabric producer, exhibitor at both *Moda In* and *Première Vision*)

Discussion: An Etic Account of Concertation

Concertation as collective enactment of the environment

In the global fabric industry, competition is conducted by strategic networks with strong territorial affiliations that "fight" against similar networks located elsewhere. The success that French and Italian producers are still enjoying in spite of the emerging competition from Middle and Far East rivals may be seen as the result of significant differences in the way these networks interpret their challenging environment. The concertation mechanism may be considered as a category of interpretive behavior based on enactment (Daft and Weick, 1984; Smircich and Stubbart, 1985), where the network of cooperating organizations and the environment in which they operate are co-created through the social interaction of key actors. Interpretation, in this case, occurs at the interorganizational level and requires the development of shared understanding and conceptual schemes among members of the learning network.

Enactment, as described by Daft and Weick (1984), reflects a high level of intrusiveness in the environment and the assumption that the environment is unanalyzable. This definition may seem at odds with the way the activities realized by *Première Vision* and *Moda In* are usually described by insiders, that is, as "trend forecasting" or "trend identification." Implicitly, these terms suggest that novel developments in society exist and can somehow (by intuition or trained observation) be spotted. When employing an interpretive approach, however, these activities cannot be considered as the discovery of "correct" trends in an existing, fixed world, but more as the selection of some among many possible alternatives and the rejection of most of the others. Put in different words, the directions for innovation that are enacted reside more in the cognitive schemes shared and harmonized among those who sit at the concertation tables, than in some "external" environment. Hence, "[t]he interpretation may shape the environment more than the environment shapes the interpretation" (Daft and Weick, 1984: 287).

When the trends enacted during the concertation meetings are communicated to *Première Vision* and *Moda In* exhibitors, a context for collective sense-making is created. Instead of a chaotic, unanalyzable environment, participating companies are provided with a shared vision of the future that makes organized behavior possible. During *Première Vision* and *Moda In*, the enacted trends are no longer an intangible vision, but have a concrete nature, since they are visible to (and touchable by) all visitors in the trend areas, where they are presented in a suggestive and visually appealing way, and on exhibitors' booths in the form of new collections. Visitors will return to their offices with the fabric samples, pictures, the documents that synthesize the trends. Those who have not physically attended the trade fairs will read about the trends in the press. Apparel producers will buy fabrics and accessories that embody such trends. For competitors, customers, suppliers, journalists, collateral producers, etc., interpretation of the environment in this phase is much less open and moves in a direction which is favorable to exhibitors. The concertation process thus has the nature of a self-fulfilling prophecy.

The boundary of the network

European companies (in the fabric as in most other manufacturing sectors) are a good deal smaller than their overseas competitors and work in different ways. For example, (1) they sell to intermediate markets (and other companies) rather than to end-markets, and so require coordination in order to integrate diverse production skills and specializations; and (2) they mainly concentrate on traditional manufacturing, generating an enormous variety of products as a result of this fragmentation. These conditions have stimulated the emergence of organisms able to integrate the activities of the individual companies (increasingly specialized and hence possibly isolated and distant from other producers and users) within a shared network in which other companies act as elements in a complex system of technological, production, market, and relational knowledge. On the one hand, these organisms, termed "meta-organizers" (Rullani, 1998), stimulate, broaden and help to deepen the relationships among companies, while, on the other, providing the investments needed to maintain and develop the network. Among meta-organizers, professional trade fairs have a predominant (but little studied) role,[9] since they allow production which is usually fragmented across various countries to be coordinated and marketed (Golfetto, 2000).

In the case of *Première Vision* and *Moda In*, the companies wishing to exhibit (i.e., those who want to be admitted to the learning network) must meet certain quality criteria to ensure that the overall informational content of the shows is not reduced. Candidate exhibitors must show themselves to be innovators, rather than imitators, and prove that their presence will benefit visitors by enhancing the content of the event. This means that the presence of new exhibitors should not jeopardize a fair's position as an "informational" rather than "commercial" event. In other words, although the network of exhibitors has a strong geographical connotation, participating companies are not limited to French or Italian industrial districts. The two events provide a location for joint promotion to actors who share strong quality levels rather than geographical origin.

There is, however, an important difference between the inclusion/exclusion patterns of the two exhibitions. In the case of *Première Vision*, the original 15 weavers who launched the initiative in 1973 soon extended the fair to other French producers and, soon after, to Italian companies, mostly operating in Italian districts, that are more numerous but smaller in size, and thus represent a greater variety in supply. In 1989 other European weavers were also invited to join the concertation process. More recently, in September 2002, *Première Vision* adopted a selective opening to a few non-European weavers who could demonstrate compliance with the product quality and innovative criteria required for admission (see Figure 6.4). At present, *Première Vision* exhibitors include companies from countries that are traditionally associated with low-cost mass-market products and tend to be considered imitators of Western companies' creativity and innovation efforts (e.g., Turkey, Taiwan).

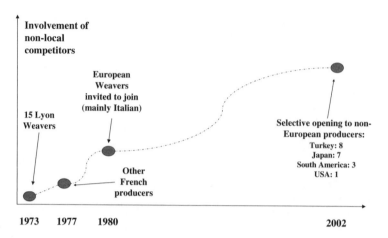

Figure 6.4 *Première Vision*: pattern of network expansion 1973–2002. *Source*: The authors.

Table 6.2 *Première Vision* and *Moda In*: exhibitors by country of origin (February 2004)

Exhibitors' country of origin	Première Vision	Moda In
Italy	339	310
France	137	40
Western Europe	195	49
Eastern Europe	3	–
Middle East	15	–
Far East	12	–
North America	1	–
South America	4	–
Total exhibitors	706	399

Source: Elaborations on data from trade fair catalogs.

An inclusion pattern of this kind should not be taken for granted, particularly given that *Première Vision* is backed by French entrepreneurial associations. In such situations, a protectionist attitude among trade fair organizers is not uncommon, leading to high entry barriers for foreign companies (Golfetto, 2004). Considering exhibitors' countries of origin, we discover that a similar pattern has not emerged in the case of *Moda In* (Table 6.2), where exhibitors are entirely west European. In part, however, these differences in internationalization levels are due to the greater accessibility for visitors offered by Paris, which induces non-European exhibitors to prefer *Première Vision* to provide international visibility to their collections and penetrate the mature European market.

Rituality and cooperation among competitors

The concertation mechanism sheds light on dynamics of value creation versus value appropriation in networks. Exhibitors at both *Première Vision* and *Moda In* are direct competitors, yet they cooperate to create value. These companies face a challenge, that of "sleeping with the enemy," which is increasingly common in today's world. When looking at this paradoxical situation from an anthropological viewpoint, it is easy to detect ritual elements in the meetings and workshop that, season after season, gather together different actors to perform meaningful activities again and again. Concertation meetings and workshops for exhibitors can be considered interorganizational rituals. Theorists from different perspectives have long highlighted the fact that rituals permit participants to imagine themselves as members of a community (Durkheim, 1995), a feeling often termed *communitas* (Turner, 1969) and also refers to a temporary suspension from the social structures that constrain behaviors. Rivalry, we argue, is temporarily suspended during concertation meetings and exhibitor workshops. The competitive pressures coming from Asian countries have facilitated the cohesion of European high quality producers. The symbolic degradation of enemies and the creation of scapegoats is a function of rituals long noted (Navarini, 1998). The common references to "imitators" and the "dangers coming from China" have substituted the intra-European hostilities among some national groups (e.g., Italian versus French, French versus German) as the "common enemy" helps discovering similarities and common problems and the construction of a European identity.

Individual differences among individuals and their companies are, for a while, superseded as an inclusive community is constructed: a community that, over the years, has broadened its boundaries to also include companies from different parts of France, Europe, and the world. When the cohesion felt during these gatherings ends as individuals come back to their offices and factories, feelings of rivalry return. However, by ritually separating the times and places of collaboration from those of competition, the collective creation of value is facilitated and the conflicts that would create obstacles to cooperation are made less severe. Beyond fostering internal cohesion, however, rituals also make visible the status and legitimacy of those that, during the ritual, are celebrated (Navarini, 1998). *Première Vision* and *Moda In* are important trade fairs in the fabric industry, well attended at the global level. The strict admission criteria guarantee visitors that exhibiting companies are the "best" producers worldwide. This may be interpreted as an ideological enterprise that fosters a social stratification in the fabric industries: that is, a hierarchy is established between exhibitors/innovators/leaders and non-exhibitors/imitators/followers. Even *Première Vision*'s inclusion of Turkish fabric producers among its exhibitors in 2002, to a great extent contributes to the stratification of the industry. A common, emic reading of this highly publicized inclusion was that those Turkish producers had been integrated within the community of innovators, in a sort of rite of passage *à la* Van Gessap. Our interpretation is, however, that of a rite of institution (Bourdieu, 1990): only very few Turkish producers have been admitted. All the others have not, and probably never will be. And this, too, contributes to put European producers in a higher position in front of the world.

Conclusion

In this chapter, we have described how French, Italian, and other selected fabric producers establish their new products as the dominant design in fashion and consequently enjoy significant gains in status within the industry. While our emic research findings do not have validity beyond the field we investigated, our etic results lend themselves to a theoretical generalization. Concertation is essentially an interpretive enterprise, where a favorable business environment is socially constructed through the interaction of key actors. An outcome of the concertation mechanism is a social stratification of the market place, that is, leaders versus followers and innovators versus imitators, which has implications in terms of premium prices and marketplace status.

Our ritual reading of the concertation mechanisms sheds light on one of the three key challenges explored in this book: How can companies that are rivals cooperate effectively? Or rather, how can they cooperate long enough to jointly create value before starting to compete again? In this chapter, we propose that a ritual separation of the special times and places of cooperation from those, more mundane, of competition is one possible solution. Individuals in key organizational positions for innovation have much in common with their colleagues from different companies: by gathering them together, imagined occupational communities may easily be formed, and benefits linked to the sharing of knowledge and the creation of informal networks accrue to all participating companies.

Another managerial implication of our ethnography regards the role of events as trade fairs and other collective events in the social construction of the market place. These events are usually conceived as mirrors of the underlying markets. From our perspective, these events stage a representation of the market, its evolution, and its actors. It is not a neutral representation, since it produces effects for those who are depicted as protagonists or simple walk-ins. Representations thus create in spectators a preferred manner of looking at the world. In every industry, to continue our metaphor, different "directors" coexist that try to impose their worldview on their customers. Not all of them are equally effective. *Première Vision* and *Moda In* have invested in their credibility for several decades and thus provide an effective context for their exhibitors' value creation strategies.

Notes

1 "L'accès est réservé . . . sur des critères de qualité des produits, de créativité (avec une obligation de renouvellement des collections tous les six mois) ainsi que la santé financière de l'entreprise." (author's translation)

2 Cappetta et al. (forthcoming) have recently highlighted the similarity between style innovation in fashion and the patterns of technological innovation described by Abernathy and Utterback (1978) and Anderson and Tushman (1990). Also in fashion, innovation cycles include both phases of radical and incremental innovation, with ferment phases (where many new styles are proposed) followed by the selection of dominant designs. However, because of the symbolic properties of fashion goods with respect to consumers' need for distinction, the dominant design co-exists with market niches for products which are radically different, but are nevertheless highly appreciated by some consumers. For example, Chanel tailleurs or Armani tuxedos are classics that do not vary with seasonal fashions.

3 As a whole, in the EU-15 there are almost 170,000 companies in the textile and clothing industry, most of which are located in Italy and France (Source: Euratex on Eurostat data).

4 In this chapter, emic expressions and terms employed by our informants are put in quotation marks. Concertation is an emic term, but since we, as researchers, have employed it also in our etic interpretation, it will not generally be put in quotation marks.

5 In the yarn production sector, important trend forecasts also come from another trade fair, *Pitti Filati*, held in Florence, which develops trends that are equally a point of reference for downstream sectors (Golfetto and Mazursky, 2004).

6 Style bureaux, which emerged in France in the mid-1980s, are "small-sized organizations, specialized mainly in the production and sale of information on fashion trends which is gathered together in the so-called *cahier de tendance*" (Guercini and Ranfagni, 2003), typically representing trends in terms of both colors and concepts. Style bureaux often carry out consultancy activities for textile companies, thus helping the latter to interpret such trends and to incorporate them into their new collections.

7 The quotes that follow provide an idea of competitor's motivations. It should be noted that "imitation"/competitive intelligence issues are generally downplayed by visitors-competitors, and emerged more from our observations and from exhibitors' comments.

> It's important to walk around here, because we see how companies facing the same problems we face solved them: if they found a solution, we could do the same. (Fabric producer, visitor at *Première Vision*)
>
> We don't really copy what we see here . . . exactly as we see it. There is always an elaboration . . . (Fabric designer, visitor at *Moda In*)

8 Again, the following quotes are representative of recurring themes.

> Exhibitors here are my customers: I want to understand how my customers have used my yarns, how they have processed them, their final use . . . (Italian yarn producer, at *Première Vision*)
>
> These trade shows are not useful only to those who work in the apparel industry, but also . . . to those whose job involves new trends: for example, those who work in furniture, interior design, jewels, cars . . . (Style Bureau at *Moda In*)
>
> I'm a furniture designer . . . the trends here are informative also for me . . . I get new ideas on what colors will be in next year . . . (Furniture designer, at *Moda In*)

9 If European SME have survived global competition, this can be seen as a result of the cooperative mechanisms which the market has identified: the industrial districts for the organization of production and the trade fairs for commercial organization. While the industrial districts have been the subject of many studies, and their important aggregation function has been recognized by both scholars and policy makers, it is little known that the districts alone cannot achieve commercial visibility, reach and assess end markets, and obtain efficient information on supply markets and global competitors. All these latter functions are realized by trade fairs.

References

Abernathy, W. J. & Utterback J. M. (1978) Patterns of industrial innovation. *Technology Review* (June–July), 40–7.

Anderson, P. & Tushman, M. L. (1990) Technological discontinuities and dominant designs: Cyclical model of technological change. *Administrative Science Quarterly*, 35, 604–33.

Arnould, E. J. & Wallendorf, M. (1994) Market-oriented ethnography: Interpretation building and marketing strategy formulation. *Journal of Marketing Research* 31, 484–504.

Bellon, B. & Chevallier J. M. (1983) *L'industrie en France*. Paris: Flammarion.

Borghini, S., Golfetto, F. & Rinallo, D. (2004) Using anthropological methods to study industrial marketing and purchasing: An exploration of professional trade shows. *Proceedings of the Industrial Marketing and Purchasing Conference*, Copenhagen, September 2–4.

Bourdieu, P. (1990) Rites of institution. In: P. Bourdieu (Ed.) *Language and Symbolic Power*, 117–26. Cambridge: Polity Press.

Cappetta, R., Cillo, P. & Ponti, A. (forthcoming) Convergent designs in fine fashion: An evolutionary model for stylistic innovation. Under revision in *Research Policy*.

Cermes-Bocconi (2004a) *The Trade Fair Industry in Europe*. Unpublished research report, Bocconi University.

Cermes-Bocconi (2004b) *Communication in B2B Trade Shows: Messages and Interpretations*. Unpublished research report, Bocconi University.

Daft, R. L. & Weick, K. E. (1984) Toward a model of organizations as interpretation systems. *Academy of Management Review* 9, 284–95.

Durkheim, É. (1995) *The Elementary Forms of Religious Life*, trans. K. Fields. New York: Free Press. (Orig. pub. 1912: *Les Formes élémentaires de la vie réligieuse*. Paris: Alcan).

Golfetto, F. (2000) Reti di imprese e meta-organizzatori: Il ruolo delle fiere. *Sinergie* 18, 189–211.

Golfetto, F. (2004) *Fiere e Comunicazione: Strumenti per le Imprese e il Territorio*. Milan: Egea.

Golfetto, F., Gibbert, M. & Zerbini, F. (2004) Impartive capacity: Towards a view of supplier as a competence provider. Paper presented at the Strategic Management Society Conference, Puerto Rico, October 31–November 3.

Golfetto, F. & Mazursky, D. (2004) Competence-based marketing. *Harvard Business Review* (December), 26–7.

Golfetto, F. & Rinallo, D. (2003) Consocia et impera: How the Italian and French textile producers cooperate in order to affirm the "dominant design" in fashion. Paper presented at the Strategic Management Society Conference, Baltimore, November 9–12.

Guercini, S. & Ranfagni, S. (2003) The role of bureaux de style in the entrepreneurial network for textile product innovation. *Proceedings of the Industrial Marketing and Purchasing Conference*, Lugano, September, September 4–6.

Navarini, G. (1998), Tradizione e post-modernità della politica rituale, *Rassegna Italiana di Sociologia*, 39(3), 305–32.

Pike, K. L. (1967) *Language in Relation to a Unified Theory of Structure of Human Behavior*, 2nd edn. The Hague: Mouton.

Première Vision (2003) Première Vision: A permanent evolution. Online document accessed July 14, 2003: http://www.premierevision.fr.

Rinallo, D. & Borghini, S. (2003) A fair(y) tale: The semiotics of B2B communication. *Proceedings of the Industrial Marketing and Purchasing Conference*, Lugano, September.

Rullani, E. (1998) Dal fordismo realizzato al postfordismo possibile: la difficile transizione. In: L. Romano & E. Rullani (Eds.) *Il Postfordismo. Idee per il Capitalismo Prossimo Venturo*. Milan: Etas.

Smircich, L. & Stubbart, C. (1985) Strategic management in an enacted world. *Academy of Management Review*, 10(4), 724–36.

Spiggle, S. (1994) Analysis and interpretation of qualitative data in consumer research. *Journal of Consumer Research* 21, 491–503.

Turner, V. (1969) *The Ritual Process: Structure and Anti-Structure*. Chicago: Aldine.

CHAPTER SEVEN

Online Social Networks and Knowledge Exchange

Siyuan Huang and Gerardine DeSanctis

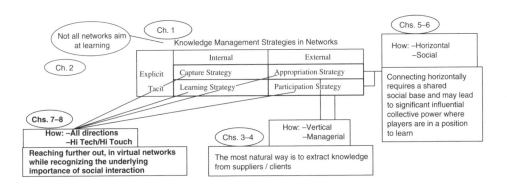

Abstract

Internet-supported communication allows individuals from across the boundaries of time, location, and organizational membership to engage in interactions, build relationships, share information, and request and extend assistance to each other. As social networks formed through face-to-face communication, resources are embedded in the online social networks. Such resources are often referred to as social capital. What types of social capital are embedded in the online social networks? How are they mobilized by the social network members? What structural properties of the online social networks are associated with the access and mobilization of social capital?

To explore these questions, we take a network perspective in studying social capital, postulating that capture and mobilization of social capital online is contingent on the social network structural properties of the online environment. In this chapter we provide an overview of online social networks using a social capital framework, explaining how the structure of online social networks can act to either inhibit or promote knowledge sharing. Using data from professional online forums devoted to knowledge management, we illustrate how different network properties are associated with different levels and types of knowledge sharing online. We further discuss social networks established through new forms of online communications. Specifically, we investigate examples of corporate blogs and social networking websites. We draw implications for designers and users of online communication and propose several propositions for future research.

An Overview of Online Social Networks

When televisions first entered the living rooms of US families, concerns were raised about television isolating people from each other. The logic is that if people spent most of their leisure time in front of their televisions, they had no time left socializing with each other. The surge of Internet has naturally spawned the same worries. A social network researcher once took a picture inside a coffee house in Cleveland, Ohio (Figure 7.1). None of the guests in the coffee house were talking to each other, shaking hands, or chatting about weather. Instead, all of them were sitting alone, busy surfing on the web, sending instant messages, and reading from their palm pilots. Is Internet the same evil as television that draws people away from parties and gatherings, and fixes them in front of computer screens?

Fortunately, although those people in the coffee house appeared to be loners, they may not be so alone on the virtual spaces. As it has been shown by numerous researches, Internet-supported communications such as emails, online chat rooms, and discussion boards allow individuals to interact with each other in the absence of acquaintance, physical proximity, group membership, a history of prior relationships, and demographic similarity (Constant et al., 1996). In cyber space, people can engage

Figure 7.1 A coffee house in Cleveland, Ohio

in interactions, build relationships, share information, and request and extend assistance to each other. These networks of relationships built online are often referred to as online social networks or cyber social networks. In online social networks, relationships may be built and maintained, and resources may be captured through social relations (Wellman et al., 1996; Lin, 2001; Wasko and Faraj, 2005).

Resources associated with social relations are conceptualized as social capital. Drawing upon the notion of capital, sociologists generally depict social capital as the investment in social relations with expected returns (Lin, 2001). There are many efforts to give a clear and operational definition of social capital. Bourdieu (1980) defines social capital as the sum of the resources, actual or virtual, that accrue to an individual or group through a network of institutionalized relationships of acquaintance and recognition. Coleman (1990) defines social capital by its function and argues that it consists of some aspect of a social structure that facilitates certain actions of individuals who are within the structure. In our study, we adopt a network-based definition, which defines social capital as "resources embedded in one's social networks, resources that can be accessed or mobilized through ties in networks" (Lin, 2005: 2).

While many researchers treat social capital as equivalent to social network structure and interactions (e.g., Oh et al., 2004; McFadyen and Cannella, 2004), we think doing so might be a source of confusion. We stay with Lin's (2001, 2005) network-based definition of social capital as resources embedded in social networks. In this way we are able to differentiate social network structural properties from social capital itself. Lin (2005: 4) puts it this way:

> While social capital is contingent on social networks, they are not equivalent or interchangeable terms. Networks provide the necessary condition for access to and use of embedded resources . . .. Yet networks and network features by themselves are not identical with resources. Rather, variations in networks or network features may increase or decrease the likelihood of having a certain quantity or quality of resources embedded. Thus, network features should be seen as important and necessary antecedents exogenous to social capital.

As such, social networks should be treated as conduits through which resources/ social capital can flow. Therefore, social capital, including material goods such as land, cars, and money and symbolic goods such as education, honors, titles, and reputation, is not equivalent to, but rather contingent on social network properties.

Social Capital Embedded in Online Social Networks

In social relationships built by face-to-face communication, hot chicken soup prepared for you by your friend when you are sick may be a valuable form of social capital. However, the major form of social capital embedded in online social networks is information. Much of online network communication involves exchange of information (Wellman et al., 1996), and it is widely agreed by researchers in the field of social networks and social capital that information is a form of resource (Coleman, 1990; Lin, 2005; Burt, 1992). While information benefits include creating new ideas and exchanging existing knowledge, the information benefits of online social networks are grounded most of all in the possibilities for transfer of information (Matzat, 2004). Therefore, many studies of online networks are centered on the issue of information sharing and transmission (e.g. Wasko and Faraj, 2005; Matzat, 2004).

Electronic communication technologies make it possible to share information quickly, globally, and with large numbers of individuals. Using the social capital concepts, we can say that informational social capital embedded in the social networks occurs as knowledge possessed by individuals participating in the interaction. They "represent a potential pool of resources capable of generating returns available to the actor, indicating the capacity of social capital" (Lin, 2005: 5). As in traditional social networks, information embedded in online social ties can be obtained in two major ways. First, information can be actively sought. The information holder, being contacted, can then disseminate the requested information. Second, information may be passively received (Lai and Wong, 2004). Seeking and distributing information by the participants are processes of mobilizing the embedded social capital.

In online settings, it is technically easy to ask for and provide information. A question is sent to a group and answers are available to the whole group as well. Feedback is shared by making both initiating messages and all responses available to all participants (Finholt and Sproull, 1990). Most online communication tools provide data storage facilities to store previous communication in an organized form that can be sorted, searched, and retrieved. Thus information repositories are created for online social networks. In this way, individual expertise and experience are turned into shared knowledge. Online communication is subject to fewer constraints in terms of information storage space than conventional communication methods. Additionally, the asynchronous nature of communications in online settings allows participants to be freed from time constraints. Therefore, the amount and range of information spread online is potentially enormous, thus raising the concern of information overload.

Information overload is the state of an individual in which not all communication inputs can be processed and utilized, leading to cognitive breakdown (Jones et al., 2004). When information is provided in excess of what has been requested, individuals may be unable to process the information adequately. In the extreme form of excessive information providing, the communication becomes pure announcement, instead of exploration, rich discourse, and exchange. However, the more prominent potential problem may be inadequate response to the requests for information and assistance. If a member of a social network sends out requests for information but receives no responses, this basically means that the member failed to mobilize the informational social capital embedded in the social network. A wide gap between information seeking and information providing indicates the failure of the social network to generate information resources. Thus if an online social network has more requests for information than responses, it has relatively low value in terms of sharing knowledge.

Some types of knowledge are more readily exchanged in online social networks than others. Generally speaking, the content of knowledge may be fairly explicit, detailed, and communicated without much difficulty, or more tacit, more time consuming, and difficult to transfer (Espinosa and Clark, 2004). Tacitness of knowledge is sometimes considered a continuous term as the degree to which knowledge is difficult to codify or articulate (Reagans and McEvily, 2003). Previous research found that tacit knowledge is more time consuming and difficult to transfer. Learning the tacit aspects of a task most often requires some increased level of interaction. Also, tacit knowledge is more susceptible to being lost or incorrectly translated from member to member.

Online Social Network Structure and Information Sharing

Social network size

Unlike social networks formed through face-to-face communication, online social networks, especially those whose access is open to the public, are often not defined or bounded by memberships to specific organizations or groups. For example, an email group list can be seen as a social network. An individual can join the list by writing a very short message to the administrator of the list. An online discussion forum can be treated as a social network as well. Membership to the discussion forum may simply be obtained by filling out basic demographic information. Therefore, such social networks can easily span across formal boundaries of organizations, and geographic locations (DeSanctis et al., 2003).

Although the expansion of online social networks is less restricted than conventional social networks, their sizes may vary remarkably from one another. For example, in the dataset we collected on online discussion forums devoted to knowledge management, the sizes of forums range from 11 to 184 members. The size of online social networks may have effects on information sharing in several different ways. Most intuitively, large size may imply a wide range covered by a social network (Wellman et al., 1996). Consequently, information may be sought and obtained by more people. Moreover, larger social networks are more likely than smaller ones to include a wider variety of participants. As a result, the information shared in larger social networks may be more diversified and thus of higher quality. Another argument regarding the importance of size as an indicator of properties of information sharing on social networks has to do with the notion of critical mass, that is, the minimum number of people to be available for the solving of various problems (Jones et al., 2004). Group size threshold may exist for sustainable interactions online (Palme, 1995). When the size of an online social network is lower than that required for a critical mass, participants may fail to obtain useful information, and information may be unable to reach a sufficient number of people that it is intended to. Ultimately, the social network, be it supported by an email group list, an online forum, or a chat room, may cease to exist.

Social network density

Social networks are not only defined by the number of participants, but also the connections among them. A fundamental construct in describing the connection among actors in a social network is its connectedness. The connection in online settings among actors is often represented by participation in the same thread of discussion. Operationally, a reply to an email message, answers to a question posted on an online forum, and simply saying back "hi" to someone on instant messenger may be considered the establishment of a social tie. In social network analysis, density is used to measure connectedness. The density of a social network is the extent to which its members are in direct contact with each other (Koku and Wellman, 2002). It was measured as the proportion of the existing number of ties in a network to the maximum possible number of ties (Scott, 1991).

Online social networks may sustain both dense and sparsely knit connections. On the one hand, increasing bandwidth and low cost of communication allow frequent, reciprocal, and often supportive contacts, thus building dense social networks. On the other hand, participants may choose to join or exit an online social network purely based on their interest. Compared with conventional social networks, there is less pressure in online settings for participants to be bound in a social network, resulting in a loose network. Differences in how connected actors are can tell stories about critical properties of social networks. Previous research has emphasized the role of density in shaping a network's communication pattern. Some researchers have postulated that in online settings, the information flow rate and quality at least partly depends on density of a network (Koku and Wellman, 2002). Given the maximal connectedness among members of dense social networks, close contact may have been established through comparatively frequent interactions. Additionally, the connectedness creates opportunities for actors to bring their concerns to the notice of other participants. As a result, requests for information in dense social networks are more likely to receive responses than in loosely knit social networks (Coleman, 1990). Following this logic, we may postulate that dense networks may be associated with more effective mobilization of information in online social networks. The ratio of information seeking to information providing is more likely to approach 1 when there is high density, namely, the actors in the social network are fully connected with each other.

With respect to the diversity of information shared in online social networks, network density is an inverse measure of range (Koku and Wellman, 2002). Dense and closed interpersonal environments typically contain less diverse resources (Marsden, 1990). As such, information resources accessed from a dense network may be less diverse than when the social network is loosely knit (Burt, 1992). However, relationships established through a dense network may allow actors to focus on certain topics, consequently leading to a deeper level of discussions. Actors may be more willing to spend time to share their thoughts, opinions, and insights. Therefore, dense networks may facilitate the sharing of tacit information which is more time consuming and difficult to transfer. In comparison, loose networks may be associated with a lower level of information sharing – explicit information sharing, although in a more diverse range of topics.

Centralization

In addition to connectedness, how the actors are connected is an important indicator of network structural properties and may have meaningful effects on information sharing as well. A widely discussed network property is centralization. Network centralization indicates the extent to which certain network members are prominent in a given network in terms of connectivity among network members (Koku and Wellman, 2002). The most centralized network is a "star" network where there is a central actor (star) that is connected to every other actor, and all other actors are only connected to the

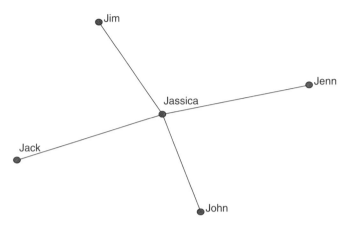

Figure 7.2 Star network structure

star (see Figure 7.2). From an ego-centric perspective, possessing a central position in a social network may be associated with such positive effects as innovativeness, power, and access to a wider range of information (Becker, 1970; Klein et al., 2004; Ahuja and Carley, 1999). However, when considering a whole network as a unit of analysis, research has found that decentralized networks provide opportunities for task-related communication and information exchange (Rulke and Galaskiewicz, 2000).

According to Burt (1992), two actors in a network are structurally equivalent to the extent that they have the same contacts. Redundancy is associated with structural equivalence, because the information acquired from the same contact is likely to be redundant. In a centralized network, many nodes except for those possessing the central positions are subject to structural equivalence because they are all connected to the central nodes. Thus the information exchanged in such a network is likely to be redundant and of less value as a resource. Meanwhile the node at the centered location is exchanging information at the cost of maintaining contact with many people. The high cost may lower the efficiency of communication as well (Burt, 1992). The central nodes may be overwhelmed as they work to maintain the large number of connections to engage in high quality information exchange. Overall, then, we expect high centralization in the network structure of an online social network to negatively affect the exchange of knowledge in the forum. This negative effect should hold whether the type of knowledge being exchanged is explicit or tacit.

Tacit knowledge is characterized by causal ambiguity and difficulty of codification (Choo, 1998; Polanyi, 1966). Because it is not readily articulated as a set of facts or rules, tacit knowledge is difficult to transfer (Sorenson et al., 2004). This is in contrast to explicit knowledge, which can be expressed formally as a system of symbols and facts, and therefore readily communicated (Nonaka and Takeuchi, 1995). Although centralization is likely to hinder both tacit and explicit knowledge sharing, the effect is likely to be more harmful in the case of tacit knowledge transfer. Consider the extreme case of centralization of a social network in which all communication is directed to and from one central actor, the star. The star node is likely to become overburdened

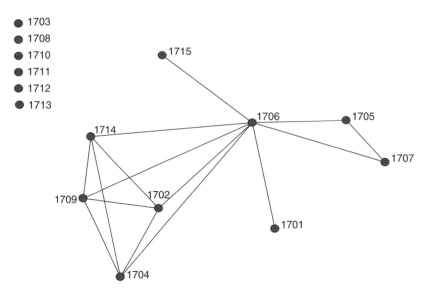

Figure 7.3 Social network visualization of "Intellectual Knowledge Management Discussion"

with the volume of communication required for both tacit and explicit knowledge distribution. But because tacit knowledge is particularly time consuming and difficult to transmit (Espinosa and Clark, 2004), the star node will find it easier to pass on explicit rather than tacit knowledge when queried for information. The non-star nodes are limited in their opportunity to communicate tacit information since their interactions are limited to those with the star only. Therefore, we expect the negative effect on information sharing associated with centralization in the online social network to be stronger for tacit knowledge than explicit knowledge. In our dataset of online forums devoted to the same topical theme, knowledge management, the average centralization score is 0.15. "Intellectual Knowledge Management Discussion," one of the forums in the dataset exhibiting the most centralized network structure, has a centralization score of 0.50. Using the Netdraw Visualization tool (Borgatti, 2002), we were able to graph its social network matrix (Figure 7.3).

As shown in Figure 7.3, among the connected actors, most interactions are centered on actor 1706. This actor may be comparative to the star in Figure 7.2. The star is kept busy to maintain communication with eight actors, and thus may not be able to engage in deep level discussion with any of them. Moreover, the informational resources obtained by the non-star actors are limited and most likely redundant because they are all connected to the same actor, the star. According to our statistics, in this forum, only 17 messages involve explicit knowledge, and only 7 messages are communicating tacit knowledge. The average numbers of messages involving explicit and tacit knowledge in the dataset are 30 and 17 respectively. Evidently, the social network formed on this forum is far below average, both in terms of explicit and tacit information sharing.

Core-periphery structure

Another important social network structural construct is the core-periphery structure. Typically in this type of structure there exists a dense, cohesive core with a sparse or unconnected periphery (Cummings and Cross, 2003). An intuitive notion of core-periphery structure consists of a two class partition of nodes in which one class is the core and the other is the periphery. In the cohesive subgroup (the core), actors are connected to each other in some maximal sense and, in another subgroup (the periphery), actors are more loosely connected to the cohesive subgroup and each other, lacking any maximal cohesion (Borgatti and Everett, 1999). An example is shown in Figure 7.4.

In conventional social networks, core-periphery structure has been shown to be negatively related to group communication and performance, because of the uneven distribution of cohesiveness (Cummings and Cross, 2003). However, in electronic networks, members of core subgroups can readily communicate with and broadcast to peripheral members (Koku and Wellman, 2002; Smith, 1999) and so greater core-periphery structure may facilitate group communication rather than disturb it. The logic for this is as follows. A core subgroup is a network structure with high closure, that is, everyone in the subgroup is connected to each other; in operational terms, this means there is a dense network inside the core. According to advocates of network closure, network closure improves communication, results in more reliable and coordinated exchange of information, and even facilitates trust and norms (Coleman, 1990). For well-connected individuals, they may become more aware of the information requests sent by others. Also, members of the dense and cohesive subgroup may be more willing to share their expertise as well as respond to the information seeking request of others, because relationships, trust, and norms may have grown from the dense connection. Moreover, from the perspective of the overall network, the core subgroup may be playing the role of discussion leader, initiating interesting topics, broadcasting responses to questions, and expressing opinions. The members of

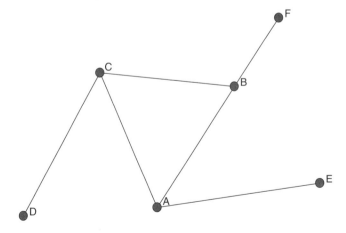

Figure 7.4 Core-periphery structure

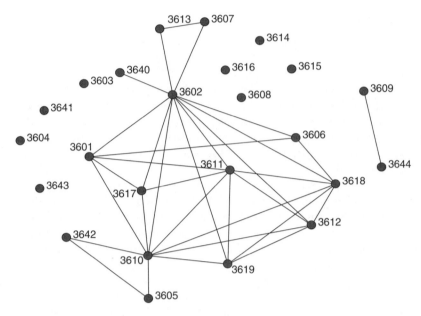

Figure 7.5 Social network visualization of "Knowledge Management Initiatives"

the peripheral subgroup benefit from the discussion as well by observing and reading what has been posted out there. When the responses exceed the amount of requests, it implies that a question may receive multiple answers. Thus participants seeking information are provided with the opportunity to scrutinize and choose from a range of options. Overall, we expect the core/periphery structure to be associated with more effective mobilization of informational social capital in the online setting, such that members of the online forum will readily provide information to those who seek it.

"Knowledge Management Initiatives" (KMI) is one of the online forums in our data set that exhibit high core-periphery social network structure. Figure 7.5 is the visualization of KMI's social network matrix. As shown in the figure, nine actors in the center form a core subgroup, with the rest of the actors sparsely connected to each other and to the core actors. According to our observation, the core members are most active participants in most of the discussions. Two of the core members initiated discussions in the forum by sending out a "Welcome" message and providing answers regarding issues relating to the forum itself. Some core members are experts in the field of knowledge management and actively share their expertise on the forum. Requests for information and assistance receive quite prompt responses often from more than one source.

Our statistics show that KMI has a core-periphery score of 0.85, higher than the dataset average of 0.75. In our sampled messages retrieved from the forum, 7 messages had been posted to ask for information of various kinds, and 24 messages provided information. Overall, the ratio between information seeking and information providing is 0.24, below the average of the dataset, 0.89. The network structure and learning behavior on this forum show support to our speculation that core-periphery structure is associated with effective mobilization of information resources online.

New Developments in Social Networking on the Internet

Weblogs

Most online forums and chat rooms are publicly accessible spaces on the Internet. They are rarely owned or hosted by any individuals. Some Internet service providers and organizations (i.e. universities) allow users to apply for small segments of virtual space on the Internet to create and maintain their own web pages. However, one must be trained to use web design tools (i.e. Microsoft Frontpage, MacroMedia) or even web programming languages (i.e. HTML, XML, Java Script) to successfully run a web space. While some gurus are able to make their personal pages rich in audio, images and even animation, most users find it overwhelming even to maintain only basic features. Blogs, short for webblogs and sometimes written as weblogs, relieve users from the burden of creating a website from scratch, while still allowing them to maintain their own space on the Internet. A blog is a personal website that can be virtually "owned" and run by a user. On a blog, the owner can publish journals in the form of dated logs. The owners can also control the accessibility to their blogs by making them open to the public or to readers with prior authorization only. Readers can leave their comments, which are published on the website as well. Besides written texts, graphs, audios, and even videos can also be uploaded to blogs.

From the social network perspective, blogs serve to expand and strengthen one's social network. Visitors establish social ties with a blog owner by leaving their comments on the website and maybe further exchanging information and other resources. Some blog owners publish a list of web links to the blogs of their social contacts. Readers may follow such links to find information about the people they intend to establish social contact with, thus expanding their social networks. Such interactions may also strengthen existing social ties with their families, friends, classmates, colleagues, etc. Blog owners can update their logs frequently so that their social contacts can easily keep track of what is going on. People can share their thoughts and insights on topics they are interested in.

From the social capital perspective, resources are embedded in the social networks established and maintained on blogs. As other online social networks, information may be the most important forms of resources shared on networks of bloggers. This is probably why blogs have drawn enormous attention from corporations as a way of launching a public relation campaign. Corporate executives create blogs to expand social networks with customers, existing ones and potential ones. They also strengthen social networks with employees and suppliers. Corporate executives can broadcast information about new products and company policies on their blogs. Compared with messages broadcast by traditional media, the information disseminated this way may be more personalized, detailed, and focused, and may reach the intended audience more effectively. It should be noted that the communication is not necessarily from one direction. The information obtained from their blogs can be valuable resources for the corporations as well. They may reflect the most direct concerns and opinions of their customers, employees, and suppliers. The literally unlimited space online for written texts allows visitors to provide feedback that is at a deep level, such as thoughts and insights that could hardly be obtained from marketing reports and analysis.

Social networking websites

There are websites whose mission is exactly to facilitate social networking for users. These websites normally do not require any fee from users for registration to become a member. An existing member can send out an invitation email to his/her social contact. The email includes a link. By clicking the link, the recipient of the email automatically joins the website and is listed as a node in the social network of the person who sends out the invitation. The recipient can further invite his/her own contacts to join him/her on the website. Thus one can expand one's social network through the social network of his/her existing contacts. These websites provide a searching function by which users can search through links that connect them with individuals with whom they may want to establish social ties.

Unlike weblogs, social networking websites do not provide means for communication and information sharing. They are analogous to online phonebooks only with common members of networks as links that connect various social networks. Therefore, it may be fair to say that these social networking sites expand social networks, but could not strengthen existing social ties for users.

Propositions for Future Research

Social network studies can be approached from two perspectives. One is to treat each individual as the unit of analysis. The position individuals take in their social networks and the characteristics of their connections with their social contacts are treated as attributes of these individuals. The other perspective makes comparison across whole social networks. The former is referred to as the egocentric perspective and the latter is referred to as the network perspective (Wellman et al., 1996). In this chapter, we adopt the network perspective, focusing on the variances in structural properties of different social networks. Egocentric analysis can be very useful in understanding attributes of social relationships associated with an individual. When studying new forms of online social networks, such as weblogs and social networking sites, focusing on individuals and the properties of their social networks may give important insights into how one should form and shape his or her online social networks to realize the most effective information sharing.

Our study is cross sectional and thus cannot account for evolution of the social network and the corresponding impact on knowledge exchange. Future studies should consider a longitudinal approach and analyze the network structures in a more dynamic way, examining how relationships are built, sustained, and in some cases fail over time. Whereas we treated network structures as exogenous variables, more fine-tuned dynamic analyses can reveal the causes of network structural properties which, in turn, can be treated as outcome variables. We also recommend that network analyses be complemented with interviews or surveys of the participants. In this way researchers might reach into the nuances of how informational social capital is mobilized and applied in the professional work of those who participate in online discussion forums.

Summary

Recent advancement in communication technologies brings unprecedented connectivity, with "literally millions more people and machines linked together via local, wide-area, and Internet based networks" (Fulk and DeSanctis, 1999: 8). Our findings suggest that people are not only connected using communication technologies, but also form social networks with embedded social capital, most noticeably in the form of informational resources. Similar to conventional social networks, social networks online vary in social capital embedded in and mobilized from them. We employed a network approach to identify the connection between social network structural properties and informational resources embedded in and mobilized from online social networks. We argued that several structural properties, size, density, centralization, and core-periphery structure may be associated with the effectiveness and levels of information sharing online. In the final part, we discussed the new developments in Internet-supported communication, and their implications for social networking on the virtue space.

References

Ahuja, M. & Carley, K. (1999) Network structure in virtual organizations. *Organization Science*, 10(6), 741–57.

Becker, M. (1970) Sociometric location and innovativeness: Reformulation and extension of the diffusion model. *American Sociological Review*, 35(2), 267–82.

Borgatti, S. P. (2002) *NetDraw: Graph Visualization Software*. Harvard, MA: Analytic Technologies.

Borgatti, S. & Everett, M. (1999) Models of core/periphery structures. *Social Networks*, 21, 375–95.

Bourdieu, P. (1980) Le capital social: notes provisoires. *Actes de la Recherche en Sciences Sociales*, 3, 2–3.

Burt, R. (1992) The social structure of competition. In N. Nohria and R. G. Eccles (Eds.) *Networks and Organizations: Structure, Form, and Action*, 57–91. Boston, MA: Harvard Business School Press.

Choo, C. (1998) *The Knowing Organization*. New York: Oxford University Press.

Coleman, J. (1990) *Foundations of Social Theory*. Cambridge, MA: Harvard University Press.

Constant, D., Sproull, L. & Kiesler, S. (1996) The kindness of strangers: The usefulness of electronic weak ties for technical advice. *Organization Science*, 7(2), 119–35.

Cummings, J. & Cross, R. (2003) Structural properties of work groups and their consequences for performance. *Social Networks*, 25, 197–210.

DeSanctis, G., Fayard, A.L., Roach, M. & Jiang, L. (2003) Learning in online forums. *European Journal of Management*, 21(5), 565–77.

Espinosa, J. & Clark, M. (2004) Structuring team knowledge: Dimensions, beliefs, distribution, and coordination. Paper presented at the Academy of Management Annual Meeting, Honolulu, HI.

Finholt, T. & Sproull, L. S. (1990) Electronic groups at work. *Organization Science*, 1(1), 41–64.

Fulk, J. & DeSanctis, G. (1999) Articulation of communication technology and organizational forms. In G. DeSanctis and J. Fulk (Eds.) *Shaping Organization Form: Communication, Connection, and Community*. Newbury Park, CA: SAGE Publications.

Jones, Q., Ravid, G. & Rafaeli, S. (2004) Information overload and the message dynamics of online interaction spaces: A theoretical model and empirical exploration. *Information System Research*, 15(2), 194–210.

Klein, K., Lim, B., Saltz, J. & Mayer, D. (2004) How do they get there? An examination of the antecedents of centrality in team networks. *Academy of Management Journal*, 47(6), 952.

Koku, E. & Wellman, B. (2002) Scholarly networks as learning communities: The case of TechNet. In: S. Barab and R. Kling (Eds.) *Designing Virtual Communities in the Service of Learning*, 299–337. Cambridge: Cambridge University Press.

Lai, G. & Wong, O. (2002) The tie effect on information dissemination: The spread of a commercial rumor in Hong Kong. *Social Networks*, 24, 49–75.

Lin, N. (2001) Cyber networks and global village: The rise of social capital. Chapter 12 of *Social Capital: A Theory of Social Structure and Action*. Cambridge: Cambridge University Press.

Lin, N. (2005) A network theory of social capital. In: D. Castiglione, J. van Deth and G. Wolleb (Eds.) *Handbook on Social Capital*. Oxford: Oxford University Press.

Marsden, P. (1990) Network data and measurement. *Annual Review of Sociology*, 16, 435–63.

Matzat, U. (2004) Academic communication and Internet discussion groups: Transfer of information or creation of social contacts. *Social Networks*, 26, 221–55.

McFadyen, A. & Cannella, A. (2004) Social capital and knowledge creation: Diminishing returns of the number and strength of exchange relationships. *Academy of Management Journal*, 47(5), 735–46.

Nonaka, I. & Takeucki, H. (1995) *The Knowledge-creating Company: How Japanese Companies Create the Dynamics of Innovation*. New York: Oxford University Press.

Oh, H., Chung, M. & Labianca, C. (2004) Group social capital and group effectiveness: The role of informal socializing ties. *Academy of Management Journal*, 47(6), 860–75.

Palme, J. (1995) The optimal group size in computer mediated communication. In: J. Palme, *Electronic Mail*. London: Artech House Publishers.

Polanyi, M. (1966) *The Tacit Dimension*. London: Routledge & Kegan Paul.

Reagans, R. & McEvily, B. (2003) Network structure and knowledge transfer: The transfer problem revisited. Working paper, Columbia University, New York.

Rulke, D. & Galaskiewicz, J. (2000) Distribution of knowledge, group network structure and group performance. *Management Science*, 46(5), 612–25.

Scott, J. (1991) *Social Network Analysis: A Handbook*. London: SAGE Publications.

Sorenson, O., Rivkin, J. & Fleming, L. (2004) Complexity, networks, and knowledge flow. *Research Policy*, 33(10), 1615–34.

Smith, M. A. (1999) Invisible crowds in cyberspace. In: M. A. Smith and P. Kollock (Eds.) *Communities in Cyberspace*, 195–219. New York: Routledge.

Wasko, M. M. & Faraj, S. (2005) Why should I share? Examining social capital and knowledge contribution in electronic networks of practice. *MIS Quarterly*, Special Issue on IT and Knowledge Management, 29(1), 35–57.

Wellman, B., Salaff, J., Dimitrova, D., Garton, L., Gulia, M. & Haythornthwaite, C. (1996) Computer networks as social networks: Collaborative work, telework, and virtual community. *Annual Review of Sociology*, 22, 213–38.

CHAPTER EIGHT

Bramble Bushes in a Thicket: Narrative and the Intangibles of Learning Networks

Cynthia F. Kurtz and David J. Snowden

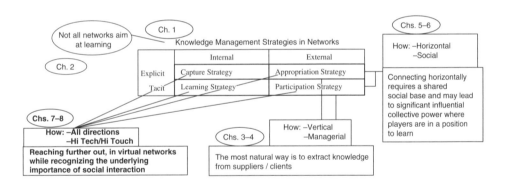

Abstract

In this chapter we explore how interorganizational learning networks affect three systemic attributes of well-functioning organizations which are not often considered in value propositions for such networks: identity management, trust negotiation, and productive conflict. We approach the topic from the standpoint of a naturalistic sense-making paradigm, in which complexity, uncertainty and the stimulation of natural processes are emphasized over idealism, control, and expert opinion. Since narrative and networks are two fundamental elements of human collective functioning and as such are integral to the naturalistic paradigm, we bring them together in this chapter. We consider how narrative participates in each of the network effects of identity, trust, and conflict, and how that participation can best be supported to maximize these intangible yet strong elements of value afforded by interorganizational networks.

This chapter is a contribution to a growing body of work that takes a *naturalistic* approach to research and intervention in organizations. Probably the best-known correlate to our approach is the naturalistic approach to decision making pioneered by Klein (1998), on whose work we have drawn in our own work (Kurtz and Snowden, 2003). We also draw on the schools of action research (e.g., Masters, 1995) and grounded theory (e.g., Glaser and Strauss, 1967). Here we contrast the naturalistic with the *idealistic* sense-making approach.

- In the idealistic approach, the leaders of an organization set out *an ideal future state* that they wish to achieve, identify the gap between the ideal and their perception of the present, and seek to close it. This is common not only to process-based theory but also to practice that follows the general heading of the "learning organization." Naturalistic approaches, by contrast, seek to understand a *sufficiency* of the present in order to act to stimulate evolution of the system. Once such stimulation is made, monitoring of emergent patterns becomes a critical activity so that desired patterns can be supported and undesired patterns disrupted. The organization thus evolves to a future that was unknowable in advance, but is more contextually appropriate when discovered.
- Idealistic approaches tend to privilege *expert* knowledge, analysis, and interpretation. Naturalistic approaches emphasize the inherent un-knowability of current and future complexities, and thus they de-privilege expert interpretation in favor of enabling emergent meaning at the *ground level*. (This upsets the modernist and postmodernist in management theory alike: the former seeking to mandate the future, the latter seeking to deconstruct source material.) In this respect we concur with the philosophy of the participatory school of action research (e.g., Wadsworth, 1998), which refuses to separate researcher from researched and from researched *for* (usually those in control) and attempts to bring all parties together into a common group of co-researchers, co-subjects, and co-actors.
- Idealistic approaches *separate* diagnosis (and thus research) from intervention, seeing the former as preceding the latter. The purpose of research in the ideal paradigm is to discover best practice by an analysis of the past that will inform and direct gap-closing interventions in the future. Research in the naturalistic paradigm is *intertwined* with practice, and sees all diagnoses as de-facto interventions and all interventions as providing an opportunity for diagnosis. An example can be found by contrasting Social Network Analysis (e.g., Cross and Parker, 2004), which seeks to analyze networks in order to allow informed management intervention, with Social Network Stimulation (Snowden, 2005a) which seeks to catalyze the ramification of cross-silo networks.

Two of the most important elements of the naturalistic sense-making approach are *narrative* (as one of the primary mechanisms of complex knowledge transfer, creation and interpretation in human society) and *networks* (as one of the primary realities of human life – we are still, unless artificially constrained, tribal and clan-like in our needs and perspectives). It follows that the intertwined threads of narrative and networks will feature prominently in any naturalistic consideration of human endeavour.

With that foundation in mind, let us consider the application of naturalistic sense-making to learning networks. Interorganizational learning networks are valuable yet intangible: while participants feel that they and their organization have benefited, they struggle to explain what exactly those benefits are and how they can be expressed. Some proof of such value has been provided, for example, in the areas of increased speed of innovation diffusion (e.g., Strang and Soule, 1998) and improved knowledge creation (e.g., Hamel, 1991; Riggins and Rhee, 1999). We would like to suggest three additional benefits of such networks that seem to us to be at least as important as these if not more so. Interorganizational learning networks bring to organizations improved negotiation of multiple identities, increased discourse regarding trust and rule structures, and greater productive conflict. All of these benefits improve the systemic functioning of the organization as a complex entity, and all involve strong narrative elements. We will consider each of these benefits in turn and suggest approaches that can help to support each benefit.

Negotiation of Multiple Identities

Human beings are masters of identity management, negotiating (without integrating) a constantly fluctuating constellation of identities. We may, for example, chat about politics (as a citizen) with a colleague (as a professional) while driving (as a motorist) our child (as a parent) to a school meeting (as a community member). These observations are well represented in the sociological literature by the related schools of identity theory (e.g., Stryker, 1987), social identity theory (e.g., Tajfel and Turner, 1986), and situated identity theory (e.g., Alexander and Wiley, 1981), which all emphasize the importance and influence of multiple roles and identifications in complex social interactions. Some part of each individual's effectiveness depends on his or her ability to manage these multiple identities in a fluid, effortless way, the way a master craftsman manages his or her tools and materials.

Collectively, organizations also have multiple identities – as producers of shareholder value, as providers to employees, as players in industries, as creators of trusted products or services, as resources for customers, as agents of social change, as partners in local communities. These multiple organizational identities influence and are influenced by the multiple identities of their members.

Juarrero (2002) explains that the problem of identity has a long history in philosophy, generally distilled into two questions: *What makes something the same thing as it was before?* and *What makes two things the same kind of thing?* She raises the question of how organizations, which are decoupled from a physical location, can maintain identity. In the context of complex adaptive systems theory she creates a vivid and appropriate image (and we acknowledge her contribution to the title of this chapter) that is worth quoting in full:

> whereas strong dynamic links among components (characterized as nodes) result in a "strong cluster," weak links between strong clusters give rise to a community or a world. Since any node can simultaneously belong both to a strong cluster and to a larger networked community, society, or world, boundaries become diffuse, but also dynamic and creative. Complex dynamical systems thus begin to look more like bramble bushes in a

thicket than like stones. And it is extremely difficult, as any outdoorsman will tell you, to determine precisely where a particular bramble bush ends and the rest of the thicket begins.

Organizations (and the individuals that make them up) are much like "bramble bushes in a thicket," and the nature of their many interacting and co-evolving identities is self-similar as well as deeply contextual and ambiguous. Idealistic approaches (such as "best practices" and the "balanced scorecard") are not best suited to handling such ambiguity, but naturalistic approaches (such as those we will describe below) are designed to deal with it.

Identity resilience

The collective identity resilience of an organization, or its ability to manage its multiple identities smoothly and without breaking down (and also to maintain a sufficient diversity of those identities) is supported by the identity resilience of its employees. For example, say an organization must make a radical change to its product line to compensate for a sudden drop in demand for a previously rock-solid product. Or say an organization decides that devolving greater decision-making capabilities to members of its field staff will reduce the faux pas based on misunderstandings of local conditions that have beleaguered its sales efforts. To the extent that its employees are able to manage their identifications both to the particular products or services they support and to the larger identities of the organization (for example as a provider of jobs to the local area), the organization will be able to reinvent itself more successfully. If employees cannot flex their identification to a particular process or product ("I only know how to run this machine," "We only market to this sector"), the transition will require more effort and may be less successful.

Organizations seem to recognize the fact that employees must manage multiple identities, creating "work-life" programs to help them juggle activities. However, too often only lip service is given, painting the picture as a simple choice of how much time to allocate to different tasks, when the issue, and the ability, can penetrate more deeply into many aspects of behavior. For example, employees often have to juggle customer relations with product development with industry outreach with project planning, and often some of these functions (and identifications) can be underserved because of inadequate training or even a denial (by the employee or others) that such functions are within the scope of work. Many employees do their work without being able to answer the question, "Who are you in this organization?" (And possibly just as importantly, "Who are the others in this organization?" and "Who is this organization?").

When identity is considered from a perspective in which the taking on of mutually exclusive roles is paramount and human activity is categorized into atomistic particles without reference to context, individuals and organizations are constantly presented with dilemmas as to which identity to support. The idealistic approach assumes that there must be some ideal resolution of such dilemmas, while naturalism prefers a paradox to a dilemma. For example, people often resolve identity conflict through ritual, which can manifest in small apparently insignificant acts that allow people to change the patterns through which they filter data. A pilot entering the cockpit of an aircraft goes through a set pattern of ritual activity that causes his or her identity as pilot to dominate his or her identity as a particular individual.

Martin and Meyerson (1988) identified three perspectives on organizational identity in contemporary research on corporate culture. According to the *integration* perspective, organizational identity is strongest when it is shared and reflects the goals and beliefs of its founders or managers. From an integration point of view, "alignment" between expressed values and informal beliefs is desirable, leading to increased loyalty and coherence. This perspective is particularly prominent in the popular literature on culture and leadership. By contrast, the *differentiation* perspective highlights subcultures and sub-identities within the organization, derides efforts at false unification, and believes that it is necessary to recognize differences of class and power within the organization to make sense of its identity. The *ambiguity* (or fragmentation) perspective views the organization more like a web in which coherent sub-identities are always appearing and disappearing and in which fluctuating elements of organization-wide identity form and dissolve on particular issues. Martin and Meyerson emphasize that none of these perspectives is entirely correct, but that all three must be considered when viewing the organization. Thus an organization is a coherent body (integration) that is divided against itself (differentiation) and always changing (ambiguity). In other words, organizations collectively manage multiple types of coexisting identities.

Silos as organizational identities

One often-quoted problem of organizational identity is the infamous "silo mentality." "Silo thinking" is blamed for many organizational ills, and horror stories abound of groups working meters away from each other, unaware of mutually critical information and unable to consider the perspectives and needs of other groups. The problem can be real, but the solution is often worse than the problem: a "change initiative" to remove barriers and force people to share all knowledge equally, in effect forcing multiple sub-identities to merge into one grand identity. This rarely works, mainly because organizational silos do provide useful advantages: rapid communication through shared language and social context, consistency, and coherent response. In fact, one could say that simultaneous prescriptions for "removing silo mentalities" and "supporting team-based organizations" are at odds.

Actually, silos are a poor metaphor for overly isolated organizational identities. If we take a cursory look at actual silo design, we see that the two most important considerations are (a) avoiding "stagnant zones" and "bridges" in which material ceases to flow, ages and decays even while new material is being added; and (b) ensuring the proper release of material for release without "flooding" (too strong flow) or lack of flow. There is also much to be read about designing silos to handle particular types of materials with different flow properties. In addition, silo design extends to many considerations exterior to the silo itself – its location in relation to water sources and buildings; its foundation and shielding; its access and inspection methods; its vapor exchange provisions; its response to rain, wind, frost, and heat; the preparation of material for storage; and the proper retrieval of material for use. In fact, silos are as much about interaction and flow (between fields, between seasons, between production and consumption) as they are about isolation and storage.

A well-functioning team within an organization is actually much like a well-designed silo: it concentrates its energy and expertise (and identity) into the tasks it is best suited for, yet maintains context-appropriate connections and flows that maintain its relationship with the entire farm complex. Silo design metaphorically corresponds not only to the internal functioning of the team, but also to its awareness of its place in the enterprise and its relationships with other teams and with the "fields" from which and to which its "content" flows in an unending rhythm. If we look at teams in this way, the most effective organization is made up of teams that are not entirely "transparent" or entirely "knowledge sharing" but aware of and capable of constantly negotiating internal and external connections between identities – some strong, some weak – in ways that make them and the entire organization more effective.

Identity resilience is not simply stability, but the ability to thrive in the face of environmental fluctuation and transformation. A resilient identity is *effective*, but it may not always be *efficient*. In nature, stability sometimes improves resilience and sometimes destroys it – and which of these is true changes unpredictably. Species tend to "choose" evolutionary "strategies" (actually, fall into canalized pathways) that range from succeeding best in periods of stability (as with "living fossils" such as horseshoe crabs and coelacanths which have remained essentially unchanged for hundreds of millions of years) to succeeding best in periods of instability (as in the famous story about nineteenth-century moths adapting their coloration to coal-blackened trees within decades). In different circumstances each of these extremes can be life-saving or deadly, but looking across evolutionary history few species that optimize stability have survived (which is why "living fossils" are so notable and amazing – and vulnerable). In organizations, the focus on efficiency that has dominated management theory for some decades and creates such practices as stripping away "surplus" functionality may pose dangers to survival. The most effective systems leave a sufficient level of inefficiency in order that they can be resilient in changing contexts.

Interorganizational networks and multiple identities

Interorganizational networks help organizations manage their multiple identities by holding up a mirror and helping them to achieve descriptive self-awareness. They also change the nature of identities within the organization. Balmer and Wilson (1998) describe how a network of radio stations provides several coincident types of affinity, with for example professional, geographic, generational, and ethnic-origin identity affiliations forming across stations. Rometsch and Sydow (2003) describe how a fast food franchise affects the identity perceptions of not only its franchisees but also its suppliers, who see their own role in upholding the vision of a network of "family restaurants" as critical. As people begin to see their organization and their place in it "from the outside," that is, from other perspectives, they begin to be more able to evaluate and navigate their identities with respect to it. In our own experience, one of us participated in such an interorganizational "learning network" and found that our most revealing experiences did not have to do with encountering new ideas but in seeing that the obstacles we faced in organizational life were not unique to our own organization but were widespread and generic. These revelations permanently changed our view of our relationship to the organization and our place in it.

These experiences match with Martin et al.'s (1983) "uniqueness paradox": the finding that stories were often told by people at different organizations to demonstrate how their organization was unique – but those stories were widely similar among organizations. For example, employees at all the organizations studied told stories in which the uniqueness of their organization was demonstrated by its willingness to promote people on merit (or not), to rise to meet obstacles (or not), and to forgive mistakes (or not). What interorganizational networks provide is the opportunity for employees to discover this paradox for themselves through learning about the experiences of people at other organizations, and in the process to change how they manage their own constellation of identities in relation to their organization. Stryker and Burke (2000) describe how identities can influence the patterns of chosen social affiliations, which can in turn change the identities that caused them to form. This means that identification with a broader network will alter the identities of individuals and groups within organizations.

These perspective-enlarging experiences are necessary to human sense-making. A particular context or contrast can stimulate a latent identity, resolve a longstanding conflict, or create a conflict where it is needed. In conditions of unexpected contrast (for example extreme stress or extreme release) we can achieve common purpose with a diverse range of individuals with whom we might have no previous or expected affiliation. The resulting coevolutionary processes are irreversible: our pre-existing and latent identities and those of the people with whom we have interacted are now altered.

Identity and narrative

One of the ways people have always talked about identity has been through the telling of identity stories which feature the individual or group as a coherent character with certain highlighted characteristics – the lone genius, the band of principled rebels, the misunderstood nobility. Stories told for purposes of identity negotiation (both individually and collectively) are fundamentally different from stories told for other purposes. Crites (1997) calls these stories "sacred stories" and describes them thus: "Such stories, and the symbolic worlds they project, are not like monuments that men behold, but like dwelling places. People live in them . . .. [They] inform people's sense of the story of which their own lives are a part, of the moving course of their own action and experience." All other stories are what he calls "mundane stories" about norms, expectations, and experiences.

Evidence for the participation of identity stories in the process of organizational identity negotiation is easy to find. Says Wilkins (1984), "When I interviewed managers and employees at a successful major electronics firm they could not define in mere words what the 'company way' was but they could define it using stories which were well known in the company." The most important words here are "well known." Identity stories are not necessarily told often, but they are known by everyone who identifies with the organization. Such "lived-in" stories create filters by which the organization creates its identity and through which it filters data from its environment. An illustrative example of such a story is the "nine-day fortnight" story observed by

Wilkins (1984):

> most employees at one company I researched have been told the story about how the company avoided a mass layoff in the early 1970s when almost every other company in the industry was forced to lay off employees in large numbers. Top management chose to avoid a layoff of 10 percent of their employees by asking everyone in the company, including themselves, to take a ten percent cut in salary and come to work only nine out of ten days. This experience became known as the "nine-day fortnight" by some and is apparently used as a script for the future of the company. In 1974 the company was again confronted with a drop in orders, and it went to the "nine-day fortnight" scheme for a short period. When other companies in the industry began layoffs, the old-timers used this story to quiet the anxiety of concerned newcomers . . ... Employees occasionally tell [this] story to communicate that this is the "company with a heart." Everyone I talked to in the company knew the story, which is used both as a symbol and a script.

Sacred stories of organizational identity represent an *ideational* component of organizational culture (Keesing and Strathern, 1998) and as such are quite different from mission statements and organizational value statements, which represent *rule-based* culture and tend to reduce the complexity of sacred stories to platitudes.

Another important aspect of identity stories is their dramatic or performance nature, which mundane stories rarely exhibit. Czarniawska (1997) uses the term "autobiographical acts" to refer to the processes of negotiating organizational identity stories and links them to Goffman's (1959) concept of the construction of the self through performances before audiences (including oneself). The organization performs its identity stories differently to different audiences: to its customers, its shareholders, its employees, its competitors, and its partners. It makes sense to say, then, that employees participating in interorganizational networks will be required to represent the organization's identity stories to an external audience, and that those tellings will impact the process of negotiation and the identities themselves. The properties of an audience made up of individuals from a parallel organization meeting for ostensibly cooperative purposes will have a different impact on organizational identities than the properties of other audiences (possibly those the organization is more institutionally prepared to address, through marketing and communications departments). A question we have often heard in interorganizational gatherings, when social time is permitted, is, "So what's it like to work for Company X?" (with the implied extension "as opposed to Company Y"). Outside such a context, people might not hear such a question, and such a performance before such an audience may not have a chance to impact the nature of the organization.

A third aspect of identity stories is their apparent uselessness: they may appear to be "about" nothing. Anyone looking for concrete evidence of "knowledge transfer" or "peer learning" – or even truth – may discard these stories, which are in some ways the most important to retain. Bauman (1986) describes how stories may be patently untrue at a purely factual level, but may reveal much deeper truths about the community in which they are told. Bauman quotes one man, during "an exploration of storytelling and dog-trading in Canton, Texas" who says, "when you get out there in the field with a bunch of coon hunters, and get you a chew of tobacco in your mouth, and the dogs start running, you better start telling some lies, or you won't be out there long."

In other words, among coon-hunters lying is a mark of truthfulness, that your word, deep down, can be trusted: that you belong.

Such storytellings are critical determinants of identity negotiation. Says Bauman:

> Since at least the time when a distinctive body of American folk humor first emerged during the early years of the American republic, the hunter and the trader have occupied a privileged place in American folklore. Dog trading at Canton is a thriving contemporary incarnation of this American folk tradition. The tall tales and personal narratives of its participants place them in unbroken continuity with the generations of hunters, traders, and storytellers that have given American folklore some of its most distinctive characteristics.

In other words, these hunters tell the stories they tell to "place" themselves within the "unbroken continuity" of a larger cultural identity. When one coon hunter told Bauman, "any man who keeps more'n one hound'll lie to you," he was representing his identity as a member of a noble group, not complaining or bragging. You can imagine that someone observing storytellings like these in an interorganizational network and looking for evidence of "best practices" transferred would conclude that the group performed no function and should not be supported, when in fact they could be on the verge of reinventing the organization.

One of the paradoxes we have observed in our work is something we call the paradox of truth: If you ask someone to tell the truth, they will lie; but if you allow them to lie, they will tell the truth. However, this key aspect of narrative does not mean that we have to fall into the epistemological uncertainty of relativism. People, like the coon hunters in the example above, are "canny" when it comes to knowledge of truth and learning in day-to-day discourses; we are highly tolerant and indeed thrive on contextual ambiguity. People routinely concatenate events and subtly change the material of experience to create appealing mechanisms for the transfer of learning. Narrative in human systems does not fill the role of what can be termed *fact-objectivism* (Boghossian, 2006) or epistemic truth, but instead supports the rapid transfer of learning and failure avoidance. This is why so many naturally occurring stories are negative (and why "best practices" is so limited in usefulness). Whole forms such as urban myths have developed to spread learning and warning without any need for literal truth.

Supporting narrative negotiation of identity

Our recommendations for supporting the exchange of identity stories in interorganizational networks include one caveat and two devices.

The caveat is this: *organizational identities are emergent properties* of complex systems, and as such are slippery creatures. Outsiders cannot easily see them; they can be destroyed by contact or even direct reference; and they cannot be created or controlled by mandate. The "extraction" of such stories by "experts" is guaranteed to be an exercise in illusion, as is their "design" by "leaders." Say Boje et al. (1982): "In their attempts to examine the organization's myth system, OD [Organisational Development] consultants often substitute their own myths for those of the client organization." Actually, though we agree with Boje's statement, there is a degree of hypocrisy in it, since Boje himself, in his deconstruction of "organizational fragments," imposes his own expert ideology in an attempt to remove ideological bias. By contrast, our narrative methods attempt no expert interpretation of collected anecdotes and only *connect* people and anecdotes into dynamic ecologies of sense-making (on which more later). In a very real sense the postmodernist approach to narrative (of which Boje is an exemplar) represents a Hegelian antithesis to the thesis of managerial modernism: that which they criticize they also practice. In rejecting managerialism, we can equally discover the tyranny of the expert, as in Orwell's nightmare the animals look through the window of the farm to see the pigs dressed as men.

Saying that identity processes cannot be controlled (either by managers or by experts) does not mean that they cannot be *influenced*; it means that the methods used must be participative and emergent rather than analytical and prescriptive. For example, a shock to the system (such as the surfacing of a negative identity story) may be useful in order to create the conditions for breaking up unhealthy rigidity and renewing self-organization; but as with all complex systems such interventions are not entirely predictable in their outcome. Pursuing multiple small interventions and seeing which seed desirable patterns works best: this is naturalistic evolution, not idealistic goal seeking.

Archetypes for narrative negotiation of identity
The first device we will mention that is particularly useful in supporting narrative exchange for identity negotiation is the *archetype*. We are all familiar with archetypes from the stories of our childhood: the "fairy tales" of the Brothers Grimm, the myths and legends of the Greek and Norse Gods, the animal stories of the Aborigine people of Australia, the myths of Native America. As people tell and retell stories about their environment, their beliefs and values as expressed through the characters within those stories gradually become more extreme. Eventually each character represents one aspect of the culture, and collectively the characters and the stories that reveal those characters provide a profound set of cultural indicators. In the modern age, we can see archetypal characters emerge in the form of cartoons such as the Dilbert series, in which the various characters are instantly recognizable in a modern corporate environment. Just as a Dilbert cartoon resonates with its audience, so an archetype or archetypal story has immediate resonance with the unarticulated collective identities of the organization's members. At their simplest, archetypes can help a group articulate understandings that have previously remained beneath the surface. At their most sophisticated, archetypes can form part of a complex network of cultural integration.

We help people to construct sets of archetypes (Snowden, 2005b) that represent their understandings about themselves and about other groups, and then help them use those sets to reveal commonalities and conflicts. These comparisons have led to some truly revealing insights about "who we are" and "who they are." For example, we have seen senior management discover that while they see themselves as hardworking, their subordinates see them as free riders on the work of others; we have seen salespeople discover that they hold their customers in contempt; we have seen educators discover that they have labeled truly creative (if unconventional) people as unproductive; we have seen managers discover that they themselves are the largest obstacle their people face. Often these discoveries are painful, but they are always useful.

Issues of identity can be sensitive subjects, and archetypes provide an indirect route to disclosure and discourse that can be much more powerful than surveys and direct questioning, which rarely produce truthful answers. Archetypes also resonate with experience, and as such persist to create a shared language with which identities can continue to be reappraised as the organization changes. In one example, an archetype constructed in one part of an organization surfaced a year later in another organization halfway across the world in a group speaking a different language. It was still meaningful and resonant, which is why it survived. This has been the function of storytelling for countless centuries.

Archetypes also represent a means of negotiating identity among groups. For example, when two organizations are merging, the atmosphere is fraught with narrative. Identity is never stronger than when it is under threat. One of us experienced the takeover of a company by IBM. Prior to the IBM takeover, the organization had three competing identities (and associated stories) that could be traced back to a previous merger of three groups to create a single division of a larger organization. After the IBM takeover those competing identities merged for the first time, threatened by the larger identity of IBM.

Our methods use narrative to help people negotiate meaning among groups. Extraction of the archetypes that precede a merger in both organizations not only provides a valuable indicator of culture and a means of informing managerial decisions (if we do X how will each of the archetypes react?), but also a means by which new *common* stories can evolve quickly. Interventions in which employees from one organization re-tell their stories through the eyes of the other organization's archetypes and vice versa in effect merge the underlying myth structures of the organization. In conflict resolution, displacement of real world issues into a semi-fictional world of archetypes allows discussions to take place without threat. Telling a story about a set of archetypes allows me to tell a story about myself without allocation of responsibility for the story. We use the same technique in crisis management to allow disclosure of failure without allocation of blame.

Sense-making databases

A second device we use to support narrative exchange for identity negotiation is the *sense-making database*. This contains anecdotes (raw, naturally occurring stories), but can also contain drawings, pictures, sound files: anything that allows people to make sense of complexity. A sense-making database is emphatically not an expert system, a knowledge base, a content management repository, a case-based learning system, or a best practices collection, although it may work in close collaboration with such systems. It is a matrix for storytelling as a mode of discourse. A few distinguishing characteristics:

- Anecdotes in the sense-making database have multiple interpretations and perspectives. They are not "codified" as having one meaning or "truth," but may have several competing interpretations preserved, which adds to their negotiation value. For example, if I can see that a group of product designers said a particular story was an unfounded rumor and a group of factory staff said the same story was "something the head office doesn't want known," I can learn a lot more from the story than I can if I am only told the story is factually true or false from an official point of view.

- Anecdotes in the sense-making database are contextually situated. They preserve as much contextual detail about the "story of the story" as is possible – Where did it come from? Why was it told? How was it told? Who told it? How did the audience respond? How was it different in another telling? How has it changed since the early days? When is it told? Who can tell it? What happens when it is told? This type of contextual situating gives users a greater ability to evaluate the story in a fine-grained way that is more useful to their navigation of identities than the simple facts of date, location, and subject matter. One might, for example, see that anecdotes represented as personal experience increasingly tend to be about customer satisfaction, while anecdotes represented as second-hand increasingly tend to be about unhappy customers, which might lead one to investigate the possibility that accountability is suffering.
- Anecdotes in the sense-making database are intimately linked with conversation in a complex ecology of communication. They are not "captured" as "knowledge" and locked away forever, but are given the opportunity to participate in ongoing dialogue, perhaps growing or changing over time. In this way the sense-making database in use becomes something larger than its software, larger than its content, and larger than its user community. Such databases are more like online communities such as epinions.com or eBay than they are like encyclopedias. They allow patterns to emerge, which are very like the mechanisms for learning and knowledge transmission that take place in oral history. As people encounter anecdotes in different combinations in different circumstances, new stories (refined, purposeful) and anecdotes (raw, naturally occurring) emerge in the context of need.
- Anecdotes in the sense-making database enable pattern detection and sense-making. They are indexed by socially relevant abstractions such as archetypes, themes, values, conflicts, and other social constructs that permit people to use the body of stories not atomistically, for look-up only, but as a pattern detection device. For example, we have seen people discover parallels between their behaviour and that of historical figures and thus reveal a new perspective on how their actions must appear to others. Importantly, these discoveries are not handed down by outside experts but are discovered by people embedded in the context of the problem for themselves, which makes them infinitely more valuable (and acceptable).
- Anecdotes in the sense-making database are indexed by their tellers, as only they know the full context. If the anecdotes cannot be indexed by the storyteller, their indexes are socially constructed by groups of people representative of the community. They are never interpreted by an external expert. Thus the indexing structure (which can include archetypal characteristics) forms a mediation device between the individually situated context of an anecdote and the meaning of that anecdote in interaction with different contexts. The indexing structure, which is itself emergently derived through the process of archetype construction, creates a grammar of narrative interaction which sets into motion the narrative ecology mentioned above.
- Anecdotes in the sense-making database create new anecdotes, which emerge from the serendipitous (not taxonomic) encounter between people and the

database and each other. The net result is the evolution of ecology rather than the compilation of a resource. Identity management is an ongoing, social, interpretive, communicative, and complex process. Supporting it requires attention to all of these elements, whether using software as a tool or not. The easiest way to support the narrative negotiation of identity is simply to allow people to do it, because they naturally will if the activity is legitimized. Even something as simple as altering the schedules of interorganizational meetings to allow time between presentations for free discussion can have an impact on the effectiveness of such meetings in supporting the identity-management function of the network. Recognition of the importance of identity negotiation, and not considering it merely a nicety, is half the battle.

Trust and Rule Structures

If we take a systemic view of trust in organizations, it is not about who can ask whom to do what, but how well the organization is able to cohere as it flows over obstacles in its path. A bicyclist encountering a rough patch will call upon her balance, her strength, her quick response time, her muscle memory – and her bicycle's design, and her built relationship with the bicycle, and even her built relationship with the road she is riding on – to trust that she will be able to ride over the patch without falling.

Trust is a feature of well-functioning systems that is "bigger on the inside than the outside" – that is, it looks simpler than it is. For example, it is commonly believed (and reported) that the winners of the Tour de France bicycle race are individuals, but in fact they are nine-person teams called "pelotons" whose intense coordination is essential to the success of the "winner." No single rider can hope to win a race against such teams, which use aerodynamic shielding, or a "common slipstream," to support the leader's progress. According to a *New Yorker* article on the success of Lance Armstrong (Specter, 2002):

> Cycling is, above all, a team sport, and the tactics involved are as complicated as those of baseball or basketball. ...there is usually at least one team rider positioned in front of his leader. Riding directly behind another man – which is called drafting – can save a skilled cyclist as much as forty per cent of his energy. . . . The team members take turns "working," or pulling, at the front to give each other a rest.

A well-functioning organization, like a well-functioning peloton, is made up of people who give each other reciprocal "rests" via networks of mutual trust, and thereby help the organization cover ground without falling behind or falling apart. In a peloton rushing down a mountain there is no time to discuss the rules of coordination, and clashes can be literally life-threatening, so the rules must be understood by all and built over time. In an organization rushing down a recession curve, a similar argument can be made.

Much has been written about the "unwritten rules" (routines, norms, standards) of organizational culture and how people learn about these rules and the consequences of upholding and breaking them (e.g., Schein, 1985; Johnson et al., 1994; Weick, 1995). Not only does it take time for new employees to learn the rules (themselves having prior assumptions and beliefs to reconcile), but also the rules themselves are a moving target, evolving over time. Rules take various forms, from those specifically stated in policy, to those written but ignored, to those unwritten but often mentioned, to those unwritten and never mentioned (but still critical), to those unwritten and only loosely applied, to those that serve mainly for cohesiveness or initiation and have very little actual consequence beyond group acceptance. Rules can arise from many sources (from below as well as above), for many reasons (for self-protection, for team cohesiveness, for conflict avoidance), and in various relationships to each other (some rules are about the applicability of other rules). Some are imposed, some form out of attempted imposition (as backlash or as twisting of original intent) and some emerge on their own (sometimes to the consternation of those in charge, but sometimes wonderfully fortuitous).

Obviously there is much complexity to be navigated here, and much of it must be done informally. In a study of stories told about employees "not knowing the ropes" in over 500 organizations, Gilsdorf (1998) found that "Stating clear policy would have helped head off 20 percent of the problems narrated by this study's respondents." That leaves 80 percent of problems to be anticipated through direct experience: through conversation, storytelling, observation, and interaction. Gilsdorf also collected estimates of what these incidents of "not knowing the ropes" cost organizations, and found accounts of lost time, lost employees, lowered productivity, and ill will, not to mention monetary losses ranging from tens of thousands to millions of dollars per incident. The strength of unwritten rules is that they are habitual within the group and thus both adaptive and resilient. Good management practice creates habits rather than rules. Coming back to our bicycle-team metaphor for organizational effort, the more individual members have transformed rules into habits, even as they are renegotiated, the more smooth is the performance of the group overall. To outsiders (consultants, the new manager?) it may look like there are no rules at all, as though the entire group merely thunders down the mountain in perfect synchrony.

Interorganizational networks and trust

Interorganizational networks help organizations sustain productive rule networks within their boundaries by making the rules and the negotiations around them more visible and better understood. When members of such networks trade experiences, they compare not only facts and procedures, but also "how we do things around here." In the same way that children find out that their dialects and accents are not universal, and thus learn more about the dialects they use, members of organizations find out that the unspoken rules they live by are not universal, and thus bring those rules into a closer scrutiny and a deeper understanding. To give a simple example, participants in one learning network pooled their experiences by telling each other stories with the theme of boundaries they encountered at work. Several generic themes emerged, such as "tunnel vision," "oversimplifying," "breaking the mold," and "rolling with the punches," with stories from disparate industries intermixed. This set of stories helped members to place their experiences within a broader range.

The importance of trust in the development of strategic alliances between organizations has been examined in a broad literature (e.g., Dyer and Chu, 2000;

Bachmann, 2001; Das and Teng, 2001). Generally, the development of norms and understandings *among* organizations is considered most fully, and not their impact on intraorganizational trust. For example, say Child and Faulkner (1998), "The fact that partners from different countries . . . follow different assumptions of 'what can be taken for granted' places particular difficulties in the way of creating trust-based relationships between them, over and above the tensions which might be expected to arise within strategic alliances in general." At the same time such cultural boundary crossings create a challenge for organizations to negotiate new mutually agreeable norms, they also provide a unique and valuable opportunity to make visible "what can be taken for granted" within each organization.

Skule (1999) describes how an interorganizational group of workers from five food-and-drink companies were taken through a training program that included "practice in other companies." Says Skule:

> Most of the skilled operators described [the experience] in terms like "see things differ-ently," "opened my eyes," "think more about what I am doing," "more alert" and "think more about the consequences." These new perspectives or ways of seeing in turn made operators attend to features in their work situation in a new way. From a former habitual way of working according to minimum standards, many skilled operators developed a more reflectively skilled way of performing their job, within the limits of existing job structures and routines.

We believe this kind of benefit may not be as often used as is possible.

Trust and narrative

Attention to the importance of storytelling as a means to negotiate and make sense of collective rules has a long history of study (e.g., Wilkins, 1983; Boje, 1995; Gabriel, 2000). To give just one example, Jameson (2001), in a study of management discourse in a restaurant chain, tells a fascinating story of how several managers went through a process she calls "storybuilding" to make sense of a new corporate directive. The directive specified that managers would be subject to a "three-strikes-and-you're-out" system for complying with requirements to submit timely information on new employ-ees. If the paperwork was missing or delayed three times, the managers would lose their jobs. In one meeting a group of operations managers was discussing the three-strikes directive with their regional executive. First, the executive told a story about how the rule would apply, using the terms "you" (the managers) and "they" (the corporate office). He then realized the managers were threatened by the use of "you," so he retold the same story with a third-person protagonist. At that time he also introduced the elaboration that even if a subordinate was in charge of submitting the paperwork (if the manager was out of town on business), the manager, not the subordinate, would be fired. This elaboration launched a series of hypothetical stories told by the managers in which the directive was "tried out" in various situations – the paperwork got lost by the corporate office, was called in but not mailed in, was mis-faxed, was hard to get from the new employee. In each case the executive kept repeating the same denouement – they, and no one else, would be fired. The managers used these fictional narratives to make sense of the new directive (which they knew they could not influence), to communicate to the executive their difficulties in complying with the directive (and thus perhaps getting him on their side in any dispute), and to come up with strategies to protect themselves and reduce the threat to their jobs. For example, they discussed saving fax records to prove they had submitted records on a timely basis. This is a compelling example, but by no means unique, of how people naturally use narrative on an everyday basis to negotiate rules, whether official or informal.

People also use narrative to safely express differing opinions about rules and their effects on them. For example, Gabriel (1995) gives an account of an accident in which a fire extinguisher exploded in a research laboratory. Four collected accounts of the incident varied widely. One employee gave only a "detached description emphasizing the material damage"; another employee half-seriously presented the incident as a "personal attack" on her by the management; another employee concentrated on making clear that he was not rattled by the explosion; and a fourth jokingly represented the event as a failed opportunity to inflict damage "upstairs" (on the management). In each of these cases, the storytellers used the story as a vehicle in which to embed sub-texts about negotiations of power and procedure. In the three-strikes story mentioned above, the operational managers populated their fictional narratives with fragments of actual experiences in order to "test" the directive from a perspective that made sense to them. Many such organizational stories embed rule negotiations inside accounts of seemingly unimportant events such as rearranging office furniture, scheduling time off, purchasing petty cash items, using the telephone and e-mail, and even making seating arrangements at meetings. Often these stories are not about what they appear to be about. As with identity stories, the importance of these rule stories may not always be obvious if looking for transferred knowledge or best practices; but without a free trade in such stories it is difficult for trust to emerge.

Supporting narrative negotiation of trust

As with the previous section on identity, our recommendations for supporting the exchange of rule-negotiation stories in interorganizational networks include one caveat and two devices.

The caveat is possibly the most important in working with narrative: *respect the power and danger of narrative.* We have found that people just beginning to consider the possibilities of narrative pass through a predictable first stage of storytelling: they think that telling a good story will affect the change they want to see. This perception is partly based on a literature that says mental models determine action and are created by stories. The mental-models view is an attractive but unrealistically simplified view of human cognition. For example, patterns of experience, either encountered directly or vicariously through stories, create complex patterns in long-term memory that dramatically affect (indeed may form the basis of) decision making. This is a far more complex phenomenon than simple "mental models" which imply a more structured and manageable process than is actually possible. For this reason we find the work of some people who advocate telling stories in organizations (the so-called "organizational storytellers") dangerous.

Those who are seduced by the assumed quasi-deterministic attractions of organizational storytelling are led into seeking replicable recipes and focusing on intervention and prescription rather than description. For example, they might hire a professional scriptwriter or storyteller to help them craft a story that they believe will fill people with enthusiasm for the vision they want to expand, and they might see narrative primarily as a device for "cultural change" or other euphemisms for control.

This telling-stories phase soon passes when people realize that narrative doesn't work that way; instead it is a complex system that can be influenced but not controlled. "Official" stories that don't reflect the perspectives and realities of different people in the organization tend to sprout other stories that more accurately do so. Particularly dangerous are "anti-stories," or cynical reaction stories, which often warp the original story to negate its message. One famous example from IBM history is the story of how T. J. Watson, famous for his nasty temperament, decided that he would institute an "open-door policy." He told his employees that he wanted to see lots of heads poking in his office door. The story soon got around that lining the inside of his office was a row of heads – on spikes.

We call such out-of-touch official stories "Janet and John stories" (so they are called in England; in the USA it is Dick and Jane, in Canada Bob and Betsy, in Wales Sion a Sian), after those sanitized manners tales told to children in which the good quiet little angels bear no resemblance to real children. We like to say that the ethics of narrative work is self-policing, because if you try to control the narrative system in an organization, it will punish you without any external force needing to do so. Still, we use a three-point set of ethical heuristics for narrative work: (1) always declare up front the use of narrative techniques (no stealth story work); (2) if asked any question about what sort of narrative intervention you are doing (such as instructing executives in how to tell stories for cultural change), answer honestly; and (3) appoint an independent arbitrator for any dispute over the use of narrative techniques in organizations. It is also important to understand that because narrative processes in organizations are complex systems, all diagnoses are interventions (thus "extracting" the stories of an organization is not an effect-free observation) and all interventions are diagnoses (thus monitoring of any narrative activity provides useful new insights).

Disruptive metaphor
The first narrative device we recommend for the support of narrative trust and rule negotiation is *disruptive metaphor*. Metaphor can provide a common reference for the group that moves them away from current concerns and prejudices into a safer space, but a space that is disruptive, and even disorienting, in the association of ideas that it stimulates. It can be used for several purposes, including eliciting stories in sensitive areas, getting people to see things from different perspectives, and breaking up rigid entrained beliefs. For purposes of rule negotiation metaphor is most useful to help people talk about issues they are not able to discuss directly. People often use metaphor naturally in conversation, but deliberate support of it can be even more helpful, especially if people are at an impasse and unable to begin dialogue.

A particularly apt choice of metaphor can break down barriers to discussion of difficult subjects, putting aside literal truths to get at deeper cultural truths. For example, the book *Longitude* by Dava Sobel (1998) describes how the British government offered a rich reward to anyone who could discover a means to measure longitude at sea, which would dramatically improve the safety of seafaring. A furniture maker in the English Midlands proposed that longitude could be measured by constructing a clock that would keep accurate time on shipboard, and thus longitude calculated by examining the time difference from Greenwich Mean Time at midday. Though the solution was obviously correct, the "experts" in London denigrated the furniture maker's solution for decades and never fully paid him the substantial reward. Their science locked them into solutions based on measurement of the distance of the moon from the earth and creating tables based on the day of the year, in effect replicating the established method for measuring latitude with a sextant and a calendar.

Given that story, it is much easier to ask people to think of instances when someone under their management has been treated like the furniture maker than to ask the same people to think of instances when they have mistreated people out of ignorance and prejudice. The metaphor allows people to understand and discuss the issue at a deeper and less personally threatening, but still disruptive level. It allows people to "own up" to bad practices that they might otherwise attempt to excuse, and it allows people to safely "accuse" others of similar practices. Common childhood stories, examples from other industries and disciplines, science fiction, and historical accounts can all provide useful disruptive metaphors. Such metaphors can even be woven into group exercises in which people are confronted with the characteristics of their own organizations in metaphorical form, perhaps exploring an alien planet or negotiating an ancient treaty. If we contrast this type of exercise with the "fall into each others' arms" trust exercises that are typically anti-storied about in organizations, we can see that disruptive metaphor allows the real issues to be discussed rather than papered over with pretensions to trust. Some of our more elaborate methods based on metaphors involve creating displaced environments (artificial life universes, alternative histories, contrasting industry sectors) designed based on a study of the organization, but with the problems displaced to the metaphorical environment. In a game environment employees are thus able to explore novel solutions without the encumbrances of current best practice and responsibility for outcome.

Story construction

A second narrative device for the support of narrative trust and rule negotiation is support for '*story construction*' as a sense-making activity. Note that we say "as a sense-making activity" in deliberate contradiction to the usual expectation of story construction as a creator of persuasive material. The use of story construction for propaganda is entirely legitimate (indeed, the term "propaganda" need not have any negative connotation – it is merely the spreading of some information rather than others), but is less amenable in a complex system of narrative exchange. We help people construct purposeful stories out of collected anecdotal material, using age-old fable forms, to negotiate meanings among different perspectives. Such fables are grounded in the reality of the organization and create a shared language people can use as a shorthand for oblique reference. For example, we once helped a group to create lessons-learnt stories about a large construction project, the first of its kind for the corporation. The stories were taught to improvisational actors and were performed at a global annual meeting. The audience then interacted with the actors, adding and creating new variations of the original form. Humor and resonance with actual experience embedded the story in the group. The story title was "and then the corporate seagulls come in and shit all over you," the language reflecting the culture of the group. The target of the story was to allow managers in the company to explain unique aspects of their organization to partner companies on large construction projects. Some years later on another project we were gathering stories in the field from a water utility company that had just started a project with the construction company. The corporate seagull story returned without alternation, years after its creation, with the same purpose.

The reader will now be able to link these interventions back to earlier examples of the creation of new myth form stories in a merger. Different networks need different stories to create their identity and the nature of their interconnection. As in a religious community, a set of stories provides a moral framework to which disparate activity can be referenced to resolve differences (think of the parable of the good Samaritan). Socially constructed stories can be used to create a sustainable and (due to necessary ambiguity) resilient framework by which the different parts of the bramble bush (and the thicket) can interact and maintain coherence.

Productive Conflict

Deutsch (1973) defined conflict as arising when two parties have incompatible goals and obstruct each other in meeting those goals. Kabanoff (1985) pointed out that conflict can arise when group members have compatible goals but approach the situation differently based on diverse backgrounds and value systems. Thomas (1992) defined conflict as arising when one party feels pain or discomfort, projects its cause (correctly or incorrectly) onto another party, and (critically) does not accept the situation. Thomas' definition brings perspective to the forefront by distinguishing situations in which parties have differing goals but accept the difference or simply do not care about the outcome.

Recent years have brought a growing interest in the positive nature of intragroup conflict, though its roots go back to Follett (1942) and Coser (1956). The old idea that all conflict is negative (thus the importance of "conflict resolution") has been replaced by a distinction between desirable and undesirable conflict (thus the importance of "conflict management"), though the diffusion of this distinction to the popular press has not been complete. Deutsch (1973) compared cooperative conflict, in which group members see the conflict as a group problem that requires common effort to solve, and competitive conflict, in which group members see the conflict as a win-lose struggle. This distinction was subsequently enlarged on by many authors and variously termed positive versus negative, constructive versus destructive, productive versus unproductive, and functional versus dysfunctional. Ravn (1998) poses the interesting possibility that Thomas' definition of conflict includes in it both productive and unproductive conflict, because productive conflict stops before it gets to the third phase of non-acceptance, instead using the energy of conflict as a positive force.

Many authors (going back to Guetzkow and Gyr, 1954) have distinguished between *cognitive* conflict over how tasks should be carried out and *affective* conflict over interpersonal relationships. Jehn (1997) added a third type of conflict – *process* conflict, over who should do what – and found that group members differentiate between these three types of conflict in practice, even in the middle of conflicts. Several authors (e.g., Jehn, 1994; Amason, 1996) have found cognitive conflict to be helpful, and affective and process conflicts to be detrimental to group performance. Amason and Shweiger (1997) point out how difficult it is to separate these types of conflict in real life: for example, conflicts about task strategies are often "taken personally" and so lead to affective conflicts. So conflict is a double-edged sword: the good comes with the bad. It is dangerous to concentrate energy too strongly on reducing affective conflict because cognitive conflict might also be reduced, leading to groupthink and repression; and it is dangerous to promote cognitive conflict without regard to the effect it has on reciprocal trust relationships.

Amason and Shweiger (1997) suggest that groups which maximize cognitive conflict while minimizing affective conflict have two characteristics: *openness*, or the accepted practice of openly airing "diverse and dissenting viewpoints," and *mutuality*, or norms of cooperation that prevent such diverse exchanges "from being misinterpreted as personal attacks or political manoeuvring." Thus shared behavioral norms that represent the cooperative nature of the group provide a sort of boundary mechanism to separate positive from negative conflict. Jehn (1997) empirically found that group norms were used in practice to allow cognitive conflict ("We need to fight about this") while disallowing affective conflict ("Leave that out of the office"). George and Stern (2002) give an excellent example of such separation norms in their description of the "four rules for not killing each other" used by three high-level defence officials in the US President Clinton's cabinet: (1) "no friendly fire," or refrain from criticizing each other publicly; (2) "walk ourselves back," or retreat voluntarily from an unreasonable stand; (3) "presume innocence," or talk to your colleague before you believe he or she has done something dishonest; and (4) "no policy by press conference," or agree to things before announcing them. These rules all served to keep cognitive conflict from "crossing over" into personal attacks and power plays.

We find Alper et al.'s (2000) concept of "conflict efficacy" useful: it says that conflict should be measured not by its nature or origin, but by its contribution to the perception among group members that conflicts can and are dealt with productively. In other words, whatever works for a particular group at a particular time is what works, and the group has to find this out in practice. Say Alper et al., "Teams that are confident they can deal with their conflicts are likely to work productively; teams that doubt their conflict management abilities may become demoralized and ineffectual." Thus the value of any particular conflict depends on the history, context and dynamics of the group (which seems a more valid systemic view). Our own work also indicates that conflict, particularly if individuals are protected by ritual practices of formal conflict, increases the scanning capabilities of a group.

Interorganizational networks and productive conflict

Interorganizational networks help organizations improve productive conflict within their boundaries in two ways: first, by increasing the productive conflict experienced by groups and individuals of the organization who are in contact with the outside network; and second, by making each internal group's norms for conflict management more visible in comparison. It does not seem that much work has been done specifically on the types and natures of conflict in interorganizational networks to date. Certainly there has been discussion of how conflicts of interest can arise between partners in business ventures, but there has not been strong attention to how inter- and intragroup conflict plays out in interorganizational learning networks.

We see some propensity in the literature on interorganizational networks to believe that members of such networks succeed best when they maximize their exposure to "best practices," which are universally agreed upon, universally applicable, and free of conflict. However, the evidence shows something different and more interesting. Beckman and Haunschild (2002) studied the effect of interorganizational networks on acquisition premiums, as quantitative measures of "good deals" reached for the future success of the firm (lower premiums meaning better deals). They found lower premiums paid when interorganizational networks were diverse in experience, reporting experiences of high and low premiums paid, than when networks were universally low in premiums paid. This contradicts the idea that organizations work by imitating others and gives support to the idea that the communication of experiences, of as wide a range as possible, produces the best informed decision making. Those experiences are inevitably going to produce conflicting advice and opinions, which are useful expansions of an organization's experience.

There is some debate about how best to increase productive conflict. Some authors have developed "conflict stimulation" methods (e.g., Van de Vliert and de Dreu, 1994) meant to increase productive cognitive conflict in groups. Macy and Neal (1995) describe classroom activities that use devil's advocacy (deliberate dissent), dialectical inquiry (tension between ideas) and reverse brainstorming (criticism of previously generated ideas). However, these methods have their limits: George and Stern (2002) point out that devil's advocacy, in which one group member is temporarily given the role of voicing unpopular opinions, is much less effective in a homogenous group than the inclusion of a "genuine dissenter" who embodies the role fully.

Our own work involves breaking a group into several sub-groups, each of which works on a problem in parallel. At strategic points a representative of each sub-group presents their solutions to another sub-group who are instructed to be passive during the presentation. The presenter then turns their chair so that they cannot maintain eye contact and now has to passively receive and take notes as the audience "savage" their ideas. Participants are instructed to be unfair, unreasonable, and unforgiving. (This technique will be recognized by those in writing groups as a variant of the "fly on the wall" approach.) If you have five such sub-groups, an idea can go through four such baptisms of fire. The fact that everyone is involved, and the ritualization (lack of eye contact, instruction to be unfair) removes personal threat and encourages greater scanning capability in the group. An external "devil's advocate" can be rejected by the group as an outsider, but the taking up of the role by a member of the group is always constrained by the prior participation of that individual in the decision processes of the group.

All of this would argue for true diversity in group membership, including diversity of cultural and learning backgrounds, as a way to stimulate productive cognitive conflict. For example, groups composed only of people with particular degrees from particular regional schools in particular subjects are likely to produce less constructive conflict than groups of people with varying educational experiences in various fields from around the world.

So a genuinely wide range of experiences and backgrounds is the best contributor to productive interorganizational conflict, which brings more than "best practices" to network members: it brings a radical re-vision of existing practices and knowledge structures. Armstrong (1990) says this well:

> One way of demystifying the seeming naturalness of a set of beliefs or interpretive practices is to juxtapose them against opposing conventions that organize the world according to different principles that may seem equally obvious to their adherents. . . . Confronting presuppositions radically different from one's own may lead one to become clearer about what one believes and why, or the challenge of rigorous opposition may compel adherents of an approach to refine their methods or to clarify their hypotheses with more subtlety and precision than they might have developed if they had not met resistance.

Holmquist (2003) makes the case that learning in intraorganizational and interorganizational networks is intermingled and that conflict is a critical ingredient in this intermingling: "The explorative character of much interorganizational learning does not occur by itself; it occurs as a result of a confrontation and a combination of single organizations' experiences." He also makes the point that because interorganizational networks typically have a less centralized structure than the organizations themselves, employees who participate in such networks are exposed to "conflicts and instability as a result of the lack of formal authority," which can increase productive conflict within their own organization. All of these signs point to the utility of interorganizational networks as a source of not only new knowledge but also of productive conflict that improves the organization's ability to reinvent itself from within.

Productive conflict and narrative

Narrative is intricately linked with conflict in two ways. First, all stories include conflict between opposing forces. Bal (1992) gives the example that "a man won a race" is not a story – but "a man with a limp won a race" is. The man's limp is a negative force, and his victory implies a positive force (possibly his determination) that struggles with the negative force. As a more detailed example, consider this Indian folk tale (Ramanujan, 1991):

> Once a lamb was drinking water in a mountain stream. A tiger came to drink the water a few yards above him, saw the lamb, and said, "Why are you muddying my stream?"
> The lamb said, "How can I muddy your water? I'm down here and you are up there."
> "But you did it yesterday," said the tiger.
> "I wasn't even here yesterday!"
> "Then it must have been your mother."
> "My mother has been dead for a while. They took her away."
> "Then it must have been your father."
> "My father? I don't even know who he is," said the desperate lamb, getting ready to run.
> "I don't care. It must be your grandfather or great-grandfather who has been muddying my stream. So I'm going to eat you," said the tiger. And he pounced on the lamb, tore him to pieces, and made a meal of him.

Conflict occurs at three levels inside the story: intrapersonal, in the tiger's explanation of his actions to himself; interpersonal, in the conflicting goals of the tiger and lamb; and environmental, in the "way of things" which means that tigers will eat lambs whether or not they can explain it. Conflict occurs at even more levels outside the story, in its inevitable multiple interpretations. Why did the tiger feel the need to justify his action? Who and what is this story really about? Is it about injustice, rationalization and duplicity, or is it about natural order and the political correctness of artificial apology? Narrative does not give answers to these questions, as logical analyses might, but maintains a necessary ambiguity.

This brings us to the second link between narrative and conflict: people use narrative reasoning to understand and negotiate conflict. According to Fisher's (1984) "narrative paradigm," we make sense of the world by comparing the many different and possibly competing narratives we encounter throughout our lives, and we use "good reasons" at least as much as "evidence" as the basis for decision making. "Good reasons" are determined by two uniquely narrative criteria of which humans, as "storytelling animals," are uniquely aware: *narrative probability* (or coherence), or whether the story hangs together, and *narrative fidelity*, or whether the story rings true. For example, the tiger and lamb story coheres because it has a beginning (possibility), middle (tension), and end (resolution), creating a larger unified idea than a simple string of events would. And it has fidelity because it resonates with our experience, leading us to quickly think of several analogous situations in our own lives.

Bennett (1997) describes a similar pattern of narrative reasoning in his observations of how jurors piece together evidence in criminal trials: "[E]ven when evidence is introduced in the often disjointed 'question-answer' format in a trial, the key elements generally will be abstracted by jurors and arranged in story form during deliberation." According to Bennett, jurors have to decide two things about a case: plausibility, or "Could it happen that way?" and verifiability, or "*Did* it happen that way?" Facts and evidence provide some of the proof as far as verifiability, but jurors also test narratives for plausibility and adherence to their own experiences of the world. For example, if the car was running for five minutes already, could it have been cold, as the defendant says it was? Indeed, we use the term "story" colloquially to talk about negotiations surrounding conflicting versions of the truth – "your story doesn't hold up" or, "that's my story and I'm sticking to it."

Supporting narrative negotiation of conflict

Our most important recommendation for supporting the exchange of narratives surrounding conflict (its revelation, management, negotiation, resolution, and even useful escalation) is to simply appreciate it. People seem to have a powerful belief that competing stories ought not to exist and make strong efforts to resolve such conflicts. What do you do, for example, if one group's "best" practices are another group's "worst" practices? If you are looking at knowledge as a thing that can be captured and transmitted, you might resolve such disputes (with force if necessary) so that one "answer" is available. But if you look at knowledge as a socially constructed, contextually situated, and constantly renegotiated phenomenon, and especially if you are trying to help people maintain productive conflict as a source of inspiration, creating such an artificial resolution would throw away something of great value. (This is a mistake made by countless textbooks.) Rather, you would want to provide people with full access to such conflicts, rich in contextual detail, so that they can make the most of them.

The value of conflict is one of our reasons for not being enthusiastic about narrative techniques that have been derived from therapeutic practice and seek to privilege one type of story over another. An example of this would be appreciative inquiry (e.g., Whitney et al., 2003), which seeks to encourage behavior change by directing the emergence of (only) positive stories. Similarly, facilitation techniques based on avoiding conflict and encouraging consensus can reduce the capacity of a group to act in the real world, by reducing the range of options considered and failing to detect opportunities or threats in the environment whose potential is represented by weak signals.

Narrative for conflict exploration

We often design narrative systems and narrative interventions that specifically work with conflict to make it more visible, as with the juxtaposition of competing sets of values and themes. We might, for example, help an organization collect a set of "raw" stories from their employees and/or customers, then have separate groups index the stories according to the same criteria (truthfulness, origin, intent, for example), and present the competing interpretations in sense-making databases so that people can use conflict as a visible device for pattern sensing. Or we might have different groups of people construct fable stories on the same subject and show them to both groups. This is especially useful when two or more groups of people need to come together, such as in an acquisition, or are interdependent, such as staff and customers. This is another reference to our argument for the creation of conditions for the rapid evolution of cross-boundary stories.

Openness and mutuality

Another set of recommendations comes from Amason and Shweiger's (1997) observation that groups which maximize cognitive conflict and minimize affective conflict create an atmosphere of openness and mutuality. Each of these qualities is well known to be supported by narrative exchange, and as such can be augmented using narrative techniques.

An atmosphere of *openness* is one in which unpopular opinions can be put forth without fear of reproach. The use of narrative to safely express such opinions has been widely studied and demonstrated. Stories tell of experiences, not of arguments. Still, it can be difficult to tell stories one knows will not be well received, and there are ways to make this easier. Anonymity helps people tell stories that need to be told but that may hurt them personally and therefore are dangerous to tell. Anonymity can be achieved via online communities, public kiosks, proxy interviewers, or even something as simple as giving storytellers pseudonyms that only they can link to their actual names. Anonymity has benefits for both tellers and listeners; executives may hear things in an anonymous online community that would never cross the power barrier in "real life." Another type of anonymity is the attribution of stories to fictional characters such as archetypes. Fictional explorations, such as alternative histories and speculative futures, help people to indirectly tell stories about the present or recent past. All of these are ways of providing masks that allow people to reveal themselves.

An atmosphere of *mutuality* is one in which people recognize the cooperative nature of their endeavors and respect each other as equal players. Mutuality requires that people see things from each other's point of view so that actions can be interpreted with understanding rather than with rushes to judgment and blame. Here again narrative can play a strong role: one of the oldest uses of the art of storytelling is providing a different perspective. Indeed, the very act of listening to a story requires the willing suspension of one's own perspective to temporarily entertain another view of the world. Folk tales abound with stories where the third worthless son slays the dragon, where the dragon is an enchanted prince, where the handsome prince is a nasty thief, and where the thief saves the day. The purpose of such stories is to remind us that we should not take things for granted and that we should keep our minds open to possibilities that may seem foolish at the time. Thus a clever person maintains multiple informal networks with large amounts of diversity, rather than just clustering with like-minded individuals.

The value of conflict among narratives
Storytelling (and even narrative self-description) is not a magic cure-all for misunderstandings and blinkered perspectives. Sometimes it can provoke as much blindness as it can remove. There are dangers when one uses narrative without adequate attention to the unique qualities of stories as communicative devices. These dangers have to do mainly with the fact that the creation of any narrative downplays some aspects of reality and highlights others as it condenses experience.

- The danger of *vividness* is shown by an experiment carried out by Reyes et al. (1980). Mock jurors were given either "vivid" or "pallid" statements supporting claims that a defendant was or was not drunk when he ran a stop sign. A pallid statement might be: "On his way out the door, Sanders staggered against a serving table, knocking a bowl to the floor." A vivid statement might be: "On his way out the door, Sanders staggered against a serving table, knocking a bowl of guacamole dip to the floor and splattering guacamole on the white shag carpet." Judgments of innocence or guilt were unaffected by vividness when the statements were first presented; but 48 hours later, people who had been shown vivid statements judged the defendant significantly more guilty than did people who were shown pallid statements. Thus if stories about "us" are vivid and stories about "them" are pallid – even if both sets contain positive messages – the vivid stories will win out. The creation of a vivid or pallid story is such a subtle point that people may do it even without knowing they are doing so.
- The *fundamental attribution error* (Ross, 1977) is important to affective conflict and can be exacerbated by storytelling. When attributing causes to behavior, people tend to attribute their own behavior to situational causes ("I'm tired this morning") and the behavior of others to dispositional causes ("You are a bad driver"). This has been well demonstrated in the field (e.g., Jones, 1979). Thus if stories about "us" contain more situational detail than stories about "them," people may continue to blame the actions of the other party solely on dispositional causes.
- The problem of *framing* has also been well demonstrated (Kahneman and Tversky, 2000). The way in which a question is framed – the way in which

a story is presented – has a measurable effect on the beliefs people form after reading it. For example, if stories about "us" mention that we saved half of the earthquake victims, and stories about "them" mention that they lost half of the earthquake victims, which group will seem more successful? Which will seem more heroic? You can see this subtle perspective constraint in television news: we "strategically withdrew" while they "were routed out"; we "regretted collateral damage" while they "slaughtered civilians."

Thus, creating a sense-making database or other storytelling device can be nothing more or less than creating a propaganda machine – intentionally or unintentionally – if these factors are not taken into account. Such an artifact will do nothing to improve conflict management and may even make matters worse. There are many ways to ameliorate this possibility, from collecting stories using impartial or naïve interviewers or observers to requiring that no story be indexed by an outsider or even by one group.

One practice we have had success with, which essentially entails creating conflict *within* a sense-making database, is to merge a "disruptive/simulative database" of stories from another domain into the narrative database. These might be stories about historical conflicts or from science fiction or alternative history ("counterfactuals"). If these stories have been collected from multiple perspectives and indexed along with those of the group, they can provide unexpected comparisons that show group stories in a new light. For example, perhaps a manager's action in the last quarter showed an eerie resemblance to Napoleon's march on Moscow, with similar disastrous consequences. Or perhaps everyone has been sure that a rapid expansion initiative will succeed, but they find their own stories about how this type of thing has been a sure-fire win throughout history contrasted by actual historical accounts of several organizations believing the same thing just before they went bankrupt. Especially when people from different organizations are telling stories together, having some independent stories in the mix can help to provide a wider perspective than just "how we do things" and "how they do things."

Conclusions

In picking up Juarrero's (2002) delightful metaphor of brambles in a thicket, we have sought to situate naturalistic approaches to learning networks in a naturalistic approach that reflects the realities of human life. We have de-privileged the expert interpreter (by argument and by practice), be they the analysts of modernism, or the de-constructivists of postmodernism. We have also called a *plague on both your houses* to the claimed universalism of process engineering and systems dynamics alike.

Human society evolved using narrative as a means of creating meaning and communicating knowledge within a network of families, clans, and tribes. We have therefore taken an approach that uses narrative as a prime sense-making capability, and as such we have used it as both a conceptual and practical lens through which we can look at identity management, trust negotiation, and the use of productive conflict. We have shown how narrative techniques based on naturalistic approaches to diagnosis and intervention can improve the systemic functioning of organizations; we also claim that this approach provides results that idealistic approaches cannot hope to achieve.

Naturalism works because unlike idealism it is aligned with the ground truth of organizational life. Contrast the "management" of a children's party with that of an organization. Can you imagine providing detailed work plans with formal learning objectives to each child on arrival at the party? Would you produce a milestone-based project plan for the party? Maybe a formal set of values, accompanied by motivational posters (you know the sort of thing, water dropping into ponds, eagles soaring over valleys with platitudinous statements of idealistic intent)? Not even the most committed management consultant would make those mistakes in their identity as parent. We manage the party by creating boundaries that restrict dangerous play (and they had better be elastic; rigid boundaries have a habit of becoming brittle) and we encourage play with catalysts such a football, party games, a swing, a DVD. We seek to stimulate beneficial self-organization, as any more formal option would result in cognitive overload. And of course we seek to create, use, and live that experience as a story. It is our natural impulse, but unfortunately we leave our natures at the door as our identity shifts from parent to manager, and we assume that behavior that would never be tolerated by our children (or indeed by ourselves) will be accepted by our adult workers.

Common perceptions of the work world as machine-like and ordered, and thus subject to the rules of order, are cultural legacies of the industrial revolution that still blind us to the fact that organizations are in fact complex adaptive systems. As an example, consider the etymology of the term "manage" itself. According to Williams (1983) the English verb "to manage" was originally derived from the Italian *maneggiare*, meaning to handle and train horses. The *manege* form of horseback riding, a more involved and time-consuming form than modern dressage (which was meant to replace manege with something more accessible to the unskilled) is a similar use of the word. In this earlier meaning the emphasis is on learning with, abiding with, adapting to, respecting, and working with another complex entity: the horse and rider as coevolving brambles in a wider thicket of social traditions surrounding beauty and form. Around the early eighteenth century, this original meaning merged with the French term *menage*, or household, making it easier to adapt the meaning of the combined term *manage* to the metaphor of the obedient machine, to the corridors of power, and to the actions of controlling and directing. The naturalistic approach we have advocated, in effect a return to *manege* rather than *menage*, is the most effective way to achieve results in organizations made up of real people. Its practice in the generation and management of learning networks is not difficult; it simply requires us to unlearn the practices that arise from a *menage* directorial tradition of management theory and relearn what we already know to be true of the *manege* multiplex world we live in.

References

Alexander, C. N. & Wiley, M. G. (1981) Situated activity and identity formation. In M. Rosenberg & R. H. Turner (Eds.) *Social Psychology: Sociological Perspectives*, 269–89. New York: Basic Books.

Alper, S., Tjosvold, D. & Law, K. S. (2000) Conflict management, efficacy and performance in organizational teams. *Personnel Psychology*, 53, 625–42.

Amason, A. C. (1996) Distinguishing the effects of functional and dysfunctional conflict on strategic decision making: Resolving a paradox for top management teams. *Academy of Management Journal* 39(1), 123–48.

Amason, A. C. & Schweiger, D. M. (1997) The effects of conflict on strategic decision making effectiveness and organizational performance. In C. K. W. de Dreu & E. Van de Vliert (Eds.) *Using Conflict in Organizations*, 101–15. London: Sage.

Armstrong, P. B. (1990) *Conflicting Readings: Variety and Validity in Interpretation*. Chapel Hill: University of North Carolina Press.

Bachmann, R. (2001) Trust, power and control in trans-organizational relations. *Organization Studies*, 22(2), 337–65.

Bal, M. (1992) *Narratology: Introduction to the Theory of Narrative*. Toronto: University of Toronto Press.

Balmer, J. & Wilson, A. (1998) Corporate identity: There is more to it than meets the eye. *International Studies of Management and Organizations*, 28(3), 12–31.

Bauman, R. (1986) *Story, Performance, and Event*. Cambridge: Cambridge University Press.

Beckman, C. M. & Haunschild, P. R. (2002) Network learning: The effects of partners' heterogeneity of experience on corporate acquisitions. *Administrative Science Quarterly*, 47(1), 92–124.

Bennett, W. L. (1997) Storytelling in criminal trials. In L. P. Hinchman & S. K. Hinchman (Eds.) *Memory, Identity, Community: The Idea of Narrative in the Human Sciences*. Albany, NY: State University of New York Press.

Boghossian, P. (2006) *Fear of Knowledge: Against Relativism and Constructivism*. Oxford: Oxford University Press.

Boje, D. M. (1995) Stories of the storytelling organization: A postmodern analysis of Disney as "Tamara-land". *Academy of Management Journal*, 38(4), 997–1035.

Boje, D. M., Fedor, D. B. & Rowland, K. M. (1982) Myth making: A qualitative step in OD interventions. *Journal of Applied Behavioral Sciences*, 18(1), 17–28.

Child, J. & Faulkner, D. (1998) *Strategies of Cooperation: Managing Alliances, Networks, and Joint Ventures*. Oxford: Oxford University Press.

Coser, L. A. (1956) *The Functions of Social Conflict*. Glencoe: Free Press.

Crites, S. (1997) The narrative quality of experience. In L. Hinchman, S. Hinchman and S. Hinchman (Eds.) *Memory, Identity, Community: The Idea of Narrative in the Human Sciences*. Albany, NY: State University of New York Press.

Cross, R. & Parker, A. (2004) *The Hidden Power of Social Networks*. Boston, MA: Harvard Business School Press.

Czarniawska, B. (1997) *Narrating the Organization: Dramas of Institutional Identity*. Chicago: University of Chicago Press.

Das, T. K. & Teng, B.-S. (2001) Trust, control, and risk in strategic alliances: An integrated framework. *Organization Studies*, 22(2), 251–83.

De Dreu, C. K. W. & Van de Vliert, E. (Eds) (1997) *Using Conflict in Organizations*. London: Sage.

Deutsch, M. (1973) *The Resolution of Conflict*. New Haven: Yale University Press.

Dyer, J. H. & Chu, W. (2000) The determinants of trust in supplier-automaker relationships in the U.S., Japan and Korea. *Journal of International Business Studies*, 31(2), 259–85.

Fisher, W. R. (1984) Narration as human communication paradigm: The case of public moral argument, *Communication Monographs*, 51, 1–22.

Follett, M. P. (1942) Constructive conflict. In H. C. Metcalf and L. Urwick (Eds.) *Dynamic Administration: The Collected Chapters of Mary Parker Follett*. New York: Harper Collins.

Gabriel, Y. (1995) The unmanaged organization: Stories, fantasies, and subjectivity. *Organization Studies*, 16(3), 477–501.

Gabriel, Y. (2000) *Storytelling in Organizations: Facts, Fictions, and Fantasies.* Oxford: Oxford University Press.

George, A. L. & Stern, E. K. (2002) Harnessing conflict in foreign policy making: From devil's to multiple advocacy. *Presidential Studies Quarterly,* 32(3), 484–508.

Gilsdorf, J. W. (1998) Organizational rules on communicating: how employees are – and are not – learning the ropes. *Journal of Business Communication,* 35(2), 173–201.

Glaser, B. G. & Strauss, A. L. (1967) *The Discovery of Grounded Theory.* Chicago: Aldine Press.

Goffman, E. (1959) *The Presentation of Self in Everyday Life.* New York: Doubleday.

Guetzkow, H. & Gyr, J. (1954) An analysis of conflict in decision-making groups. *Human Relations,* 7, 367–82.

Hamel, G. (1991) Competition for competence and inter-partner learning within international strategic alliances. *Strategic Management Journal,* 12, 83–103.

Holmquist, M. (2003) A dynamic model of intra- and interorganizational learning. *Organization Studies,* 24(1), 95–123.

Jameson, D. A. (2001) Narrative discourse and management action. *Journal of Business Communication,* 38(4), 476–507.

Jehn, K. A. (1994) Enhancing effectiveness: An investigation of advantages and disadvantages of value-based intragroup conflict. *International Journal of Conflict Management,* 5, 223–38.

Jehn, K. A. (1997) A quantitative analysis of conflict types and dimensions in organizational groups. *Administrative Science Quarterly,* 42(3), 530–57.

Johnson, J. D., Donohue, W. A., Atkin, C. K. & Johnson, S. (1994) Differences between formal and informal communication channels. *Journal of Business Communication,* 31(2), 111–22.

Jones, E. E. (1979) The rocky road from acts to dispositions. *American Psychologist,* 34, 107–17.

Juarrero, A. (2002) Complex dynamic systems and the problem of identity. *Emergence,* 4(1/2), 94–104.

Kabanoff, B. (1985) Potential influence structures as sources of interpersonal conflict in groups and organizations. *Organizational Behavior and Human Decision Processes,* 36, 113–41.

Kahneman, D. & Tversky, A. (Eds.) (2000) *Choices, Values, and Frames.* Cambridge: Cambridge University Press.

Keesing, R. & Strathern, A. (1998) *Cultural Anthropology: A Contemporary Perspective.* Orlando: Harcourt Brace & Co (3rd edn, 1st edn published 1976).

Klein, G. (1998) *Sources of Power: How People Make Decisions.* Cambridge, MA: MIT Press.

Kurtz, C. & Snowden, D. (2003) The new dynamics of strategy: Sense making in a complex-complicated world. *IBM Systems Journal,* 42(3), 462–83.

Macy, G. and Neal, J. C. (1995) The impact of conflict-generating techniques on student reactions and decision quality. *Business Communication Quarterly,* 58(4), 39–50.

Martin, J. & Meyerson, D. (1988) Organizational cultures and the denial, channeling, and acknowledgement of ambiguity. In L. R. Pondy, R. J. Boland & H. Thomas (Eds.) *Managing Ambiguity and Change,* 93–125. New York: John Wiley & Sons.

Martin, J., Feldman, M. S., Hatch, M. J. & Sitkin, S. B. (1983) The uniqueness paradox in organizational stories. *Administrative Science Quarterly,* 28, 438–53.

Masters, J. (1995) The history of action research. In I. Hughes (Ed.) *Action Research Electronic Reader.* University of Sydney, online at http://www.behs.cchs.usyd.edu.au/arow/Reader/rmasters.htm

Ramanujan, A. K. (1991) *Folktales from India: A Selection of Oral Tales from Twenty-two Languages.* New York: Pantheon Books. (The referenced folk tale is "If It Isn't You, It Must Be Your Father", 92–3.)

Ravn, I. (1998) Understanding conflict as a (missed) opportunity for social development. *Proceedings of the International Association for Conflict Management Annual Conference,* June 7–10, University of Maryland.

Reyes, R. M., Thompson, W. C. & Bower, G. H. (1980) Judgmental biases resulting from differing availabilities of arguments. *Journal of Personality and Social Psychology*, 39, 2–12.

Riggins, F. J. & Rhee, H. S. (1999) Developing the learning network using extranets. *International Journal of Electronic Commerce*, 4(1), 65–83.

Rometsch, M. & Sydow, J. (2003) Identities of networks and organizations: The case of franchising. *Proceedings of the International Conference on Economics and Management of Networks* (EMNet), Vienna. Available online at: http://www.univie.ac.at/EMNET/program.htm

Ross, L. (1977) The intuitive psychologist and his shortcomings: Distortions in the attribution process. In L. Berkowitz (Ed.) *Advances in Experimental Social Psychology* (Vol. 10). New York: Academic Press.

Schein, E. H. (1985) *Organizational Culture and Leadership*. San Francisco: Jossey-Bass.

Skule, S. (1999) Organizational routines, occupational standards and industry recipes: The role of rule-following in organizational knowledge and learning. In M. Easterby-Smith, L. Araju & J. Burgoyne (Eds.) *Organizational Learning*, 3rd International Conference, Conference Proceedings, Vol. 2, Lancaster University.

Snowden, D. (2005a) From atomism to networks in social systems. *The Learning Organization*, 12(6), 552–62.

Snowden, D. (2005b) Stories from the frontier. *E:CO*, 7(3–4), 155–65.

Sobel, D. (1998)*Longitude: The True Story of a Lone Genius Who Solved the Greatest Scientific Problem of his Time*. London: Fourth Estate.

Specter, M. (2002) The long ride: How did Lance Armstrong manage the greatest comeback in sports history? *New Yorker*, July 15.

Strang, D. & Soule, S. A. (1998) Diffusion in organizations and social movements: From hybrid corn to poison pills. *Annual Review of Sociology*, 24(1), 265–90.

Stryker, S. (1987) Identity theory: Developments and extensions. In K. Yardley & T. Honess (Eds.) *Self and Identity: Psychosocial Perspectives*, 83–101. New York: Wiley.

Stryker, S. & Burke, P. J. (2000) The past, present, and future of an identity theory. *Social Psychology Quarterly*, 63, 284–97.

Tajfel, H. & Turner, J. C. (1986) The social identity theory of inter-group behavior. In S. Worchel & L. W. Austin (Eds.) *Psychology of Intergroup Relations*. Chicago: Nelson-Hall.

Thomas, K. W. (1992) Conflict and negotiation processes in organizations. In M. D. Dunnette & L. M. Hough (Eds.) *Handbook of Industrial and Organizational Psychology*, 651–717. Chicago: Rand McNally.

Van de Vliert, E. and De Dreu, C. (1994) Optimizing performance by conflict stimulation. *International Journal of Conflict Management*, 5, 211-22.

Wadsworth, Y. (1998) What is participatory action research? *Action Research International*, Paper 2. Available online: http://www.scu.edu.au/schools/gcm/ar/ari/p-ywadsworth98.html

Weick, K. E. (1995) *Sensemaking in Organizations*. Thousand Oaks, CA: Sage Publications.

Whitney, D. Trosten-Bloom, A. & Cooperridder, D. (2003) *The Power of Appreciative Inquiry: A Practical Guide to Positive Change*. San Francisco: Berrett-Koehler.

Wilkins, A. (1983) Organizational stories as symbols that control the organization. In L. Pondy, P. Frost, G. Morgan & T. Dandridge (Eds.) *Organizational Symbolism*. Greenwich, CT: JAI Press.

Wilkins, A. L. (1984) The creation of company cultures: The role of stories and human resource systems. *Human Resource Management*, 23(1), 41–60.

Williams, R. (1983) *Keywords: A Vocabulary of Culture and Society*. London: Fontana Press.

CHAPTER NINE

Competing and Collaborating in Networks: Is Organizing Just a Game?

Max Boisot and Xiaohui Lu

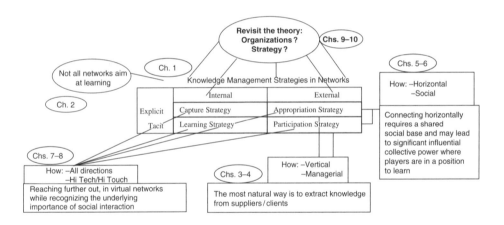

Abstract

In the organizational and management literature, networks are hailed as a new organizational form. In the natural and social sciences, however, networks are a form of description that can be applied to any organized form. In this chapter we argue that the network concept, by allowing a more fine-grained analysis of organizational processes, is more useful as a general description of organizational form than as an organizational form in its own right. We show how concepts drawn from game theory can combine with network thinking to generate different institutional and organizational forms.

In the natural sciences, networks have become a valuable descriptive resource for studying the structure of physical interactions at the level of cells, molecules, or elementary particles (Watts, 1999). In the social sciences networks are used as a descriptive resource to study phenomena as varied as entrepreneurship, international trade, community processes and migration (Smith-Doerr and Powell, 2004). In many organization science applications, however, we see networks taken as a new *organization form* made possible by evolving information and communication technologies (ICTs), a form that is contrasted with earlier organizational forms such as the multidivisional or functional structure, or the matrix organization (Baker, 1992). The managerial literature, for example, views the network as a form of organization that is intermediate between markets and hierarchies and characterized by higher levels of connectivity, more permeable boundaries, and flatter job hierarchies than alternative forms of organization (Williamson, 1985; Smith-Doerr and Powell, 2004). Podolny (1999) defines a network form of organization as any collection of actors ($N > 2$) that pursue repeated, enduring exchange relations with one another without a legitimate organizational authority to arbitrate and resolve disputes that may arise during the exchange. Joint ventures, strategic alliances, business groups, franchises, research consortia, relational contracts and outsourcing agreements, all qualify as networks (Smith-Doerr and Powell, 2004). Thus while the natural and much of the social sciences take networks to be a *form of description* (Erdös and Renyi, 1959), much of the organizational and managerial literature take them to be *an organizational form* (Baker, 1992).

In this chapter we shall argue that the network concept is more useful under the first interpretation than under the second. The network-as-description, by allowing the more fine-grained and discriminating ways of thinking about competitive and collaborative processes that have been advocated by Tsoukas and Knusden (2002), extends the reach of organizational theory in general and of organizational economics in particular. The network-as-organizational-form, by contrast, whilst recognizing the validity of the network-as-description approach (Baker, 1992), confines the application of a powerful concept to a small subset of organizational phenomena. In what follows, we first discuss three of the metaphors that have guided theorizing on organizations. We then explore the difference between a network as an organizational form and a network as a form of organizational description. In the next section we briefly show how a few simple concepts from game theory can combine with network thinking to account for different institutional forms. We then discuss the implications of our analysis for how organization theory should approach networks. A conclusion follows.

From Mechanical to Organismic and Ecological Perspectives on Organization

Human organizations are not visible as entities in their own right even if many of their various manifestations are. We see products, we see factory and office buildings, we see badges, we see uniforms, we see logos, we read press articles on an organization's stock prices. But we do not actually see the organization that occasions all these. Human organizations are social constructs through which we align our actions (Tsoukas, 1996). We often apprehend such constructs through the use of metaphors. Here we briefly compare three of these: the organization as mechanism

(Morgan, 1986); the organization as organism (Gersick, 1991); and the organization as ecology.[1]

- *The organization as mechanism*: The last third of the nineteenth century saw the birth of the giant corporation, first in the United States and then later in Europe (Chandler, 1977; Marris, 1964). This new organizational form, made possible in part by the development of the railways and the telegraph, was largely under the control of engineers. Increased powers of managerial coordination in the large corporation gave rise to an ever-finer division of labour accompanied by a progressive mechanization of lower-level organizational tasks. The bureaucratic perspective on organizations independently elaborated by Weber for state organizations, and by Fayol, and Taylor for commercial ones, took the need for the formalization of organizational tasks to be an adaptive response to a technological imperative that conceived of labor as means rather than as ends (Burns and Stalker, 1961). An organization chart corresponded to a blueprint for building a social machine that could control physical or social processes by mechanical means. Like most machines, the organizational one required *tight coupling* as well as a stable and predictable environment – that is, the factory – in which unintended variations could be eliminated through control of the organizational boundary and a careful application of formal command-and-control principles. For this purpose, then, organizations were best described by their authority structures, which, through a process of delegation, generated a command hierarchy. The flow of authority down a hierarchy corresponded to the flow of a mechanical force.
- *The organization as organism*: In *The Division of Labour in Society*, Durkheim distinguished between mechanical and organic solidarity, but associated the first with less developed social formations and the latter with the division of labor to be found in advanced industrial society (Durkheim, 1933). Mechanical solidarity reflected both a simple and unchanging social order as well as simple tasks to be performed. Organic solidarity was the product of both complexity and change. Yet it was not until the 1960s that the organismic metaphor first emerged in organization theory in the work of Gouldner and of Burns and Stalker, as a reaction against the mechanistic perspectives on organization of Weber, Fayol, and Taylor (Gouldner, 1954). The metaphor favors a unitary description of the firm as a living object with a corporate body, a head, limbs etc. (Beer, 1981) and capable of adaptation to a changing environment (Lawrence and Lorsch, 1967). Such a system is moderately coupled and more open to its environment than a mechanical system. But it is still *conservative*, maintaining an internal state of equilibrium through a process of *learning* from *negative feedback* (Katz and Kahn, 1978). General systems theory, focusing as it does on systems that remain open to their environment, offers a set of covering concepts for the further elaboration of this metaphor (von Bertalanffy, 1976). Here, learning, if it takes place at all, does so within the individual organism and determines its survival prospects in a changing and competitive environment (Hannan and Freeman, 1977).

- *The organization as ecology.* Toward the end of the twentieth century, the rate of technological and social change accelerated to create a more connected and turbulent world. Organizations now reached out in space and time as they had never done before, increasing the complexity of organizational tasks and often putting them beyond the direct control of the formal organization, whether mechanistically or organically conceived. Instead of viewing organizations as organisms operating within ecologies made up of other organisms, they could now be thought of as *loosely coupled* and *dissipative systems* (Weick, 1995) giving rise to *novel emergent structures* operating far from equilibrium through a process of selection and *positive feedback* (Holland, 1975) – in short, they could be conceived of as ecologies in their own right. In contrast to an organization-as-organism perspective that maintains a clear distinction between an organization and its environment, the organization-as-ecology perspective takes them to be complex adaptive systems (CAS) that maintain no such distinction. The ecological metaphor favours a *network description* of organizations, one in which they and their environment interpenetrate.

Organizations-as-organisms gives us population thinking with a focus on population averages and on normal distributions. The emphasis here is on conservation and stability based on the additivity of independently distributed phenomena. Organizations-as-ecologies, by contrast, gives us scale-free networks characterized by the interactivity of phenomena, nonlinearities, power-law distributions, and emergent events (McKelvey and Andriani, 2005; Andriani and McKelvey, 2005). The emphasis in the latter case is on novelty and evolution (Barabasi, 2002). Whereas organizations-as-organisms lead to greater predictability and exploitative learning, organizations-as-ecologies lead to higher levels of uncertainty and exploratory learning (Levitt and March, 1991).

Also, if a mechanistic approach to organizations delivers an undersocialized account of human behavior within organizations, the organization-as-organism metaphor delivers an oversocialized – that is, deterministic – account (Granovetter, 1992). Network descriptions of organizations based on the organization-as-ecology metaphor, however, supported by new powerful computing technologies, offer a middle ground that restores a role for human agency and choice (Child, 1972), a valuable source of microdiversity in organizational processes (Allen, 2001). Whereas, in the interest of parsimony, most mechanical and organic descriptions of organization focus on averages and assume away variances around the average as so much noise, a more fine-grained network-based description of organizational processes exploits the generative potential of micro-diversity and allows for the study of emergent phenomena. In the first type of description one *discovers* the mean, and through an aggregation of these, one creates the organization as an object. In the second type of description, the mean is *created* through an emergent process that does not easily lend itself to aggregation but admits of creative destruction (McKelvey, 2004).

The three metaphors are not mutually exclusive and can apply at different levels of analysis or in different circumstances. And they need not apply solely to human organizations. The Biologist John Tyler Bonner argues that all cells compete and collaborate. Where collaboration between cells predominates we see multicellular organisms emerging. Cellular slime moulds, for example, feed as separate amoebae but when their food supply is consumed they aggregate into collections of cells that form small multicellular fruiting bodies (Bonner, 2000). Under the latter regime they look like a single moderately coupled organism whereas under the former they look like a collection of loosely coupled organisms – that is, an ecology. Are slime moulds, then, in a biological version of contingency theory (Pugh et al., 1969), organizationally structured in two different ways in response to different environmental conditions? It would appear so. But it turns out that changes in the coupling strength between individual amoebae deliver different structural properties that can be described in network terms. Network descriptions can accommodate a variety of coupling mechanisms and coupling strengths – at the human scale these go by the name of strong and weak ties (Granovetter, 1973) – that reflect their reach and other relational properties. The tightest coupling yields organizations-as-machines. Loosening the coupling a bit yields organizations-as-organisms. Loosening it further increases the degrees of freedom and yields organizations-as-ecologies. With the last-mentioned perspective, the organizational boundary associated with tightly coupled or moderately coupled systems dissolves. In sum, mechanistic, organismic, and ecological approaches to organizations, each in its own way, lend themselves to network forms of description. This point is often overlooked when viewing networks as organizational forms in their own right (Baker, 1992).

This has implications for how we think of organizational governance. Under both mechanistic and organic metaphors, organizations need clear boundaries, accountability structures, rules of membership, etc. for their effective governance. To the extent that networks are seen as just another organizational form, they inherit conventional thinking on such governance issues: collaboration is what should go on within organization and competition is what should go on between organizations. Network forms of organization are thus unlikely to differ radically from other forms in their governance needs. How might an ecological perspective on organizations, together with network forms of organizational description, modify our thinking on corporate governance? As with slime moulds, we might hypothesize that competition and collaboration would emerge to shape the evolution of an organization as a function of its response to environmental munificence or scarcity. By implication, an ecological perspective would call for a variety of governance structures to match an ever-widening range of organizational possibilities.

In the next section we further explore the difference between the network as an organizational type and the network as a form of description of organization.

Networks as Type versus Networks as Description

Networks as organizational types

Developments in information and communications technologies create new possibilities for organizing political and productive activity (Chandler, 1977). The revolution in printing initiated by Guttenberg in the 1440s increased the spatial reach of political structures giving rise both to the state bureaucracies of the seventeenth and eighteenth centuries as well as to the nation state itself (Eisenstein, 1983). In the nineteenth century, the development of the railways and the telegraph brought forth the giant multilevel hierarchies of the twentieth-century corporation (Chandler, 1977). Further developments in information and communication technologies allowed these hierarchies to differentiate and decentralize through multidivisional structures (Chandler, 1962). That we are now witnessing further dramatic changes in the way that business is being organized is clear. The new ICTs are increasing organizational connectivity and accelerating the globalization of markets. By extending the scope for outsourcing and "offshoring," the Internet is modifying the spatial and legal dimensions of organizing as well as increasing the variety of forms to choose from. Associating the development and spread of ICTs with further organizational changes, therefore, seems warranted and the network form of organization would appear to be a natural next step in this co-evolution of technology and organization. This form is defined by Podolny and Page (1998: 59) as "any collection of actors that pursues repeated, enduring exchange relations with one another." In contrast to the mechanical form of organization, no common central authority is required to steer such exchanges (Smith-Doerr and Powell, 2004).

Networks as organizational description

Smith-Doerr and Powell (2004), however, observe that networks are ubiquitous. Linguists talk about semantic networks; logicians talk about logical ones. At the human scale, networks are used to describe social interaction, and social and technological interactions can be combined to produce actor-networks (Callon, 1986). Most human undertakings can effectively be described as networks of activities or people related to each other and sequenced in time. Such networks are *scalable*: their nodes can describe individuals, small groups, or whole organizations. Finally, the natural sciences have also made extensive use of network representations. Physicists draw on them to describe the interaction of subatomic particles (Feynman, 1996); chemists often describe catalytic reactions using network diagrams (Eigen and Schuster, 1979); biologists represent complex natural ecologies in network form (Kauffman, 1993). We could go on, but the point should by now be clear: *any* discrete set of elements, events, states, etc. that can be related to each other in some way can be described as a network. In support of such description we now have a general and abstract language – graph theory – to study network properties such as entropy, centrality, in-degree, out-degree, etc. (Berge, 1962).

Arguably, therefore, if networks are nothing more than a set of interrelated elements, they do not actually constitute an organization form as such but rather a way of describing an organization – *any* organization, including a market type of organization (Knorr-Cetina and Bruegger, 2002). It follows that when we associate the word "network" with the word "organization," we should be focusing less on new organizational forms than on new ways of describing either existing or possible organizational forms that offer advantages over prior descriptions. What advantages might these be? The one we will focus on is that a much larger, richer, and more flexible range of organizational representations is now made possible by our ability to capture and record complex processes through the use of ITCs. Just as today in chemistry, physics, and biology, the computer offers visualization tools that allow complex network representations of physical processes, so they offer a powerful tool to help managers handle the increasing environmental and organizational complexity they confront.

Network descriptions of organizations move us away from organic and towards ecological metaphors (Aldrich, 1999). Organisms have *boundaries*, clearly discernible barriers that separate out what is internal from what is external and that can be clearly perceived. Ecologies do not. Here, what separates the inside from the outside can often look more like a shifting set of *gradients*. Seen as an ecology, therefore, an organization may look less like an object and more like a complex, kaleidoscopic process, a complex adaptive system (CAS) whose elements interact in nonlinear and emergent ways with each other and with their environment (Kauffman, 1994). The formal authority relation that characterized earlier descriptions of organization now becomes but one of many relations that can depict the system. How, then, does such a system evolve?

Evolving networks

In any system, organization emerges out of the interplay of process and structure. The interplay can be represented in network form. In a social system, for example:

- One can look at which ties between actors – here treated as nodes and called nodal actors – are activated under what circumstances in order to capture the pattern of a *process*.
- One can study the strength and recurrence of network ties between nodal actors in order to identify a pattern of *structural relationships*.

We briefly discuss each.

Processes

The nature and density of the ties that characterize different types of networks – that is, whether particular ties describe positive or negative relationships between nodal actors; how many ties are available to nodal actors, etc. – establish the distribution of competitive and collaborative conditions within them. A nodal actor can only manage so many links at a given tie-strength without loss of efficiency. Beyond that, social bounds to rationality kick in. Where links are informal and face-to-face, for example, the number of sustainable links will be smaller than when the links can be formalized and maintained through electronic or less personal means (Boisot, 1998). Relationships with a given nodal actor will be *non-exclusive* to the extent that one relationship does not displace another. They will be *exclusive* to the extent that a relationship between A and B precludes a relationship between A and C. There may well be formal organizational requirements for such exclusivity – such as in hierarchical reporting relationships – but network properties themselves will eventually generate exclusivity when actors become saturated nodes in a network and new relationships can only be established by displacing existing ones. Nonexclusive links are more likely to be collaborative and hence positive. Exclusive links, by contrast, are more likely to be competitive and negative. Exclusive links promote a *disjunctive* logic within networks (either/or but not both). Nonexclusive links promote a *conjunctive* logic with networks (either/or/both). Thus competition and collaboration can be framed as components of a logical process that yields different computational outcomes. All organizations display a mix of positive and negative links and different network structures offer different computational potential (Prietula et al., 1998).

The network centrality of nodal actors generates linkage saturation on account of the finite transactional capacities of the relevant actors and results in two kinds of competition: (1) hierarchical competition: between nodal actors at one level for the attention of – and hence linkage with – (fewer) nodal actors at the next level up a hierarchy; (2) horizontal competition: between nodal actors for the attention of – and linkage with – other nodal actors at the same level. The first kind exploits the presence of information asymmetries across hierarchical levels to maintain a positive relationship between nodal actors located at different levels. The negative relationships implied by this kind of competition are "managed" through the hierarchical coordination of nodal actors. The second kind of competition exploits the absence of information asymmetries to allow one link to substitute for another. Linkages are then established through a process of bargaining and mutual adjustment that ends up privileging communications between a limited number of nodes to the exclusion of a wider group (Boisot, 1995a). In this way of describing interaction between nodal actors, organization becomes a *variable*, a matter of degree that reflects both the stability of the links established through recurrent interactions as well as the computational coherence that the resulting structure can deliver as an organizational output. Note that none of the above necessarily distinguishes between an organizational interior and exterior. Organization here becomes an emergent property of network interactions that varies in intensity across the network. Only under some circumstances does the organizing process give rise to closure and hence to an organization as an *object*.

Structure

The structure of any system refers to those elements and relations of the system that are relatively invariant under spatio-temporal transformations (Grünwald, 2005). Whether desired or not, structure is a source of stability and predictability in a system. In many social and organizational networks, structural stability is imparted by roles and the relationships between roles. Recurrent interactions – collaborative or competitive – between nodal actors, by mutually orienting them towards each other, strengthen and stabilize the ties that link them. The degree of organization present in the network reflects the amount of structure present in the links that constitute it. In some cases, structure is "designed" into network interactions from the outset to guide the evolution of the organization. In other cases network interactions gradually "evolve" to some given level of organization over time through a mixture of self-organizing (Luhmann, 1995) and structurating processes (Giddens, 1984). Network descriptions of organizational processes offer a fine-grained understanding of how process can give rise to structure and of how structure subsequently constrains process (Giddens, 1984). Being able to observe the metamorphosis of one structural form into another as the frequency and strength of individual interactions change yields useful insights into the dynamics of both organizational and institutional evolution. Questions that are currently not well addressed by the network-as-organizational-form literature become amenable to investigation. What circumstances, for example, give rise to the formalization of links between nodal actors, and when do informal routines give rise to formal rules and vice versa? What types of interaction promote hierarchical as opposed to horizontal linkages? What types of linkage generate organizational closure and give rise to a boundary?

With some help from game theory, network-as-description helps us to understand how competition and collaboration can give rise to different institutional forms – generic organizational structures available for the accomplishment of particular purposes. We explore this next.

Game Theory and Institutional Structures

Evolving organized networks through game theory

Aumann (1987) has argued that "Interactive Decision Theory" would be a better name for what is normally called "Game Theory." Interactive decision problems formally resemble parlour games such as monopoly, chess, poker, bridge, etc. Game theory concerns the decisions of actors (players) whose behaviors affect each other. Although the theory has found wide applications in economics, in political science, and in the social sciences in general, it has not much penetrated organizational theory. Yet its methodologies apply in principle to *all* interactive situations between actors, taken as moves in a game. Could game theory help us to understand the emergence of organization starting from interactions between nodal actors in networks? Note that in contrast to transaction cost economics, such an enterprise does not presuppose a choice between pre-extant markets and hierarchies (Coase, 1937). Neither institutional form can be taken as already available for an institutional assignment of transactions. Each has to be constructed from scratch through the interaction of nodal actors. Yet just as institutional economics, building on the work of John Commons (1934), took the transaction as its basic unit of analysis, so we can take the interaction between nodal actors as our basis unit of analysis.

Game theory describes processes of competition and collaboration between nodal actors operating in a network of interactions under different states of nature and with different strategies and payoffs available to each (Binmore, c. 1994–c. 1998). How well an actor can perform in a given game is contingent both on the states of nature and the effectiveness of the strategies adopted by other actors. A game's payoff matrix describes what each actor receives given the interaction between its chosen strategy and that selected by other actors in different states of nature. Clearly, an actor's payoff will be affected by the nature of its relationships with other actors as well as by how many of these it interacts with. Some interactions between actors will be one-off and will suggest one class of competitive or collaborative strategies. Others will be recurrent, involving actors in repeated games and suggesting a different class of strategies. Non-repeated games will give rise to random networks exhibiting little or no structure (Barabasi, 2002; Watts and Strogatz, 1998) whereas repeated games could evolve stable network structures exhibiting varying degrees of organization. Some actors within the network will have a high degree of centrality; other actors will have the capacity to reach other players right across the network, etc. An actor's payoff will also be affected by the costs of interacting with other actors – that is, the game's transaction costs, the distribution of trust across the network of participating agents, the availability of structures and mechanisms to enforce commitments, etc. The structure of communication between actors plays a crucial role in game theory since it determines what knowledge they can acquire concerning the behavior of other actors as well as what knowledge they themselves can be deemed to possess by those actors. This raises the question of how speedily and extensively information flows in networks and of how effectively it is processed by boundedly rational agents. Tacit information will flow more viscously in a network than explicit knowledge and is more likely to give rise to personal face-to-face networks than to impersonal networks (Boisot, 1995b).

The structure of a game establishes the nature of the link between different actors – positive ties versus negative ties; strong ties versus weak ties. Repeated games give rise to strong ties. The resulting network structure can in turn shape the value of future games by making some ties between actors either exclusive and zero-sum or non-exclusive and positive-sum. In an employment contract, for example, if agent *A* interacts with agent *B*, it is precluded from interacting with agent *C*. Since *A* has to make an exclusive choice between *B* and *C*, the relationship between *B* and *C* is zero-sum and competitive. Where ties are not zero sum, by contrast, *A* can increase the number of its positive ties and – sometimes by judiciously occupying *structural holes* between non-communicating agents (Burt, 1992) – achieve a greater measure of network centrality, thus extending both its choice of moves as well as the recurrence of the interactions that it engages with. This affects what we might call *A*'s *marginal propensity to compete or to collaborate*. Competitive relationships between *A* and other agents, however, will be altered when these compete in one arena but collaborate in another (Smith-Doerr and Powell, 2004). In a study of savings and loan firms, for example, Haveman and Nonnemaker (2000) noted that while firms competing in multiple domains achieve greater network centrality by having more exchange partners and more recurrence in their exchanges, they are led to temper their rivalry to avoid future reprisals for cut-throat behavior. If one's position in a network can be empowering, then it can also be constraining, since breaking strong affiliations can be a costly business. Yet there is no free lunch. One cannot just go on adding strong positive ties *ad infinitum*. Each tie consumes scarce resources of time and energy and strong ties do so more than weak ones. Sooner or later the social bounds to rationality kick in as the attentiveness required by each tie begins to erode.

Institutional structures as networks

Games are classified as being either cooperative or non-cooperative. This distinction rests not on the observed behavior of the participating actors but on the institutional structures available to them to support their respective strategies. Cooperative games presuppose the availability of institutions that can make any agreement reached by participating actors binding upon them. In the case of non-cooperative games, no such institutions exist and actors must rely on self-enforcing agreements to secure binding commitments (Harrington, 1987). A *Nash equilibrium* offers a solution concept that is self-enforcing for non-cooperative games (Kreps, 1987). A Nash equilibrium emerges when no actor can improve its payoff by changing strategy when other actors do

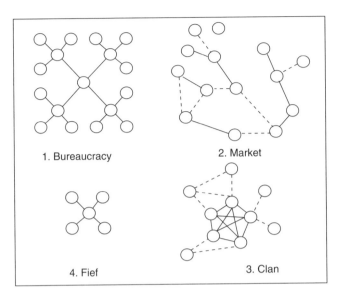

Figure 9.1 Four different network structures

not change theirs, even if that payoff is negative. Because of this, many repeated games characterized by Nash equilibria will self-organize to look like a market when the density of competitive interactions is higher than that of collaborative ones. If the reverse obtains and collaboration predominates, the emergent organization that results will look more like a firm.

If cooperative games presuppose the availability of institutions to enforce agreements, then it follows either that institutions can themselves emerge out of Nash equilibria or that they must rely on the presence of other institutions for their construction. The firm as an institution, for example, could not have developed without the prior availability of the legal system as an institution. The legal system itself, however, might initially have emerged as a Nash equilibrium in a non-cooperative "Hobbesian" game or "war of all against all." Either way, where games are generic and widely played, their different structures can often be institutionalized so as to reduce the costs to agents either of playing the game or of pursuing certain strategies within the game – that is, of speeding up the attainment of an equilibrium, whether of the Nash or other variety. Boisot (1998) identified four such institutional structures: markets, bureaucracies, clans, and fiefs. These structures, as depicted in Figure 9.1, all lend themselves to network description:

- *Market networks:* Efficient markets can be described as random networks (Barabasi, 2002) since spot-market contracting under competitive conditions does not provide enough recurrence between transactions to be predictable. There are no barriers to entry in efficient markets so that such networks have no maximum size and hence no natural boundary. Given the size of an efficient market network, the relationship between actors is likely to be quite impersonal, with each pursuing its own objectives in a non-collaborative way.

- *Bureaucratic networks*: Such networks involve large numbers of actors operating in hierarchically ordered structures with more than two levels and in which the relationship between actors located at different levels is likely to be impersonal and established by formal authority. In these networks actors engage in repeated games with each other. Formal processes and network ties have the effect of reducing the emotional intensity and the frequency of conflict (Morrill, 1995) between actors, effectively establishing "armed truces" between them (Nelson and Winter, 1982).
- *Clan networks*: Clans are nonhierarchical but limited in size by the need to maintain shared values and hence a measure of personalization through face-to-face interaction. The relationship between agents is characterized by continuous bargaining and negotiation. In contrast to market networks, there are barriers to entry into a clan networks based on the need for trust, on an alignment of values and beliefs – often signaled by some shared prior experience – and on loyalty to the group. Beyond a certain size of clan, the linking capacity of nodal actors gets saturated. To survive and attain a Nash equilibrium, this kind of network then closes in on itself, thus creating an in-group and an out-group.
- *Fief networks:* These are personalized hierarchies and hence, like clans, are limited in size by the need to share values and beliefs, and hence to maintain face-to-face relationships. But here relationships between agents are maintained not by formal authority as with bureaucratic networks, but by loyalty to one or two individuals who thus exhibit a high degree of network centrality. The central nodes in a fief network are often charismatic actors who manage to appropriate for their own purposes links that, under different circumstances, would have gone into constructing a clan.

The institutional structures just described give rise to distinctive cultures, values and ways of doing things. Danger and uncertainty, for example, have a tendency to generate densely knit networks (Rubio, 1997). These, in turn, constrain and limit the freedom to choose moves. The resulting payoff matrix is smaller and so is the number of players. Since network size and characteristics determine the variety of games a nodal actor can play in and the number of times it can play in each one – as well as its choices, costs, and payoffs – this affects the character of the equilibria that can be reached.

None of the above institutional structures, however, necessarily maps one-to-one on to any specific organization form; they could combine inside a single organization or across different organizations. Nor do they necessarily give rise to organizational closure and boundaries. The distinction between internal and external organization goes back to Marx who had contrasted the "sphere of production" and "the sphere of exchange." He argued that the two were separate. Yet instead of assuming that collaboration takes place inside the organizational boundary and that competition takes place outside it, our network description has the effect of making the definition of organization more problematic. With networks, the inside and the outside interpenetrate. One can, of course, draw legal boundaries, identity boundaries, emotional boundaries, etc. But multiple organizational boundaries create fuzziness, and, for many purposes – alliancing, knowledge-creation, trust-building – one can draw no boundaries at all. The transaction cost literature has tended to equate bureaucratic networks with internal organization and market networks with external organization. Yet if a network description renders the location of boundaries problematic, then these simple equations become dubious. One is as likely to encounter market processes at work "inside" the organization as one is to encounter hierarchical bureaucratic processes "outside" it (Boisot, 1986).

Changes in network size and configuration are continually transforming the "inside" into the "outside" and vice versa. External networks become internal networks through mergers, acquisitions, alliances, joint ventures, etc. Internal networks become external ones through spin-offs, outsourcing, offshoring, etc. A major challenge for organizational change becomes that of managing these transitions. The organic perspective on organization stresses the need to maintain a clear and stable distinction between the inside and the outside. The ecological perspective stresses the need for organizational flexibility in the face of increasing environmental turbulence, and hence the need to manage emergent phenomena.

Implications

It is a commonplace that the world is getting more complex and that organizations are struggling to match that complexity with their internal processes. This is difficult because by definition complexity is hard to describe. Supported by ever more powerful technologies of representation – that is, advanced computing and software – the language of networks can help firms to come to terms with that complexity, but not if the term "network" itself is hijacked to describe one particular form of organization alone.

Network analysis has been criticized for its focus on the structure of networks at the expense of the content of ties (Goodwin and Emirbayer, 1994). Also, the emphasis on the more durable and recurrent "structural" relationships neglects the more transient ones. The focus is on an organization's anatomy, not on its physiology. This implicitly favors structure over process or function and imparts to network analysis a rather static character (Wasserman and Faust, 1994). Yet networks are capable of "hormonal" action in which small causes have disproportionately big effects that would never be picked up by current "structural" methods. The emphasis on structure reflects the limitations of our technologies of representation as much as it does the interests of social scientists. As these technologies become ever more fine-grained – as, for example, in the ability to build networks out of email traffic – so the physiology of networks should become more visible.

The history of organizations shows us that technologies of representation matter. Modern mathematics, for example, would have been impossible if we had stuck to Roman numerals. The modern enterprise could not have evolved without accounting technologies that could fairly represent its activities to outsiders. What new possibilities, then, do network descriptions of organization open up?

Network representations of organization offer a more "postmodern" approach to thinking about them, one in which no single view is privileged. They challenge the implicit assumption that inside the organization it is all about collaboration and that outside the organization it is all about competition. Drawing on concepts from game theory, network representations offer a more fine-grained understanding of exactly where competition and collaboration are likely to take place and where zones of stability are likely to emerge, irrespective of where the organization's boundaries are drawn for a particular purpose. What implications does this point carry for the theory of the firm? Firms are deemed to be hierarchical forms of organizations that essentially collaborate on the inside and that compete on the outside. The network perspective, by substituting an ecological for an organic view of the firm, effectively dissolves its boundary and challenges the simplicity of this division of labour between competition and collaboration. For a start, if, as we have argued, organization is a property of network structure and a matter of degree then *there is no reason to suppose that the boundary of the firm constrains an organized network to having the same boundary, or, indeed, to having a boundary at all.*

The firm, viewed as a legal entity, is a distribution mechanism, a structure of claims upon an output, a system of property rights associated with different stakeholder groups (Hart, 1995). The boundary of firm is essential to a legal concept of the firm and is required to enforce property rights and accountability. Through outsourcing and alliancing, however, the organization of production is increasingly taking place across rather than within firms. As a concept, therefore, organization has effectively ceased to be a stable *object* to become instead an *attribute* of complex interactive processes in which constant shifting configuration of actors – individuals, groups, firms, etc. – simultaneously compete and collaborate with each other. But how do any of these actors appropriate value in a complex and kaleidoscopic network? How do intellectual and physical property rights function when such networks generate value in emergent and hence unpredictable ways? When value emerges inside an organization only part of which is covered by value-appropriation mechanisms called firms?

In sum, although firms and organizations mutually constitute each other, they turn out not to be co-extensive. Firms are legally structured claims on the distribution of an output – claims by employees, suppliers, banks, bondholders, shareholders, etc. – whereas organizations are productive arrangements for generating the output. The firm articulates a zero-sum competitive process between stakeholders regulated by a governance structure that establishes the rules of the game; the organization harbors a collaborative process regulated by the logic of production. The first establishes a payoff matrix for the different stakeholders in the game whereas the second determines the value of the game to be played by them, and hence what is to be distributed across the payoff matrix. Now firm stakeholders need time and energy to shape and negotiate their required payoffs. Often this time exceeds the pace at which productive opportunities come and go, and hence at which organizations – as opposed to firms – have to formulate an adaptive response. It is unrealistic, therefore, to frame the process as one of competition followed by collaboration. Both competitive and collaborative processes alternate in unpredictable ways.

What implications do network forms of representation have for how we think of strategy? Well, if things speed up, as they seem to be doing, then *making sense* of what goes on in organized yet kaleidoscopic networks is going to be ever more of a problem. Ashby's law teaches us that any organized system must match the complexity of its environment in a timely and adaptive way if it is to survive and prosper (Ashby, 1956). Yet where the environment is both complex and fast moving, any attempt to match it in all its variety can lead to disintegration. Since only some variety is of relevance to the system – much of it will be "noise" – an intelligent and organized system is selective in the variety that it responds to, and often its adapted response consists in reducing the variety confronting the system rather than adapting to it. Human beings, for example, reduce variety by converting their world into a collection of stable objects so as to tame them, make them analytically tractable and predictable, and hence controllable. At the level of institutional systems, placing productive yet kaleidoscopic organizations inside relatively stable structures called firms also aims to reduce the variety one has to deal with.

In the kind of complex evolving networks that we have been describing, however, things are now changing their identity too fast for complexity reducing strategies to be viable. Patterns shift all the time and managers often have to act before they can clearly identify them – as Tom Peters (1987) put it, "Ready, fire, aim." Certain knowledge is no longer on offer. We can anticipate, therefore, that the environment will become ever more entrepreneurial and that competitive advantage will accrue to those actors who are the first to recognize and act upon emergent patterns. Such *pattern recognition skills* will require fast learning and a willingness to engage in the creative destruction of prior knowledge (Boisot, 1995a) – that is, in forgetting. Networks, in effect, offer a new perspective on the nature of organizational learning. Studies of the brain, for example, show that in neural networks learning is not a property of the nodes alone, but rather emerges from complex interactions between nodes (Hebb, 1949). If this discovery scales up to the level of human networks, it implies that learning and knowledge are a property of organized networks rather than firms. In other words, organized networks *possess* knowledge even if legally firms *own* such knowledge (Boisot and Griffiths, 2001). To the extent that organization and firm are no longer co-extensive in the information economy this poses new problems of governance.

So what implications, then, do network descriptions of organization hold for our concepts of governance? In the traditional theory of the firm, the organization builds *down* from the ownership structure through the mechanism of agency to create a group of "internal" actors called firm employees. If, in contrast to firms, organized networks become "boundaryless," then we need to build *up* organizational capacity out of stakeholders in general instead of firm employees in particular. The stakeholder perspective creates a more complex governance problem than the shareholder one. As the cases of Enron, Tyco, WorldCom, and others have recently demonstrated, the tensions that exist between the relatively static distribution structure of firms as legally conceived and the rapid kaleidoscopic patterns of value-creation in organized networks provide plenty of scope for institutional arbitrage and for opportunistic behavior. As Williamson (1985) pointed out, the firm as an institution aims to limit both bounded rationality and opportunistic behavior. But bounded rationality itself provides scope for opportunistic behavior, and while organized networks can operate at a higher level of complexity than traditional firms, they are constrained by the bounded rationality of their stakeholders as a whole. We conclude that such networks will therefore be more vulnerable to opportunistic behavior, and we further hypothesize that such behavior will not be mitigated by measures such as the Sarbanes–Oxley Act that essentially target legal entities called firms rather than the broader organizational networks in which these operate.

Conclusion

From the earliest times, the ICTs of the day have always conditioned how we think of organization. If the development and spread of printing technologies from the sixteenth century onward helped to bring forth the rational-legal bureaucracies that underpinned the emergence of the modern nation state, the advent of the telegraph and later the telephone in the last third of the nineteenth century extended the geographical reach of managerial coordination and contributed to the construction of the giant corporation. Today, the further rapid development of ICTs, by amplifying our powers of description and dissemination, offers us new transactional and organizational possibilities. The network forms of organizational representation are an expression of these new descriptive powers. Yet, in exploiting these, we tend to draw upon extant – and increasingly inappropriate – concepts of organization.

With network forms of organizational description we extend the reach of our theorizing in much the same way as the move from Roman to Arabic numerals opened up new territory for mathematics. We make a mistake in thinking of a network as an organization form in its own right. After all, no one would think that just because they are presented differently, Roman and Arabic numerals constitute different types of numbers; they offer alternative ways of representing the same abstract concept, and we can do a lot more with one representation of the concept than we can with the other. Much talk of network forms of organization, therefore, turns out to be loose talk that deprives us of the expressive possibilities that network forms of description offer us. Network forms of description apply to *all* types of organization. It isn't the case that we now have one more organizational form that co-exists with earlier forms. What is the case is that we can now do more with whatever form of organization – functional, multidivisional, etc. – happens to suit our purpose.

Ashby's law tells us that a system needs to increase in complexity when its environment becomes more complex. Network forms of description allow us to access this complexity and perhaps even to manage it. Yet making organization a matter of degree and the property of a network rather than an object challenges all the assumptions we make about the nature of organizations. They are no longer clearly separated out from their environment as suggested by both the organic and the mechanistic metaphors and we therefore need a new way of thinking about them. We believe that a change of organizational metaphor from organism to ecology is timely.

Finally, we suggested in the section "Networks as Type versus Networks as Description" that through a mixture of competition and collaboration organizations can be thought of as carrying out computational processes. If so, we are moving from a model of organizations as serial computers operating under some centralized – or even decentralized – command-and-control regimes to one of organizations as connectionist computers operating under a distributed processing regime (Boisot and Cox, 1999). The operations of serial computers are confined to what goes on inside a single box; those of a connectionist computer are not. The Church–Turing thesis tells us that serial computers can carry out the same tasks as connectionist computers and vice versa. The only thing that changes is the efficiency of the computation (Church, 1936). The former is more efficient for tasks that are repetitive and well defined. The latter is more effective for tasks that are novel and fuzzy. In a world that is becoming more novel and fuzzy by the day, we need organizational concepts that look more "connectionist" than "serial."

Clearly, network descriptions of organizations restore to managers a measure of managerial autonomy and choice (Child, 1972). They do so at a price, however, as they now require managers to operate at a higher level of ambiguity and complexity than was implied by earlier forms of organizational description. They also have the effect of making management less of a fixed role in a static hierarchy and more contingent on the nature and distribution of network activity. In short, if organization becomes an emergent dimension of interacting networks, then, by implication, so does managing. In effect, in kaleidoscopic networks, the manager becomes a serial entrepreneur.

Note

1 The organization-as-ecology concept must not be confused with the organizational ecology concept of Hannan and Freeman (1989). The latter takes a population of firms as acting like organisms in a wider ecology.

References

Aldrich, H. (1999) *Organizations Evolving*. Thousand Oaks, CA: Sage Publications.

Allen, P. (2001) A complex systems approach to learning, adaptive networks. *International Journal of Innovation Management*, 5, 149–80.

Andriani, P. & McKelvey, B. (2005) Beyond Gaussian averages: Redirecting organization science toward extreme events and power laws. Presented at the Academy of Management Annual Meeting, Honolulu, HI, August 9.

Ashby, R. W. (1956) *An Introduction to Cybernetics*, London: Methuen.

Aumann, R. (1987) Game theory. In J. Eatwell, M. Milgate & P. Newman (Eds.) *Game Theory: The New Palgrave*. New York: W.W. Norton.

Baker, W. (1992) The network organization in theory and practice. In N. Nohria and R. Eccles (Eds.) *Networks and Organizations: Structure, Form, and Action*. Boston, MA: Harvard Business School Press.

Barabasi, A.-L. (2002) *Linked: How Everything Is Connected to Everything Else and What It Means for Business, Science, and Everyday Life*. New York: Plume (The Penguin Group).

Beer, S. (1981) *Brain of the Firm*. 2nd edn, reprint. Chichester: Wiley (1st edn: 1972, London: Penguin Press).

Berge, C. (1962) *The Theory of Graphs*. London: Methuen.

Binmore, K. G. (c. 1994–c. 1998) *Game Theory and the Social Contract*. Cambridge, MA: MIT Press.

Boisot, M. (1986) Markets and hierarchies in cultural perspective. *Organization Studies*, 7(2), 135–58.

Boisot, M. (1995a) *Information Space: A Framework for Learning in Organizations, Institutions and Culture*. London: Routledge.

Boisot, M. (1995b) Is your firm a creative destroyer? Competitive learning and knowledge flows in the technological strategies of firms. *Research Policy*, 24(4), 589–606.

Boisot, M. (1998) *Knowledge Assets: Securing Competitive Advantage in the Information Economy*. Oxford: Oxford University Press.

Boisot, M. & Cox, B. (1999) The I-space: A framework for analyzing the evolution of social computing. *Technovation*, 19, 525–36.

Boisot, M. & Griffiths, D. (2001) To own or to possess? Competence and the challenge of appropriability. In R. Sanchez (Ed.) *Knowledge Management and Organizational Competence*. Oxford: Oxford University Press.

Bonner, J. T. (2000) *First Signals: The Evolution of Multicellular Development*. Princeton, NJ: Princeton University Press.

Burns, T. & Stalker, G. (1961) *The Management of Innovation*. London: Tavistock.

Burt, R. (1992) *Structural Holes*. Cambridge, MA: Harvard University Press.

Callon, M. (1986) Some elements of a sociology of translation: Domestication of the scallops and the fishermen of St. Brieuc Bay. In J. Law (Ed.), *Power, Action, and Belief*. New York: Routledge.

Chandler, A. (1962) *Strategy and Structure: Chapters in the History of the American Industrial Enterprise*. Cambridge, MA: MIT Press.

Chandler, A. (1977) *The Visible Hand: The Managerial Revolution in American Business*. Cambridge, MA: Belknap Press of Harvard University Press.

Child, J. (1972) Organizational structure, environment and performance: The role of strategic choice. *Sociology*, 6, 1–22.

Church, A. (1936) An unsolvable problem of elementary number theory. *American Journal of Mathematics*, 58, 345–63.

Coase, R. (1937) The nature of the firm. *Economica* N.S., 4, 386–405.

Commons, J. R. (1934) *Institutional Economics*. Madison: University of Wisconsin Press.

Durkheim, E. (1933) *The Division of Labour in Society*. New York: Free Press.

Eigen, M. & Schuster, P. (1979) *The Hypercycle: A Principle of Natural Self-Organization*. New York: Springer.

Eisenstein, E. (1983) *The Printing Revolution in Early Modern Europe*. Cambridge: Cambridge University Press.

Erdös, P. & Renyi, A. (1959) On random graphs I. *Publicationes Mathematicae (Debrecen)* 6, 290–7.

Feynman, R. (1996) *Feynman Lectures on Computation*. Reading, MA: Addison-Wesley.

Gersick, C. J. G. (1991) Revolutionary change theories: A multilevel exploration of the punctuated equilibrium paradigm. *Academy of Management Review*, 16(1), 10–36.

Giddens, A. (1984) *The Constitutions of Society: Outline of the Theory of Structuration*. Cambridge: Polity Press.

Goodwin, J. & Emirbayer, M. (1994) Network analysis, culture, and the problem of agency. *American Journal of Sociology*, 99(6), 1411–54.

Gouldner, A. (1954) *Patterns of Industrial Bureaucracy*. Glencoe, IL: Free Press.

Granovetter, M. (1973) The strength of weak ties. *American Journal of Sociology*, 78, 1360–80.

Granovetter, M. (1992) Problems of explanation in economic sociology. In N. Nohria & R. G. Eccles (Eds.) *Networks and Organizations: Structure, Form, and Action*. Boston, MA: Harvard Business School Press.

Grünwald, P. (2005) Introducing the minimum description length principle. In P. Grünwald, J. Myung & M. Pitt (Eds.) *Advances in Minimum Description Length: Theory and Applications*. Cambridge, MA: MIT Press.

Hannan, M. & Freeman, J. (1977) The population ecology of organizations. *American Journal of Sociology*, 82, 929–64.

Hannan, M. & Freeman, J. (1989) *Organizational Ecology*. Cambridge, MA: Harvard University Press.

Harrington, J. (1987) Non-cooperative games. In J. Eatwell, M. Milgate & P. Newman (Eds.) *Game Theory: The New Palgrave*, New York: W.W. Norton.

Hart, C. W. L. (1995) The power of internal guarantees. *Harvard Business Review,* 64–73.

Haveman, H. & Nonnemaker, L. (2000) Competition in multiple geographic markets: The impact on growth and market entry. *Administrative Science Quarterly,* 45, 232–67.

Hebb, D. (1949) *The Organization of Behaviour.* New York: Wiley.

Holland, J. (1975) *Adaptation in Natural and Artificial Systems.* Cambridge, MA: MIT Press.

Katz ,D. & Kahn, R. (1978) *Social Psychology of Organizations.* New York: John Wiley & Sons.

Kauffman, S. (1993) *The Origins of Order.* Oxford: Oxford University Press.

Kauffman, S. (1994) *At Home in the Universe.* New York: Viking.

Knorr-Cetina, K. & Bruegger, U. (2002) Global microstructures: The virtual societies of financial markets. *American Journal of Sociology,* 107, 905–50.

Kreps, D. (1987) Nash Equilibrium. In J. Eatwell, M. Milgate & P. Newman (Eds.) *Game Theory: The New Palgrave.* New York: W.W. Norton.

Lawrence, P. & Lorsch, J. (1967) *Organization and Environment: Managing Differentiation and Integration.* Homewood, IL: Richard Irwin.

Levitt, B. & March, J. G. (1991) Organisational learning. *Annual Review of Sociology,* 14, 319–40.

Luhmann, N. (1995) *Social Systems.* Stanford, CA: Stanford University Press.

Marris, R. (1964) *The Economic Theory of "Managerial" Capitalism.* London: Macmillan.

McKelvey, B. (2004) Toward a 0th law of thermodynamics: Order-creation complexity dynamics from physics and biology to bioeconomics. *Journal of Bioeconomics,* 6, 65–96.

McKelvey, B. & Andriani, P. (2005) Why Gaussian statistics are mostly wrong for strategic organization. *Strategic Organization,* 3, 219–28.

Morgan, G. (1986) *Images of Organization.* Beverly Hills: Sage Publications.

Morrill, C. (1995) *The Executive Way: Conflict Management in Corporations.* Chicago: University of Chicago Press.

Nelson, R. & Winter, S. (1982) *An Evolutionary Theory of Economic Change.* Cambridge, MA: Harvard University Press.

Peters, T. (1987) *Thriving on Chaos.* New York: Alfred A. Knopf.

Podolny, J. (1999) Networks as pipes and prisms of the market: A look at investment decisions in the venture capital industry. Working Paper, Stanford Graduate School of Business.

Podolny, J. & Page, K. (1998) Network forms of organization. *Annual Review of Sociology,* 24, 57–76.

Prietula, M., Carley, K. & Gasser, L. (1998) *Simulating Organizations: Computational Models of Institutions and Groups.* Cambridge, MA: MIT Press.

Pugh, D., Hickson, D., Hinings, C. & Turner, C. (1969) The context of organization structures. *Administrative Science Quarterly,* 14(1), 91–114.

Rubio, M. (1997) Perverse social capital: Some evidence from Columbia. *Journal of Economic Issues,* 31, 805–16.

Smith-Doerr, L. & Powell, W. (2004) Networks and economic life. In N. Smelser and R. Swedberg (Eds.) *The Handbook of Economic Sociology.* Princeton: Princeton University Press.

Tsoukas, H. (1996) The firm as a distributed knowledge system: A constructionist approach. *Strategic Management Journal,* 17, 11–25.

Tsoukas, H. & Knudsen, C. (2002) The conduct of strategy research. In A. Pettigrew, H. Thomas & R. Whittington (Eds.) *Handbook of Strategy and Management.* London: SAGE Publications.

Von Bertalanffy, L. (1976) *General System Theory: Foundations, Development, Applications.* New York: George Braziller.

Wasserman, S. & Faust, K. (1994) *Social Network Analysis: Methods and Applications.* Cambridge: Cambridge University Press.

Watts, D. (1999) *Small Worlds: The Dynamics of Networks between Order and Randomness.* Princeton, NJ: Princeton University Press.

Watts, D. & Strogatz, S. (1998) Collective dynamics of "small world" networks. *Nature*, 393, 440–2.

Weick, K. (1995) *Sensemaking in Organizations.* Thousand Oaks, CA: Sage.

Williamson, O. E. (1985) *The Economic Institutions of Capitalism: Firms, Markets, Rational Contracting.* New York: Free Press.

CHAPTER TEN

Networks and Some Limits to Managing Them

J. C. Spender

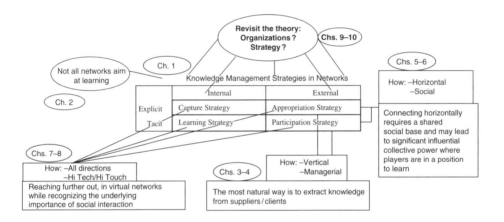

Abstract

The proposal that networks offer managers new strategic options is this book's principal theme, and its SKIN framework treats firms as knowledge complexes embedded within other complexes. Explicit and tacit knowledge is created, absorbed, applied, forgotten, and circulated within these complexes and coherent managerial strategies are needed to ensure the firm benefits rather than gets plundered by the network's other actors. But do managers have much control over this? What are the limits to their power? We still lack a good understanding of how networks differ from other socioeconomic arrangements such as firms and markets, which differ notably in terms of managerial access and control. We are also unclear about whether network means a structure or is a metaphor or verb for describing processes like exchange, communication, or knowledge flow. Whatever strategic options networks might have opened up must reflect the power arrangements within and between the networks and with those trying to manage them. In this chapter we engage these questions by exploring a more explicit theory of networks that differentiates them from both firms and markets. We conclude with comments on how managers might use networks, having come to terms with the limits to their control.

Some Current Network Theorizing

In his analysis of networking DiMaggio notes several authors, particularly Powell, Castells, Burt, and Williamson (Burt, 1983; Castells, 1996; Powell, 1990; Williamson, 1985, 1991), have made networks "the central trope of organizational change" (DiMaggio, 2001: 212). But he also writes the term "network" elides a great deal. He ponders whether networking's seeming rise is mere synecdoche, our tendency to describe things in terms of the dominant explanatory models of the day – in this case twenty-first century ones based on computers and communication systems so replacing the nineteenth-century metaphors of mechanism (DiMaggio, 2001: 236) and even earlier ones based on organisms (Durkheim, 1964; Toennies, 1971). He wonders if the move to networked forms of organization is actually a move to a new paradigm, as so many writers suggest, or just a transition on the way to some new form as yet unrevealed (DiMaggio, 2001: 239). Thus Guillén reminds us that flexible forms of organization will only be implemented to the extent they are consistent with the prevailing managerial ideology (Guillén, 1994: 304). Gerlach confirms this with his analysis of how the Japanese *keiretsu* networks reflect their social system (Gerlach, 1987, 1992).

Behind these comments lie concerns that the term "network" is used merely as a descriptor without anyone expecting it to add much understanding. That would require a theory of networks, of how they come into being, function, and are managed. But what is this theory, and would it be widely shared among those who use the term? Our conclusions line up with DiMaggio's, that networked organizational and economic forms have been evident throughout our history from Roman times through the Hanseatic League to the Hudson Bay Company, so there may be less new here than the "new forms of organization" boosters suggest. But at the same time the spreading use of the term is more than a linguistic or analytic fad; it is evidence of our attempt to break out of conceptual restraints inherited from twentieth-century organizational theorizing.

Defining Networks

Defining networks seems easy. DiMaggio suggests a network is an "analytic convenience" of a "system of actors (units, nodes, objects) connected by a set of relations or flows" (DiMaggio, 2001: 237). We might dub this the engineer's definition. In the same way as economists call the firm a "legal fiction," so this definition of network suggests a mechanical fiction, abstracted in the sense it imposes few limits on the nature of the actors or their relationships. But what we really mean by "network" as we refer to an electricity grid or a telephone system or a neurological system or a job hunt, depends greatly on the entities and relations comprising the system being considered. Autopoiesis aside, the fiction will read differently in a world of organisms than it does in a world of communications or information flows.

Organization charts show objects and entities like people or departments relating, or interfirm alliances and cross-investments; but are these networks? Organization theorists have long been interested in trust and dependence relations, incomplete con-tracts, relational contracting, interorganizational alliances, and so forth (Fox, 1974; Hart, 1988; Pfeffer and Salancik, 1978); but do such relations characterize or define a network? Scott defines networks as "cooperative connections among formally inde-pendent organizations that enable them to enjoy simultaneously the benefits associated with being small, such as rapid response, and with being large, such as economies of scale" (Scott, 2003: 13). But this definition's main components refer to theoretically framed properties of organizations – economies of scale or responsiveness – rather than to any properties specific to networks. Does Scott's network differ materially from any organization, with its own connections to particular suppliers, customers, and so forth? What is added by using the term network?

Many writers see evidence that networks are an increasingly common form of organ-ization, typically when contrasted with the bureaucratic model of the last two centuries or so (Castells, 1996; Davis, 1961). DiMaggio suggests the networked organiza-tion is a form that relaxes the basic axioms of organization theory and is new in this respect. Trust relations, and contingent, path-dependent, reciprocal, and tacit relations are more common while bureaucratic-style authority relations dissolve and goal structures become less unified. Weberian notions of rules and rational author-ity disappear behind a screen of organic forms and collective benefits reminding us of Durkheim and Toennies. There is an erosion of unity of command (Fayol, 1949). Thus Castells argues the networked enterprise arises at the intersection of autonomous systems of goals (Castells, 1996: Vol. II, 171). In this sense a networked organization may be "postmodern," multi-cephalous, and multi-logiced, contrasted with bureau-cracy, "modern" and uni-logiced, an articulation of its unified system of control and a coherent rationality-setting goal.

Powell and Williamson see networked organizations as occupying a conceptual middle ground between hierarchies and markets. Powell argues the pressures of competition, downsizing, out-sourcing, globalization, information technologies, with today's shift towards a "winner-takes-all" economy have precipitated a search for more flexible modes of organizing (Powell, 2001: 40). Greater collaboration dissolves the boundary of the firm and suppliers, customers, and even competitors are drawn into the evolving network (Hamel et al., 1989). Market forces play an increasing role, pen-etrating the rational core of rules and authority relations previously insulated from the market by boundary-spanning activities (Thompson, 1967). The distinctions between full-time and temporary employees disappear, suppliers hold stocks in the buying firm's plants and manage them with their own personnel, etc. Powell writes: "the growing involvement of firms in an intricate lattice of collaborations with 'outsiders' blurs the boundaries of the firm, making it difficult to know where the firm ends and the market or another firm begins" (Powell, 2001: 58).

Williamson likewise stresses the context-driven need for organizations to adapt and explore economical methods of dealing with bounded rationality, long-term relational contracting, and the resulting bilateral dependency and exposure to opportunism (Williamson, 1991: 280). He dubs this middle ground form "hybrid," and in the writ-ings of Powell and many others this becomes virtually synonymous with "network" (Powell, 1987, 1990). The question, though, is about the spectrum of alternatives implied by such "polar modes" or opposites. In what conceptual space can we find both markets and organizations, as well as a middle ground for this hybrid form? We are more likely to consider markets and hierarchies mutually incompatible, denying the possibility of a middle ground. Kraakman (2001) asks why it makes sense to position hybrids as half-steps between firm and market, should we not see them instead as categorically distinct and separable types?

It is noteworthy that both Scott and Williamson buttress their explanations of how hybrid forms might arise under the press of competition with a tentative theory of networks. Both draw on communication network theory to illustrate differences between wheel, line, and "all channel" networks (Scott, 2003: 161; Williamson, 1975: 46). Markets are all-channel networks, everyone speaking to everyone else, while bureaucracy is essentially wheel-shaped, with communications emanating from a central dominant hub, so "economizing" on the communication. Hybrid forms are thought to meld these differences to minimize communication losses. The idea is evident earlier in Fayol's cross-ladder interdepartmental communications, the result of delegation by the senior executives to managers whom they can trust to interpret the organization's objectives without micro-managing their interactions (Fayol, 1949). It also recalls Graicunas' diagram of 2^N communication links between N nodes (Graicunas, 1933).

While this kind of communications-based theorizing does not give us any useful rules for designing hybrid organizations – beyond structuring the communication channels economically to reduce the 2^N connections – it suggests principles managers might bear in mind as they try to adapt their organizations to the particular conditions they are experiencing. Perhaps the implication is that they should conduct "natural experiments" and explore alternative degrees of re-structuring and hybridization to see which works best. But measured against what criteria? Note also Williamson's discussion of vertical integration moves towards a form with hierarchical slices interleaved with intermediate product-market domains. We might ask whether this is a coherent form of organization at all or just a system of related mini-markets. It is clear this is not really a hybrid, in the sense of being a different form, but simply a complex laminate of pure market and hierarchical types.

Actors and Agents: Theorizing Networks

Latour is also interested in the notion of hybrids, seeing them as empirical evidence of the limitations of a modernist view that artificially separates the disciplinary domains of social enquiry (Latour, 1993). But when real social phenomena are to be grasped, these separations must be bridged and conjoined. To call an organization "hybrid" may appeal directly to observation and evidence rather than to theory, a description that bridges incommensurable theoretical bases. We often do this when the available theory does not meet our needs. But we are on especially difficult ground with the relationships between bureaucracy and the theory of the firm. It is a commonplace that one theory deals with the world inside the firm, the other with the outside. There are two different domains of inquiry, and in two early papers Simon explored their different axiomatic bases and their incommensurate-ness (Simon, 1952a, 1952b). Outside and inside analyses, emic and etic, are incommensurable by definition. Melding them may be impossible without substantially changing both.

Perhaps the most crucial differences between organization and market theory lie around the notion of agency. Micro-economics presumes people are principals acting for themselves, in their own interests and on the basis of their own utilities and valuations. The theory of the firm is essentially about the interaction of isolated economic entities. But organization theory presumes employees, persuaded by a system of inducements, abandon their personal agency to follow the instructions of others, subordinating their own interests in an act of participation with and commitment to the organization's goals and values (Simon, 1958: 110). It is as if they are persuaded to adopt a different identity; just as the subjects in Milgram's infamous experiment did (Milgram, 1974). The spectrum of these forms of socioeconomic order runs from fully atomistic independence at one extreme to utter subordination at the other.

Along these lines DiMaggio (2001: 214), citing Campbell and Lindberg (1991), offers a provocative matrix of socioeconomically ordered forms. This contrasts with the SKIN model which implies but does not highlight the inter-actor power relations. The dimensions in DiMaggio's matrix are domination and explicit coordination – more specifically a two-dimensional space defined by the extent of explicit coordination among partners and the degree to which some actors are capable of dominating others (DiMaggio, 2001: 213). DiMaggio locates spot and oligopolistic markets, and hierarchies, and long-term relational contracts in this space (Figure 10.1), though his distinction between domination and coordination is less than clear. The figure suggests domination and coordination are orthogonal. Long-term relational contracts, for instance, being explicit but involving low domination. Williamson's analysis suggests the opposite – long-term relational contracts call for additional forms of domination because of the parties' bounded rationality and their exposure to opportunism. Likewise spot markets are not really domains of low explicitness and low domination; on the contrary they are extremely explicit and necessitate a legal structure to support them and the titles they exchange.

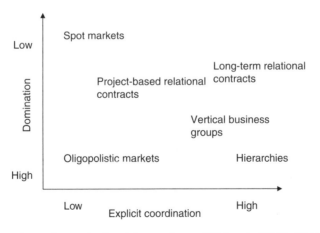

Figure 10.1 A typology of organizational forms. *Source*: DiMaggio (2001: 214).

If we go back to Commons' institutionalism we see a more sophisticated discussion of the transactions to which Figure 10.1 refers (Commons, 1957). He notes the legal and normative infrastructure which stands behind all legitimate economic transactions. This alone allows one to distinguish between the rights and obligations attendant on any transaction. The issue is not whether there is domination, for that is a characteristic of society itself; the question is, who is dominating whom? Absent a strong property rights and exchange law regime, there can be neither spot nor oligopolistic markets, and it is the presence of this kind of infrastructure that stands behind the explicit coordination dimension in Figure 10.1. Without state power, articulated through a system of laws, there is only high domination and there are no markets. Only when there is a strong legal system in place can individuals acquire and exercise independent choices, and this is the fundamental presupposition of microeconomics. But this same legal system is not a prerequisite to hierarchical forms of control, so quite different notions of societal context are being implied.

Some History of Organizations

To clarify the play of power and control we might step back to learn more of how organizations came about. Coleman's analysis of the evolution of modern society bears well on this (Coleman, 1974). Summarizing, he tells us the transition from feudal to modern democratic society was facilitated by three evolutions: (a) the institutionalization of feudal (or regal) power into the state's institutional apparatus; (b) the development of new socioeconomic entities, that is, rights-holding citizens as opposed to the previous all-powerful lords and complementary indentured vassals; and (c) the emergence of institutionalized cooperation in the form of corporate bodies. Today's corporations have evolved far from the legal forebears created by royals and lords for specific projects, for example the America-colonizing London Company of 1607 (Davis, 1961). Later, as citizens won rights of association, the corporate legal apparatus allowed them to coalesce their interests into agentic entities, able to choose their own goals and resist the state. Corporations were no longer only the arms of state, comprising the public sector, but became instruments through which citizens acted to create the new private sector. The history is important, complicated, and interesting because the forms of law and organization we have today are path-dependent and contingent on our culture and history (Horwitz, 1992).

We need not know many of the historical details to get the main point. The separation of the two prior social tiers, lords and vassals, into today's three tiers, state institutions, corporations, and citizens, involved huge social changes at every level. Note these changes are still essentially matters of description, that is, we do not yet have a theory of social change that can frame or do adequate justice to our empirical data. Likewise Commons' "old" institutionalism is grounded in empirical observations of the rights and obligations of a particular socioeconomy rather than on the kind of abstractions that underpin microeconomics and, to a considerable extent, macroeconomics also. The key to the social changes that brought today's organizations into existence was the transfer of power from feudal lords to state institutions and enfranchised citizens. With the invention of the joint-stock company and the person-like rights it acquired, we see a stable three-ring circus of citizens, organizations, and state. Citizen–citizen and organization–organization interactions are exemplified by the evolving notion of free markets and the eventual abstractions of economics (Galenson, 1989). State–citizen and state–organization interactions are the domain of politics and law (Fligstein, 1991, 2001; Herman, 1981). Citizen–organization interactions fall into the domain of organization theory, which is where we are, and organization to organization interactions constitute the heart of our markets.

Socioeconomic networks and hybrids differ from engineering networks. Social networks presuppose a power-exercising background or infrastructure which can be distinguished empirically and historically from the entities and interactions that comprise the foreground. To analyze real market behavior, as Commons and McCloskey remind us, we must know something of the legal and cultural infrastructure in which it is embedded (McCloskey, 2002). Likewise, to understand real corporate behavior we must understand the legal constraints on managerial power, the relevant employment law, and the state of the labor market, as well as the legal constraints on competitive and collaborative activity (Bain, 1968; Porter, 1979).

The communications networks invoked by Scott and Williamson imply infrastructural suppositions too, but of a quite different type. Physical networks need power to overcome the frictions and losses that arise. But communications networks also make assumptions about the meaning-systems in which they are embedded, for they move signals, data, rather than meaning (Shannon and Weaver, 1949). The infrastructure of shared meanings makes communications possible. A more troublesome matter is that engineering networks are designed from the outside, as it were, by designers whose concepts specify the network's infrastructure and its interactions with the network's components. Social networks are more emergent, and to say they are "designed" is unhelpful, given we do not know the identity of their designer. Their order is more difficult to explain.

Picturing Possibilities

At this point a graphic might help. In Figure 10.2 we see feudal society breaking into three layers, showing us the crucial third dimension missing from DiMaggio's analysis. We see an interplay between foreground and background, between the social entity and the social context in which it is embedded and on which it relies for its identity, the relationship between its rights and obligations. Likewise we do not really understand the entities at any of Figure 10.2's three "levels" without knowing something of the interactions between them, for that helps us see they are mutually constitutive as structuration theory suggests. It is important to see the notion of organization supposes both individual rights and state institutions, not simply unproblematic self-interested individuals and managers. We also see the importance, on the one side, of Simon's "decision to participate" and, on the individuals' side, the state's control over management's decisions to use or abuse those who have decided to so subject themselves.

We can move towards a third graphic (Figure 10.3) to help differentiate hybrids from networks, else we must lose the use of one or other term. We presume hybrids

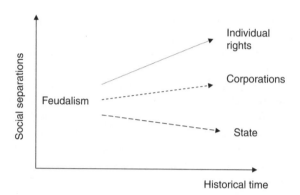

Figure 10.2 Coleman's notion of social evolution.

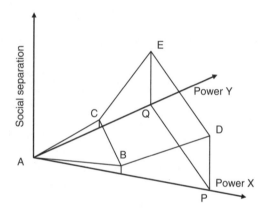

Figure 10.3 A typology of socioeconomic networks.

are empirically evident entities that seem to combine incommensurate concepts or "ideal types" and so be multi-logiced. Absent an overarching theory that explains or captures their unique features we are unable to differentiate them from other types of network. A mathematically describable network, like an engineer's, is "well formed" and uni-logiced by definition because a single logic is used to describe its system of entities and interactions. From our experience, we suspect real organizations and markets are more complicated and "ill-formed" and a variety of logics must be brought to their analysis. They might be theorized as exchange systems, or as power systems, or as communication systems, or they might be biological, or mechanical. They also persist through time and do not vanish like a spot transaction or a single command. So we shall presume hybrids are a subset of the broad family of socioeconomic networks, by which we mean any order and continuity of ongoing relations between individuals or organizations through time. Some of these are ideal types, uni-logiced, and others more complex, multi-logiced. They also inhabit multiple levels, networks of individuals at the upper level, of organizations at the middle level, and of individual–organizational relations between them. All of this is implicit in Figure 10.1

so we do no great violence to DiMaggio's analysis and our criticism is directed more directly to Powell's and Williamson's work, which has led many authors to treat networked organizations as distinct from bureaucratic organizations and markets without ever identifying the theory that would justify that treatment.

Socioeconomic networks are embedded in systems of social power. The efficient market of microeconomics assumes no power relations between the interacting principals – no one of them has the ability to interfere with the choices of any other. A long line of economists like Veblen, Marshall, and Chamberlin argued real markets exist within an imperfect politically structured context and that organizations are instruments for the pursuit and management of quasi-monopoly (Chamberlin, 1933; Marshall, 1969; Veblen, 1965). Porter likewise saw strategy as the pursuit and maintenance of quasi-monopoly (Porter, 1980). Without getting deeply into the economics of monopoly we can see an efficient spot market as a limiting notion of the term network, neither power nor ongoing-ness is implied.

As market forces penetrate the authority structure, and so present the actors within with multiple logics, they transform bureaucratic networks into hybrids. In Figure 10.3, point A is where all power is invested in the feudal lord for whom might is truly right. As the society evolves separations begin. In our Anglo-Saxon history we see the Magna Carta limiting or *distraining* the king's rights, paving the way for the legal establishment of citizens' rights. Separation accelerates the development of the society, suggested by the upward kink of the field BCED. The line DE represents the limit of the new definition of the individual. Previously constrained by birth, lineage, connections, and patronage, the Magna Carta is the origin of the notion of the citizen who stands equal with all others before the law, which is impersonal. The law becomes separated from the king whose powers are feudal and *ad hominen*, personal.

Eventually the state institutionalizes the greater part of the feudal monarch's powers. The region APQ in Figure 10.3 implies the gradual evolution of an all-powerful but rational system of law. The state, in concept, has established the necessary monopoly on the means of violence, and its citizens stand equally before its dictates irrespective of age, gender, religion, ethnicity, wealth, and so forth. Much of what one then means by crime against the state and against others is defined as acting in ways that contradict this cultural infrastructure. Meanwhile, at the limiting condition DE, citizens have freedom to engage in barter and trade with fully defined property rights without, of course, being able to diminish the rights of other citizens recklessly or shout "fire" in a crowded theater.

The point is not to explain our legal system. Like real markets, the functioning of the law is riddled with shortcomings and imperfections which, in the United States, it is the work of the Supreme Court to adjudicate. Rather our purpose is to set out a three-dimensional space in which to show some of the problems confronting Figure 10.1. The key, as noted earlier, is the treatment of human agency. By Power X we shall mean power between principals, while by Power Y we shall mean power between master and servant, between principal and agent (Pratt and Zeckhauser, 1991). Hybrids lie between these axes and mingle these forms of power.

The figure is complex, for while power is total at point A, it is both diffused and diminished for organizations and individuals as we move towards the lines BC – and yet further reduced towards the line DE. However, the power previously held centrally in the fiefdom and later institutionalized as state power increases as we move in the plane APQ toward the line PQ; the balance between the power within organizations and between organizations and the state, while contested, shifts in the latter's favor. Again, the message is that hybrids not only combine the structural characteristics of hierarchies and communities, so melding principals and agents, they also co-mingle the different types of power (French and Raven, 2001). This dichotomizing takes us back to Toennies and his distinction between *Gesellschaft* and *Gemeinshaft*, between the impersonal relations of the socially legitimated goal-directed organization on the one hand, and the pervasive sense of community identification and subordination on the other.

Bureaucracy

The pivot to the theory of bureaucracy is "legitimated power" or authority, grounded in the master–slave relationship in which one person gives up their agency and becomes the agent of another, as in principal–agent theory. This leads to other forms of power, such as the legitimated and so de-personalized position-based power of mangers over employees (French and Raven, 2001). The extent to which Power Y, that within the organization, seems legitimate to those outside the organization is a function of the relationship between the organization and the state, and the relevant law. As individuals also embedded within a community, managers and employees stand more or less equal before its power at point D. The community constrains the organization, or rather its management's choices, and in so doing may protect the employee *qua* citizen from the managers' power as we move towards point E. The networks that interest us are the independent legal-economic entities stabilized by legitimated modes of governance chosen by managements exercising their freedoms to subordinate others and engage in trade within the constraints of the relevant property rights, commerce, and employment laws. They lie in the field BCED, but with defining ties and interactions to the state and institutional infrastructure comprising the field APQ. We clarify these in Figure 10.4.

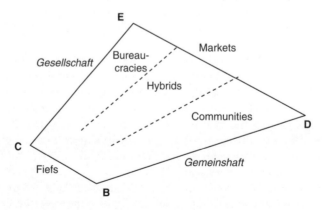

Figure 10.4 Distribution of types of network.

Conventional theorizing leads us to consider bureaucracy as little more than central control within the organization's goal-oriented logic. Our analysis shows that this simplification, ignoring the interplay of the levels in Figure 10.2, obscures important strategic levers that managers may find useful. Organizations are embedded in a sociolegal context which sets limits to their Power Y, yes, but they are also embedded in society with institutions, public goods, and an infrastructure on which the organization normally draws extensively. Its interactions with the state are frequently about its access to these extra-organizational resources, such as education, transportation, and freedom from riots and other interference with their business – and taxes to maintain these resources. Given this contextual network of resources and obligations is far from rationally designed and is partially emergent, replete with contradictions and oversights, a great deal of strategizing is about positioning the organization to take maximum advantage of it. The same tussle between interests arises within the organization which, in addition to being a field of authority (Power Y) is also an internal property-rights regime. As we know, decision rules are crucial to bureaucratic theory, but one of the most effective ways to control the organization is to control the resources people need to do their work. In medieval times only nobles could hold property, so the diffusion of power pictured in Figure 10.2 was accompanied by diffusing the rights to own property. Just so within the organization when subunits are able to keep some of the revenue they generate and cycle it back into innovation and the resources necessary to organizational responsiveness.

The movement from fiefs to markets is one of increasing actor independence and clarity of individual identity, buttressed by increasingly powerful impersonal laws and social norms (Boisot and Child, 1988; Ouchi, 1980). Historically the political and legal "invention" of the corporation's "person-hood," enabling it to appear before the law as a citizen, is crucial – for that connected it to legal precedents that would allow the law governing citizens to be refashioned into corporate law (Horwitz, 1992). Though bureaucracies are characterized by the master–servant relationship (Power Y), the subordinate's loss of identity will vary considerably depending on the extent to which the individual can resist managerial power. Thus organizations will range from near fiefdoms, such as often existed in one-company towns, in which the owners' powers over the employees' lives were almost unlimited, to the publicly rule-bound bureaucracies of today in which employees have substantial internally and externally supported rights to appeal all manner of managerial decision (Blau and Meyer, 1987).

Communities are hybrid in that they are marked by both hierarchy (Power Y) and market behaviors (Power X). Type X powers do not arise and are not imposed or apportioned through anyone's designing the community; they are emergent in and contingent on the history of the community's development. So communities will also range from near fiefdoms in which power is narrowly held, to open voluntary communities in which people are free to reject the power of others and exit the community (Hirschman, 1970; Scott, 2003). At the point at which those within an organization have as much power as its managers, even though it is based on employee rights contingent on their relationship with the infrastructure – as is the "whistle-blower's" right to act against the organization – a bureaucracy begins to approximate a market.

The purpose of our analysis thus far is to lay out a conceptual domain within which the different empirically observed socioeconomic networks might lie, and so justify our claim that network is a more useful and general term than either hierarchy or market. It embraces all their real occurrences. In this sense we can see that one of the appeals of the term "network" is that we can apply it to socioeconomic systems for which we have no other label. When we want to speak of a collaborative system, such as that observed in the Emilia-Romagna textile district, it is the only label we have (Best, 1990); likewise when we want to speak of a flexible ad hoc project team. But there are limits. The perfect market is an abstraction, a limiting condition that lies beyond the reach of the term "network." Likewise the fiefdom, the ultimate master–slave relationship in which the slave is an object to be possessed with no rights whatsoever, also lies beyond networking. The term covers the domain BCED, within a civil society in which individual, organizational, and state rights have arisen. Within these boundaries the different network types reflect Etzioni's typology (Etzioni, 1961, 1964).

DiMaggio's figure (Figure 10.1) does not take into account the legal and normative infrastructure in which his networks are embedded, and without paying attention to these we cannot understand what ultimately holds real networks together. The integrity of a designed network comes from its designer alone. Real socioeconomic networks are inevitably long term, under specified and, at least in part, emergent, and so hold together only because they are embedded in a society which itself has achieved a substantial degree of integration. First a society of social institutions, then a citizenry, and only then organizations and markets. Williamson's assertion that "in the beginning there were markets" (Williamson, 1975: 132) is ludicrous. Absent a system of enforced property laws, neither markets nor organizations can exist – which is one reason why the concept of property lies at the heart of economics and capitalist society, and its corruption is so damaging to economic growth (Berle and Means, 1968; Nedelsky, 1990).

The next step is to see how we might move beyond the primitive communication-based theory of networking that Scott and Williamson bring to bear. The point is that while we have created an analytic field in which to locate the socioeconomic networks that interest us, we have derived no analytic or design principles, nothing that we can draw on for a strategic theory. We see these networks are essentially ones of power and agency but the term "network" is still mere description. The nodes are people or organizations, the interactions are ones of decision, when principals interact, or of advice about those decisions coming from the community, or authoritative decision rules where hierarchical relations exist. But does this tell us much about whether managers need to reconstruct their firms in the face of the conditions which Powell argues drive the trend to networking? If there are principles for analyzing or organizing these networks they are either contingent on the particular kinds of node and interaction – implied in the notion of economizing communication – or they reside in the nature of networks themselves, independent of the empirical particulars of the network. The networking literature gives little support to the first. However, recent developments in network theory illuminate the second.

A New Network Theory

The notion that some social structures are emergent, not the work of a designer, and beyond the control of managers goes back centuries and largely comes into contemporary analysis through the work of Toennies (Toennies, 1971). *Gemeinschaftlich* social organizations, like those addressed by, say, Burt, Uzzi, and Castells, are un-designed by definition (Burt, 1992; Castells, 1996; Uzzi, 1997). For instance, we think of markets as largely emergent for no one actor can shape their behavior. This unmanaged or unmanageable aspect is also key to the libertarian view that markets are efficient information distribution devices and that the most efficient economy is one that is not managed directly (Hayek, 1945). Unfortunately neither sociologists nor other theorists have been able to identify unambiguously the preconditions for the emergence of a new social network or its subsequent growth trajectory. We take it to be a consequence of our being social animals. But this is mere tautology for we only know this because it seems we coalesce into networks and societies. It would appear that the business strategist has only one weapon in his armory, control and its implementation in a designed hierarchy. The alternative is *laissez faire*.

While it is too early to know its full application to business affairs, a new theory of networking is emerging from mathematical analyses of naturally occurring order, that is, order that has not been created by Man. Chaos theory has opened up some of this (e.g. Kauffman, 1995). Mathematicians understand networks as graphs within graph theory. As with the legal and historical comments above, we do not need to delve too deeply to get the underlying message. There is nothing inherently inefficient about an all-channel communication network, though its 2^N links look forbidding (Graicunas, 1933). Email and mobiles make us accustomed to speaking directly with the person targeted rather than having to channel our requests formally through intermediaries. We might say modern communications are dis-intermediated and informal in avoiding channels and chains of command. Likewise the Internet is dis-intermediating brokers such as travel agents and retail outlets. The transactions costs of the new direct methods are often so low that if we want to inform a large group of people it is often cheaper to broadcast (or spam) than to pre-screen.

But, as Adam Smith told us, organizations prosper primarily because of the beneficial consequences of the division of labor, so different people's information needs differ widely. When we think about influencing people's decisions the challenge is to manage the network so that it directs specific messages from one individual to another. This applies as much to instructions and decision rules as it does to the data used in decisions. Even though all-channel networks can share everything with everyone and are increasingly technologically viable, we cannot overlook our basic human limitations. Much of management is about managing people's attention and dealing with their bounded rationality. The concept of a network as a system for searching for information may be more appropriate than as a system for distributing information, since the former brings people's limitations rapidly to the fore. Then the question is, what kind of network and management works best if person A is seeking some information but does not know the identity of person B who has that information? Search engines, data-mining techniques, directories of experts, and so forth become increasingly valuable as the positive externalities of scale and scope increase.

Watts calls this new mathematical approach the "science of a connected age" (Watts, 2003). Its insights come from analysis of networks that are other than randomly interconnected. We seem content to say that all occurring networks seem to be hybrids in the sense developed above, partially structured and partially emergent, both formal and informal, so melding *Gesellschaft* with *Gemeinschaft*. We think of them as partially designed by management and partially evolved through the problem-seeking and problem-solving activities of the individuals and organizations networked. But we lack the theory of network dynamics which forms the heart of the new science (Watts, 2003: 50). Its fundamentals are encapsulated in the phrase "six degrees of separation"; the maxim that any two people in the world can be connected through six or fewer person-to-person links. This seems counter-intuitive but it seems to apply widely and, as a result, we discover our world may be more local than it seems. The implication might be that an "intelligent designer" is at work or, perhaps much the same thing, social networks evolve reflecting some species-specific socializing properties. But the new analysis suggests neither implication is correct.

The argument is complex but well covered in Barabási's book (2002). Many real world networks share this "small world" character (Milgram, 1967; Watts and Strogatz, 1998). Mathematically, these networks are unlike random networks whose characteristics are Gaussian (bell-curve). Instead, they are "power law" systems, which Pareto noticed and encapsulated as the 80/20 rule which bears his name – that 20 percent of the roads carry 80 percent of the traffic, for instance. Pareto was primarily interested in the distribution of wealth, but power laws have now been observed in a large number of fields: molecular, physical, and biological, as well as social and economic (Andriani and McKelvey, 2005). Ijiri and Simon (1977) dealt with the skewed (power law) distribution of firm sizes, an effect that persists in spite of their managers' best efforts to make things otherwise – linear on a log-log scale. The implication is that power-law networks, also known as "scale-free" networks, possess considerable self-organizing capabilities that at the population level overcome or at minimum severely constrain the individual firms' managers.

The puzzle is how networks do this without an external designer acting as a source of order distinct and different from the firms' managers. One thing to notice is how graph-theory networks change as the number of connections to each node exceeds two, so that a node interacts with several other nodes rather than just with its immediate neighbors. At the same time we presume networks are bounded in the sense that each node has limited capacity and cannot handle being connected with every other node. Second, even when each node is connected with others in a regular design, the average path length between two randomly chosen nodes is significantly reduced when a small number of links are added randomly, so providing additional connection paths (Barabási, 2002: 51). It turns out that scale-free networks arise only when simple design principles are interpenetrated by chance, when there is both order and disorder, neither pure randomness nor pure structure. Third, scale-free networks arise when newly arriving nodes are active agents, able to choose and select their relationships rather than having them assigned by chance. If their preference is to connect with the already most-connected nodes, highly connected hubs quickly emerge. These are characteristic of many scale-free networks (Barabási, 2002: 87).

Scale-free systems analysis can be applied in other disciplines. In sociology it illuminates Granovetter's empirical observations about "the strength of weak ties" (Granovetter, 1973). From his empirical work Granovetter concluded that while most people have a small circle of close friends, his "strong ties," they also have friends in more distant circles. These are equivalent to Barabási's random links. Granovetter dubbed these "weak ties" and found them more useful when seeking new jobs. This example shows us how scale-free networks are a powerful means for connecting A and B when A needs something that B has, but A does not know of B's existence. Watts' analysis goes on to consider epidemics, which may soon concern us greatly, and the Internet.

As Watts suggests, most of our field's network literature is paradigmatically managerialist, the assumption being that our theorizing is directed towards helping managers design systems of efficient communication and control. Scott, Williamson, and Powell adopt this paradigm. But the analysis of scale-free networks shows that when networks are emergent, enacted by those seeking information, influence, connections, signals, and so forth, under conditions of uncertainty and bounded rationality, they suggest quite different design and process principles. At the same time these networks are evidently more efficient than those that managers design, and have a robustness and survival capability the rationally designed networks do not. We have known for a while that attempts to suppress informal networking in organizations are counter-productive, even destructive. The lesson for organizational theorists is that real socio-economic networks cannot be understood without moving away from the managerialism underpinning most of organization theory. We should show more respect for the impact that solution-seeking individuals have on the organization, and the same applies in markets. Principals and firms are highly selective about those others with whom they trade, and use the term "trust" to express their preferences.

Conclusion: Strategies for Managing Networks

While this chapter's overall focus is the management of networking, our first objective was to show "network" is actually a broad term covering the spectrum between several ideal types: fully controlled mechanistic bureaucracy at one extreme, and *laissez faire* at the other. At the first pole we rely on rational design, at the second on notions of emergence. This might mean evolutionary emergence, as with organizational routines (Nelson and Winter, 1982) or social institutions (North, 1991), or alternatively some version of the mathematical approach reviewed above. Many real networks are hybrids with emergence penetrating managerially designed order. So theorists might do better to appreciate the limits to managerial control. One implication is that we might reframe our theorizing, and move on from optimized static designs to focusing on facilitating the network's dynamic adaptation. As the defenders of informal systems in organizations are quick to point out, people communicate whether their managers like it or not, and we can make a virtue out of the impossibility of total control. Second, we might pay more attention to what we mean by people, that is, just who are the agents in these networks? We see each group's or each individual's identity constantly reshaped by their relations with the organization's system of power, and with the rest of the infrastructure that enables them to claim and protect their identity. In transactions costs terms the notion of a node is tied up with having the facilities and capabilities necessary to take a vigorous constructive part in the ongoing activities of the network. Aside from having an agentic identity, there may be other tangible necessities, such as the freedom to choose who to talk to, access to the Internet, social recognition, rights of citizenship, etc.

Once socialized into the network, individuals and groups engage in a two level dynamic, as Watts points out. The first level is evident as traffic through the network. Relationships are enacted, messages moved, etc. But there is also a second-level dynamic of change in the network's structure and process as links appear and disappear, and flows refashion themselves around the problems and challenges being addressed. This dynamism is the source of a real network's robustness and survival ability in the face of disruptions. Watts tells of the Toyota manufacturing network's recovery after a catastrophic fire at the plant sole-sourcing a precision brake component (Watts, 2003: 254). The solution was not resource redundancy, the conventional mechanical and managerialist solution to guard against chance and disruption – we should note the central place of redundancy in Nonaka and Takeuchi's theory of knowledge generation (Nonaka and Takeuchi, 1995: 80). Watts is not an organizational theorist and does not focus on these issues, glossing his conclusion that the recovery resulted from the network's self-organizing properties.

But the strategic message – when disaster strikes let the system reorganize itself – seems anti-managerialist and alarming, especially when the conventional response is to centralize and tighten control. We see the partially self-organizing network presents continuing challenges to its nodes, requiring them to exercise choice and get creative. The network is then about problem-solving in the ordinary sense and about the continuous reconstruction of identity through self-referencing and channeling the nodes' creativity. In the Toyota example the way the network operated before it was damaged led to a substantial distributed reservoir of creativity. As Watts shows, it was this dynamic capability, as well as the group's ability to channel it towards solving the problem, that saved the company from disaster.

The strategic lessons are that managers can easily focus on control through rules, sanctions, or by closely managing the property rights regime within the firm, and so contrive systems that shut down the creativity of those being managed, as in the case of a strong bureaucracy (Amabile, 1998; March and Simon, 1958). But we suggest they might do better to delegate, let go, and facilitate the ongoing interpenetration of order and chaos that seems to foster distributed creativity throughout the network. The managerialist inclination is to think only managers are creative and that all the firm's strategy making must be done by them, that control is their only strategy. Under the spell of romanticism or humanism many writers inveigh against control and its evident dysfunctions (March and Simon, 1958). They search for *Gemeinschaft*, or an emergent organic theory of organizations (e.g. Burns and Stalker, 1961; Mintzberg, 1994; Senge, 1990). But we have yet to see a compelling or testable theory of this emerge (Easterby-Smith and Lyles, 2003). Scale-free networks show us that responsive and efficient networks can arise from any node that is reflexive enough to recognize its choices and be permitted to exercise them. *Inter alia*, this brings democracy to the network. This theory of networking implies a network's most strategic capability is not communication, as Scott and Powell and most other writers, suggest. Rather it is the network's dynamic self-management, its ability to channel the practice-based creativity distributed among its nodes. We might also suggest this is what Penrose's theory of the growth of the firm is ultimately about (Penrose, 1995).

References

Amabile, T. M. (1998) How to kill creativity. *Harvard Business Review*, 76(5), 76–88.

Andriani, P. & McKelvey, B. (2005) Beyond averages: Extending organization science to extreme events and power laws. Unpublished MS, Durham Business School.

Bain, J. S. (1968) *Industrial Organization*. New York: John Wiley & Sons.

Barabási, A.-L. (2002) *Linked: The New Science of Networks*. Cambridge, MA: Perseus Publishing.

Berle, A. A. & Means, G. C. (1968) *The Modern Corporation and Private Property*. New York: Harcourt, Brace & World.

Best, M. H. (1990) *The New Competition: Institutions of Industrial Restructuring*. Cambridge, MA: Harvard University Press.

Blau, P. M. & Meyer, M. W. (1987) *Bureaucracy in Modern Society*, 3rd edn. New York: McGraw-Hill.

Boisot, M. & Child, J. (1988) The iron law of fiefs: Bureaucratic failure and the problem of governance in the Chinese economic reforms. *Administrative Science Quarterly*, 33, 507–27.

Burns, T. & Stalker, G. M. (1961) *The Management of Innovation*. London: Tavistock.

Burt, R. S. (1983) *Applied Network Analysis: A Methodological Introduction*. Newbury Park, CA: Sage.

Burt, R. S. (1992) *Structural Holes: The Social Structure of Competition*. Cambridge, MA: Harvard University Press.

Campbell, J. L. & Lindberg, L. N. (1991) The evolution of governance regimes. In: J. L. Campbell, J. R. Hollingsworth & L. N. Lindberg (Eds.) *Governance of the American Economy*, 319–55. New York: Cambridge University Press.

Castells, M. (1996) *The Information Age: Economy, Society and Culture*. Malden, MA: Blackwell.

Chamberlin, E. H. (1933) *The Theory of Monopolistic Competition*. Cambridge, MA: Harvard University Press.

Coleman, J. S. (1974) *Power and the Structure of Society*. New York: W. W. Norton.

Commons, J. R. (1957) *Legal Foundations of Capitalism*. Madison, WI: University of Wisconsin Press.

Davis, J. P. (1961) *Corporations: A Study of the Origin and Development of Great Business Combinations and their Relation to the Authority of the State*. New York: Capricorn Books.

DiMaggio, P. J. (2001) Conclusion: The futures of business organization and paradoxes of change. In: P. J. DiMaggio (Ed.) *The Twenty-First Century Firm: Changing Economic Organization in International Perspective*, 210–43. Princeton, NJ: Princeton University Press.

Durkheim, E. (1964) *The Division of Labor in Society*. New York: Free Press.

Easterby-Smith, M. & Lyles, M. A. (Eds.) (2003) *The Blackwell Handbook of Organizational Learning and Knowledge Management*. Malden, MA: Blackwell.

Etzioni, A. (1961) *A Comparative Analysis of Complex Organizations: On Power, Involvement, and their Correlates*. New York: Free Press.

Etzioni, A. (1964) *Modern Organizations*. Englewood Cliffs, NJ: Prentice-Hall.

Fayol, H. (1949) *General and Industrial Management*. London: Pitman.

Fligstein, N. (1991) The structural transformation of American industry. In: W. W. Powell & P. J. DiMaggio (Eds.) *The New Institutionalism in Organizational Analysis*, 311–36. Chicago, IL: University of Chicago Press.

Fligstein, N. (2001) *The Architecture of Markets: An Economic Sociology of Twenty-First Century Capitalist Societies*. Princeton, NJ: Princeton University Press.

Fox, A. (1974) *Beyond Contract: Work, Power and Trust Relations*. London: Faber & Faber.

French, R. P. & Raven, B. (2001) The bases for social power. In: J. M. Shafritz & J. S. Ott (Eds.) *Classics of Organization Theory*, 5th edn, 319–28. Belmont, CA: Wadsworth.

Galenson, D. W. (1989) *Markets in History: Economic Studies of the Past*. New York: Cambridge University Press.

Gerlach, M. L. (1987) Business alliances and the strategy of the Japanese firm. *California Management Review*, 30(1), 126–42.

Gerlach, M. L. (1992) *Alliance Capitalism: The Social Organization of Japanese Business*. Berkeley, CA: University of California Press.

Graicunas, V. A. (1933) Relationship in organization. *Bulletin of the International Management Institute*, 7(March), 39–42.

Granovetter, M. (1973) The strength of weak ties. *American Journal of Sociology*, 78, 1360–80.

Guillén, M. F. (1994) *Models of Management: Work, Authority, and Organization in a Comparative Perspective*. Chicago, IL: University of Chicago Press.

Hamel, G., Doz, Y. L. & Prahalad, C. K. (1989) Collaborate with your competitors – and win. *Harvard Business Review*, 67(1), 133–39.

Hart, O. (1988) Incomplete contracts and the theory of the firm. *Journal of Law, Economics and Organization*, 4, 119–39.

Hayek, F. A. (1945) The use of knowledge in society. *American Economic Review*, 35, 519–30.

Herman, E. S. (1981) *Corporate Control, Corporate Power*. Cambridge: Cambridge University Press.

Hirschman, A. O. (1970) *Exit, Voice and Loyalty: Responses to Decline in Firms, Organizations and States*. Cambridge, MA: Harvard University Press.

Horwitz, M. J. (1992) *The Transformation of American Law, 1780–1860*. New York: Oxford University Press.

Ijiri, Y. & Simon, H. A. (1977) *Skew Distributions and the Sizes of Business Firms*. Amsterdam: North-Holland.

Kauffman, S. (1995) *At Home in the Universe: The Search for the Laws of Self-Organization and Complexity*. New York: Oxford University Press.

Kraakman, R. (2001) The durability of the corporate form. In: P. J. DiMaggio (Ed.) *The Twenty-first Century Firm: Changing Economic Organization in International Perspective*, 147–60. Princeton, NJ: Princeton University Press.

Latour, B. (1993) *We Have Never Been Modern*. Cambridge, MA: Harvard University Press.

March, J. G. & Simon, H. A. (1958) *Organizations*. New York: John Wiley.

Marshall, A. (1969) *The Principles of Economics* (student edn). London: Macmillan.

McCloskey, D. N. (2002) *The Secret Sins of Economics*. Chicago, IL: Prickly Paradigm Press.

Milgram, S. (1967) The small world problem. *Psychology Today*, 2, 60–7.

Milgram, S. (1974) *Obedience to Authority: An Experimental View*. New York: Harper & Row.

Mintzberg, H. (1994) *The Rise and Fall of Strategic Planning: Reconceiving Roles for Planning, Plans and Planners*. New York: Free Press.

Nedelsky, J. (1990) *Private Property and the Limits of American Constitutionalism: The Madisonian Framework and its Legacy*. Chicago, IL: University of Chicago Press.

Nelson, R. R. & Winter, S. G. (1982) *An Evolutionary Theory of Economic Change*. Cambridge, MA: Belknap Press.

Nonaka, I. & Takeuchi, H. (1995) *The Knowledge-Creating Company: How Japanese Companies Create the Dynamics of Innovation*. New York: Oxford University Press.

North, D. C. (1991) Institutions. *Journal of Economic Perspectives*, 5(1), 97–112.

Ouchi, W. G. (1980) Markets, bureaucracies and clans. *Administrative Science Quarterly*, 25, 120–42.

Penrose, E. T. (1995) *The Theory of the Growth of the Firm*, 3rd edn. New York: Oxford University Press.

Pfeffer, J. & Salancik, G. R. (1978) *The External Control of Organizations: A Resource Dependence Perspective*. New York: Harper & Row.

Porter, M. E. (1979) How competitive forces shape strategy. *Harvard Business Review, March–April*, 137–45.

Porter, M. E. (1980) *Competitive Strategy: Techniques for Analyzing Industries and Competitors*. New York: Free Press.

Powell, W. W. (1987) Hybrid organizational arrangements: New form or transitional development? *California Management Review*, 30(1), 67–87.

Powell, W. W. (1990) Neither market nor hierarchy: Network forms of organization. In: B. M. Staw & L. L. Cummings (Eds.) *Research in Organizational Behavior*, Vol. 12, 295–336. Greenwich, CT: JAI Press.

Powell, W. W. (2001) The capitalist firm in the twenty-first century. In: P. J. DiMaggio (Ed.) *The Twenty-First Century Firm: Changing Economic Organization in International Perspective*, 33–68. Princeton, NJ: Princeton University Press.

Pratt, J. W. & Zeckhauser, R. J. (1991) Principals and agents: An overview. In: J. W. Pratt & R. J. Zeckhauser (Eds.) *Principals and Agents: The Structure of Business*, 1–35. Boston, MA: Harvard Business School.

Scott, W. R. (2003) *Organizations: Rational, Natural, and Open Systems*, 5th edn. Upper Saddle River, NJ: Prentice-Hall.

Senge, P. M. (1990) The leader's new work: Building learning organizations. *Sloan Management Review*, 32(1), 7–23.

Shannon, C. & Weaver, W. (1949) *The Mathematical Theory of Communication*. Urbana, IL: University of Illinois.

Simon, H. A. (1952a) Comments on the theory of organizations. *American Political Science Review*, 46, 1130–9.

Simon, H. A. (1952b) A comparison of organization theories. *Review of Economic Studies*, 20(1), 40–8.

Simon, H. A. (1958) *Administrative Behavior: A Study of Decision-Making Processes in Administrative Organization*, 2nd edn. New York: Macmillan.

Thompson, J. D. (1967) *Organizations in Action: Social Science Bases of Administrative Theory*. New York: McGraw-Hill.

Toennies, F. (1971) *On Sociology: Pure, Applied, and Empirical*. Chicago, IL: University of Chicago Press.

Uzzi, B. (1997) Social structure and competition in interfirm networks: The paradox of embeddedness. *Administrative Science Quarterly*, 42, 37–69.

Veblen, T. (1965) *The Theory of the Business Enterprise*. New York: Augustus M. Kelley.

Watts, D. J. (2003) *Six Degrees: The Science of a Connected Age*. New York: W. W. Norton.

Watts, D. J. & Strogatz, S. H. (1998) Collective dynamics of "small world" networks. *Nature*, 393(June), 440–2.

Williamson, O. E. (1975) *Markets and Hierarchies: Analysis and Antitrust Implications*. New York: Free Press.

Williamson, O. E. (1985) *The Economic Institutions of Capitalism: Firms, Markets, Relational Contracting*. New York: Free Press.

Williamson, O. E. (1991) Comparative economic organization: The analysis of discrete structural alternatives. *Administrative Science Quarterly*, 36(2), 269–96.

Index

4I framework, 15–16
80/20 rule, 184

action research, 122
actors and agents, 174–6
advisory boards, supplier networks, 48
affective conflict, 139–40, 144
agents and actors, 174–6
Akzo-Nobel, 51
alliances, 26–7, 36
    formation, 27–9, 32–4
    link, *see* link alliances
    performance and outcomes, 30–1, 34–5
    scale, *see* scale alliances
    trust, 134–5
ambiguity perspective, organizational
    identity, 125
anecdotes in the sense-making database,
    131–3
anti-stories, 137, 138
appreciative inquiry, 144
appropriation strategy, knowledge
    management, 14, 16–17, 18–20
archetypes for narrative negotiation of
    identity, 130–1
Ashby's law, 164, 166

Becker-Acroma, 51
blogs, 117–18
Bosch, 53
bureaucracy, 174, 180–2, 186
bureaucratic networks, 161, 162, 163
bureaux de style, 96
Bürkle, 51
business plans, interfirm teams, 75, 76, 77,
    78–9, 86
    learning model, 83, 84
buyer–supplier collaboration in product
    development projects, 4, 59–63, 67–8

    maximizing transaction value, 63–4
    project-level collaboration, 65–7
    value appropriation, 64–5

capture strategy, knowledge management,
    14–15, 18–20, 21
centralization of online social networks,
    112–14
Cereal Partners Worldwide (CPW), 28
certification of suppliers, 48, 49
chaos theory, 183
chat rooms, 111
Church–Turing thesis, 166
clan networks, 161, 162
closure in online social networks, 115
coalitions, interfirm teams, 83, 84
cognitive conflict, 139–40, 144
cohesiveness of online social networks, 115
collaboration costs, scale alliances, 33, 34, 36
communication in supplier networks, 47
communitas, 90, 103
competence for governance, 83–4, 85, 86
competence leaves, 73–4
complementarity, alliance formation, 27–9
complementary competence, group learning
    model, 80–1, 84–5
complex adaptive systems (CAS), 164–5
    ecological perspective on organizations,
    154, 157
concertation in fashion industry, 88–90,
    91–3, 103–4
    emic account, 95–100
    etic account, 100–3
    innovation in fabric, 90–1
    key events, 93–5
conferences, and supplier networks, 48
conflict, productive, 123, 139–40
    interorganizational networks, 140–2
    and narrative, 142–3
    supporting narrative negotiation of, 143–6

conflict efficacy, 140
conflict stimulation methods, 141
constructivism, 73, 85
contracting costs, 63
cool hunting, 95
cooperation stage, group learning model, 79–80
cooperative games, 160–1
coordination costs, scale alliances, 34
core-periphery structure of online social networks, 115–17
corporate culture, and buyer–supplier collaboration, 66
CPW joint venture, 28
cross-functional teams, supplier networks, 47–8
cultural issues, interfirm teams, 78, 80, 82–3
cyber social networks, *see* online social networks

defining networks, 172–4
Delphi, 52, 55
density of online social networks, 111–12, 115
Department of Defense (DoD), buyer–supplier collaboration, 65
description, networks as, 152, 156–7, 159
devil's advocacy, 141
dialectical inquiry, 141
differentiation perspective, organizational identity, 125
Dilbert cartoons, 130
discussion forums, online, 119
  centralization, 114
  core-periphery structure, 116–17
  size, 111
disruptive metaphor, 137–8
dominant designs, fashion industry, 104 n. 2

early supplier involvement strategy, 59, 67
easygroup, 2
ecological perspective on organizations, 154–5, 157, 163, 164, 166
egocentric perspective, social network studies, 118
EHS NewCo, 75–84
email group lists, 111
emic account of fashion industry, 93, 95–100, 104
enactment in fashion industry, 100–1
enforcement costs, 63
engineering change orders, and value appropriation, 64, 66

engineer's definition of networks, 172
Enron, 165
Environment, Health and Safety (EHS)
  case study of learning process, 75–84
  in chemical industry, 75–6
equality principle, buyer–supplier collaboration, 65
equity principle, buyer–supplier collaboration, 65
etic account of fashion industry, 93, 100–3, 104
evolving networks, 157–9
  through game theory, 159–60
  processes, 157–8
  structure, 158–9
experimentation, teaching through, 54
explicit knowledge, 12, 13–14, 21, 22
  appropriation strategy, 16–17
  capture strategy, 15
  game theory, 160
  online social networks, 113–14
external knowledge, 12–14, 21, 22
  appropriation strategy, 16–17, 18, 20
  participation strategy, 17–18

fashion industry, concertation of French and Italian fabric producers, 88–90, 91–3, 103–4
  emic account, 95–100
  etic account, 100–3
  innovation in fabric, 90–1
  key events in concertation, 93–5
ferment phase, fashion industry, 104 n. 2
feudalism, and social evolution, 176, 178, 179
Fiat, 28
fiefdoms, 181, 182
fief networks, 161, 162
"fly on the wall" technique, 141
fragmentation perspective, organizational identity, 125
framing, and narratives, 145–6
Fuji Xerox, supplier networks, 49
fundamental attribution error and narratives, 145

game theory
  evolving organized networks through, 159–60
  institutional structures as networks, 160–3
  network representations of organization, 163–4
Gemeinschaft, 180, 183, 184, 186

General Mills, 28
general systems theory, 153
geographical dispersion, buyer–supplier
    collaboration, 66, 67
Gesellschaft, 180, 184
GILDEMEISTER AG, 59–61
global production networks, knowledge
    exchange in, 41–2
goodwill, participation strategy, 18
governance
    competence for, 83–4, 85, 86
    and network descriptions of
        organization, 165
graph theory, 156, 183, 184
grounded theory, 122
group-level learning, 74–5
groupthink, and conflict, 140

Harley Davidson, supplier monitoring and
    evaluation, 46
hierarchical competition, evolving
    networks, 158
history of organizations, 176–7
horizontal competition, evolving networks,
    158
hybrid organizations, 173–4, 177–80,
    183–4, 185

IBM
    seminars, 47
    takeover, 131
    Watson, T. J., 137
idealistic paradigm, 122, 147
    multiple identities, 124
identity, 123–4
    interorganizational networks and multiple
        identities, 126–7
    and narrative, 127–9
    resilience, 124–5
    silos as organizational identities, 125–6
    supporting narrative negotiation of,
        129–33
identity theory, 123
IKEA, supply network, 50–2, 53, 54
imitation in fashion industry, 99, 105 n. 7
indexing structure in the sense-making
    database, 132
industrial districts
    cooperative mechanisms, 105 n. 9
    knowledge exchange in, 41
informal socialization, interfirm teams, 82
information and communication
    technologies (ICTs)

interfirm team learning, 83
    knowledge management, 9, 10, 19, 20;
        capture strategy, 14–15, 20
    networks as organizational description,
        156–7
    networks as organizational types,
        155–6, 166
    new network theory, 183
    see also Internet; virtual teams
information overload, online social
    networks, 110
innovation
    buyer–supplier collaboration, 60, 63, 65,
        67, 68; geographical dispersion, 66
    centralization of social networks, 113
    fabric producers, 89, 90–1, 94, 104; emic
        account, 96–7, 98, 99; etic account,
        100, 101, 103
    link alliances, 31, 32; formation, 28, 29
    scale alliances, 32
institutionalization, learning strategy, 15–16
institutional structures as networks, 160–3
integration, learning strategy, 15–16
integration perspective, organizational
    identity, 125
interactionism, 73–4
interfirm team, learning in an, 5, 72–3, 85–6
    EHS NewCo case study, 75–9
    four-stage model, 79–85
    group-level learning, 74–5
    interactionism, 73–4
internal knowledge, 12–14, 21, 22
    capture strategy, 15, 18
    learning strategy, 16, 18
International Observatory, *Première Vision*,
    94, 95
Internet
    networks as organizational types, 156
    new network theory, 183
    online social networks, 5, 107–9, 119;
        centralization, 112–14;
        core-periphery structure, 115–17;
        density, 111–12; future research,
        118–19; new developments, 117–18;
        size, 111; social capital embedded in,
        109–11; structure and information
        sharing, 111–17
interorganizational networks and multiple
    identities, 126–7
interpartner learning, 30–1
interpersonal links, group learning model,
    81–3, 84–5
interpretation, learning strategy, 15–16
interpretive systems, organizations as, 89–90
intuition, learning strategy, 15–16

"Janet and John stories," 137
joint-stock companies, historical context,
    176–7
joint ventures, *see* alliances

key account management function, 48
Klinkner, Professor Dr.-Ing. Raimund, 59–61
knowledge-based view (KBV) of the firm, 14
knowledge exchange in supplier networks,
    41–2
  and purchasing, 42–5
knowledge management (KM), 9–12
  definitions, 10–12
  strategies, 3–4, 8–9, 14, 21–2;
    appropriation strategy, 16–17, 18–20;
    capture strategy, 14–15, 18–20;
    distinguishing between, 18–20;
    learning strategy, 15–16, 18–20;
    participation strategy, 17–18, 18–20
knowledge purchasing in supplier networks,
    41, 42
  extensive knowledge exchange, 43–4
  from a market, 42–3
  as outsourcing production, 43
knowledge types, 8–9, 12–14
Kodak, supplier evaluation criteria, 45–6
KronoPol, 51, 53
kyoryoku kai organizations, 50

learning
  in an interfirm team, 5, 72–3, 85–6; EHS
    NewCo case study, 75–9; four-stage
    model, 79–85; group-level learning,
    74–5; interactionism, 73–4
  in supplier networks, 41–2
learning strategy, knowledge management,
    14, 15–16, 18–20
legal system, 175, 176, 177, 179
  bureaucracy, 181
link alliances, 26–7, 36
  formation, 27–9, 32–3
  performance and outcomes, 30–1, 34–5
  resource-based view, 31, 32
London Company, 176

Magna Carta, 179
managing networks, 6, 171, 185–6
  actors and agents, 174–6
  bureaucracy, 180–2
  current network theorizing, 172
  defining networks, 172–4
  history of organizations, 176–7

new network theory, 182–5
  picturing possibilities, 177–80
market networks, 161, 163
mechanical perspective on organizations,
    153, 154–5
Memorandum of Understanding (MOU),
    EHS NewCo, 80
mergers, and identity negotiation, 131, 139
meta-organizers, 101
metaphor, disruptive, 137–8
Moda In, 89–90, 91–104
modern society, evolution of, 176
modularity
  buyer–supplier collaboration, 60, 62–3, 68
  fabric producers, 91
monitoring costs, 63
  scale alliances, 34
Motorola
  supplier advisory board, 47
  supplier training programs, 46–7
  and Volvo Cars, 53
multinational corporations, knowledge
    exchange, 41–2
mutuality, and productive conflict, 145

narrative, 5–6, 121–3, 146–7
  for conflict exploration, 144
  negotiation of multiple identities, 123–33
  productive conflict, 139–46
  trust and rule structures, 133–9
narrative fidelity, 143
narrative probability, 143
Nash equilibrium, 160–1, 162
naturalistic paradigm, 122–3, 146–7
  multiple identities, 124
negotiation
  costs, 34
  group learning model, 83–5
Nestlé, 28
network perspective, social network studies,
    118
new product development (NPD),
    buyer–supplier collaboration, 59,
    60–1, 62
  maximizing transaction value, 63–4
  project-level collaboration, 65–7
  value appropriation, 64–5
Nike, supply network, 47
non-cooperative games, 160–1
"not-invented-here" syndrome, 66

oligopolistic markets, 175, 176
online social networks, 5, 107–9, 119

centralization, 112–14
core-periphery structure, 115–17
density, 111–12
future research, 118–19
new developments, 117–18
size, 111
social capital embedded in, 109–11
structure and information sharing, 111–17
openness, and productive conflict, 144
Open-Source approach, 2
opportunism
    network description of organization, 165
    and transaction costs, 63, 67
    and value appropriation, 64
organismic perspective on organizations,
        153, 154–5, 157, 163, 164
organization, 6, 151–3, 163–7
    ecological perspective, 154–5, 157, 163,
        164, 166
    evolving networks, 157–9
    game theory, 159–60
    history of organizations, 176–7
    institutional structures, 160–3
    mechanical perspective, 153, 154–5
    networks as organizational description,
        156–7, 159
    networks as organizational types, 155–6,
        158–9
    organismic perspective, 153, 154–5, 157,
        163, 164
organizational ecology, 167 n. 1
outsourcing
    GILDEMEISTER, 59–60
    knowledge purchasing as, 42, 43, 44
    value appropriation issues, 64

pallidness in narratives, 145
Pareto rule, 184
participation strategy, knowledge
        management, 14, 17–20
pattern recognition skills, 165
Peugeot-Citroën, 28
Pitti Filati, 105 n. 5
Polman, Paul, 2
postmodernism, and network representations
        of organizations, 163
power-law systems (scale-free networks),
        184–5, 186
preferred supplier status, 48
Première Vision, 89–90, 91–104
principal–agent theory, 180
process conflict, 139–40
Procter and Gamble, 2

product development projects,
        buyer–supplier collaboration in, 4,
        59–63, 67–8
    maximizing transaction value, 63–4
    project-level collaboration, 65–7
    value appropriation, 64–5
productive conflict, 123, 139–40
    interorganizational networks, 140–2
    and narrative, 142–3
    supporting narrative negotiation of, 143–6
project-level collaboration, 65–7
purchasing knowledge in supplier networks,
        41, 42
    extensive knowledge exchange, 43–4
    from a market, 42–3
    as outsourcing production, 43

quality issues, fabric producers, 101, 103

re-cognition stage, group learning model,
        79–80, 84–5
redundancy in online social networks, 113
repression, and conflict, 140
resource-based view of scale alliances, 31–2
reverse brainstorming, 141
rituals
    concertation in fashion industry, 89–90,
        103, 104
    group learning model, 81–3, 84–5
    multiple identities, 124–5
routines, group learning model, 81–3, 84–5
routinization, 73
rule structures and trust, 133–4
    interorganizational networks, 134–5
    and narrative, 135–6
    supporting narrative negotiation of, 136–9

sacred stories of organization identity, 127–8
Sarbanes–Oxley Act, 165
scale alliances, 4, 26–7, 36
    aircraft production, 35–6
    formation, 27–8, 29, 32–4
    performance and outcomes, 34–5
    resource-based view, 31–2
scale-free networks, 184–5, 186
search costs, 63
self-fulfilling prophecy, concertation as, 101
seminars and supplier networks, 47, 48
sense-making databases
    for identity negotiation, 131–3
    for productive conflict, 146
service intense companies, 8
Sevelnord alliance, 28

sharing principles, buyer–supplier
    collaboration, 65
silo mentality and design, 125–6
situated identity theory, 123
six degrees of separation, 184
size
    of online social networks, 111
    of teams, and buyer–supplier collaboration,
        66, 67
SKIN framework, 3–6, 175
social capital embedded in online social
        networks, 107–11, 119
    centralization, 112–14
    core-periphery structure, 115–17
    density of social network, 111–12
    future research, 118–19
    size of social network, 111
    weblogs, 117–18
    websites, 118
social exchange theory, and buyer–supplier
        collaboration, 66
social identities, buyer–supplier
        collaboration, 66
social identity theory, 123
social networks
    historical context, 177
    online, see social capital embedded in
        online social networks
socioeconomic networks, 178–9
Sorbini, 51
sphere of exchange, 162
sphere of production, 162
spot markets, 175, 176, 179
standards, fabric producers, 89
star network structure, 112–14
story construction, 138–9
strategic alliances, see alliances
Strategic Learning Assessment Map
        (SLAM), 16
Strategic Management Society (SMS), 2
Strategy for Knowledge in Networks, see
        SKIN framework
structural equivalence in online social
        networks, 113
style bureaux, 96
Style Committee, Moda In, 95
subcontracting, and knowledge
        purchasing, 43
superiority in buyer–supplier relationships, 66
supplier associations, 50
    IKEA, 50–2
    Volvo Cars, 52–3
supplier networks
    learning in, 41–2

teaching in, see teaching in supplier
        networks
Suzuki, supply network, 47
Swedwood, 51, 53, 54
symposia and supplier networks, 47
systems theory, 153

tacit knowledge, 12, 13–14, 21, 22
    game theory, 160
    learning strategy, 15, 16
    online social networks, 110–11, 112,
        113–14
    participation strategy, 17–18, 19
teaching in supplier networks, 4, 40–2, 54–5
    knowledge exchange and purchasing, 42,
        44–5; purchasing from a market,
        42–3; purchasing involving extensive
        knowledge exchange, 43–4;
        purchasing as outsourcing
        production, 43
    teaching in networks, 49–50, 53–4;
        supplier associations, 50–2
    teaching suppliers, 45, 48–9; assistance and
        training, 46–7; cross-functional teams,
        47–8; effective two-way
        communication, 47; incentives and
        motivation, 48; monitoring and
        evaluation, 45–6
team size, and buyer–supplier collaboration,
        66, 67
tendering, and knowledge purchasing, 42, 44
theorizing networks, 174–6
Toyota, 186
trade fairs, fabric producers, 89–90, 91–104
training programs for suppliers, 46–7, 49
transaction costs
    alliance formation, 27, 33
    buyer–supplier collaboration, 63, 67
    game theory, 160
    information and communications
        technologies, 183
    institutional structure, 163
transaction value, buyer–supplier
        collaboration, 63–4
trend forecasting, fabric producers, 95, 100
trust, 123, 133–4
    buyer–supplier collaboration, 63, 68
    clan networks, 162
    and cognitive conflict, 140
    game theory, 160
    interfirm teams, 82, 83, 84
    interorganizational networks, 134–5
    and narrative, 135–9
    participation strategy, 18

truth, paradox of, 129
Tyco, 165
types, networks as, 152, 155–6, 158–9
typology of organizational forms, 175

uniqueness paradox, interorganizational
    networks, 127

value appropriation, buyer–supplier
    collaboration, 64–5, 66, 67, 68
vendor assessment programs, 45–6, 49

virtual teams
    innovative task performance of, 66
    interfirm learning, 83
visits in supplier networks, 47, 49
vividness in narratives, 145
Volvo Cars, supply network, 52–5

Watson, T. J., 137
weblogs, 117–18
websites for social networking, 118
Wicoma, 51, 53
WorldCom, 165